The Ideas of Newman

The Ideas of Newman

Christianity and Human Religiosity

Lee H. Yearley

The Pennsylvania State University Press

University Park and London

Library of Congress Cataloging in Publication Data

Yearley, Lee H
    The ideas of Newman.

    Includes bibliography and index.
    1. Newman, John Henry, Cardinal, 1801–1890.
I. Title.
BX4705.N5Y4   230′.2′0924   77-13894
ISBN 0-271-00526-2

To My Father and Mother
Bernard C. Yearley and Mary H. Yearley

Contents

Preface

John Henry Newman's life spanned almost all of the nineteenth century. More important, he lived many of the intellectual tensions of that century—tensions that are still with us—in an especially profound way. Most important, he stood, or tried to stand, in two worlds at once, a traditional Christian world and a modern world. Almost all of his major works attempt to relate traditional Christianity to some aspect of modernity. In *An Essay on the Development of Doctrine,* it is historical change and doctrinal continuity. In *An Essay in Aid of a Grammar of Assent,* it is philosophic skepticism and religious assent. In *The Idea of a University Defined and Illustrated,* it is secular education and religious nurture. In the *Apologia pro Vita Sua,* it is human beings as creatures who change and self-consciously perceive their own beliefs and human beings as creatures who have a continuing identity and hold beliefs. Throughout his life, he worked on the problem of modernity as it affects religion. Newman is a particularly interesting figure because he tries to stand in both a traditional and a modern world; he is a particularly complex figure because his thought reflects the tensions of those two worlds; he is a particularly challenging figure because he argues that one can and must stand in both worlds at once.

This mixing of modern and traditional ideas often results in a haunting ambivalence in Newman's analysis of issues. The attempt to reconcile individual freedom with religious authority or to harmonize a revelatory message and a historically conditioned tradition are just two of many examples. This very ambivalence, however, also gives his thought a distinctive and complex texture. Like all people, Newman is bound by his times, but, like some people, he may also speak to different times. He is accessible to us because he struggles with real problems; indeed, he has a genius for uncovering what the real problems are.

Moreover, as with all great thinkers, he combines this nose for real problems with a firm sense of what he thinks it means for someone to be fully human. He attacks many in his time, especially those he calls

Liberals, because their view of humanity is superficial. This superficiality is most dangerous when religion is the issue. The possession of certain religious characteristics, for Newman, makes humans fully human. When Liberals overlook these characteristics, they create a religion that deforms human beings. Liberal religion, the religion that reveals modern people's distinctive view, leads to a deformation of its adherent's humanity.

The human religious potential that Liberal religion distorts is actualized in Catholic Christianity. Newman's conversion to Roman Catholicism, his defenses of it, his own struggles to change it, all rest in his idea that Catholic Christianity fulfills people's religious potential. Newman's religious ideas, then, can be focused by examining his view of humanity's basic religiosity and its completion in one type of religion—Catholic Christianity—and its deformation in another type of religion—Liberal religion.

This approach differs from the approaches that have been used to interpret Newman. Those approaches usually rest on a traditional Christian theological model that works with pairs of terms, such as grace and nature. I replace this theological model, using polar oppositions, with a model where everything is on a single continuum: humanity's natural religiosity, its deformation in one religion, and its fulfillment in another religion. My model does more justice to the complex interplay of elements within Newman's thought. Moreover, it allows me to analyze certain issues from a variety of viewpoints. For example, I can investigate revelation not only as an aspect of Christianity but also as an aspect of natural or Liberal religion.

My approach also differs from previous approaches (to my knowledge, all previous approaches) because it uses methods and information drawn from the comparative study of religion. Such an approach allows me to organize Newman's ideas in a distinctive fashion, as well as to highlight some areas that are otherwise hard to see. I can, for example, organize Newman's disparate ideas on Liberalism into a type of religion, Liberal religion. Viewing Liberalism as a type of religion allows us to see the full character of that alternative religious view Newman pits himself against. Moreover, this approach clarifies why Newman thinks any attempt to use Liberal religion's ideas to reformulate Christianity must lead to the destruction of Christianity and the creation of a new religion.

This analysis, employing the comparative study of religion, also allows me to separate out those two views of Roman Catholicism that operate in Newman. The fulfillment model of Roman Catholicism sees it as perfecting all aspects of religiosity. It emphasizes how Catholic

Christianity harmonizes natural religion's destructive division between the notional and the real, or how it unifies natural religion's disparate elements around a new sacred center, or how it completes natural religion's inchoate longings for efficacious mediation. The authority model of Roman Catholicism, however, stresses that the authority is the crucial fulfilling element. This model's most distinctive characteristic is its idea that a religion can set out saving truths, in specific propositional forms, that must be believed by all those who are to be members of the sacred community. I shall, using ideas drawn from the comparative analysis of religious thought, explain how Newman could hold his often puzzling ideas on dogma's importance to religion.

Separating out these two models of Roman Catholicism helps us understand different strands in Newman's thought. The fulfillment model is more flexible and irenic, the authority model more formal and divisive. Indeed, the authority model underlies Newman's most uncompromising assertions about how religious strivings find fulfillment only in Catholic Christianity, as well as many other of his more perplexing positions.

The tools provided by the comparative study of religion also allow us to penetrate Newman's view that religiosity arises from people's sense of both a sacred realm and their estrangement from it. The estrangement is most evident in the information that conscience provides. The sacred realm is most evident in the information that various religions provide, especially where similar phenomena appear, phenomena such as prayer, revelation, or sacrifice.

Viewing Newman through the perspective of the comparative study of religion enables me to organize his thought in a distinctive and revealing way. Moreover, it generates productive questions for our examination of some general topics in him, topics such as the character of conscience, or of assent, or of first principles.

The comparative perspective also allows us to focus on two more general problems: the relationship of Christianity to other religions, and the idea that a characteristically modern religion, such as Liberal religion, deforms the religious potential. The final chapter deals with these issues in a theoretical fashion. I test Newman's claims that Christianity fulfills other religions and that the religion most congenial to the modern view deforms humanity. Throughout my analysis, however, Newman's answers to these questions will surface. His answers tell us a great deal about his view of himself, his work, and his religion.

Many have contributed to this study. I am especially grateful for the help of Professor William Clebsch at Stanford University, Professor Frank Reynolds and Professor Brian Gerrish at the University of Chicago, Father Stephen Dessain of the Birmingham Oratory, Professor Edward Kelly at St. Louis University, John Carmody, Alan Miller, Hilda Kessler, Victor Lovell, William Howell, Mary Yearley, and W. L. Parker. John M. Pickering, Editorial Director of The Pennsylvania State University Press, has also given most valuable aid. The Mabelle McLeod Lewis Foundation and Stanford University provided aid for the research, writing, and typing of this manuscript. Finally, my thanks and more to Ann for reasons that we both know.

1

Natural Religion

John Henry Newman has usually been interpreted by utilizing the traditional Christian distinction between nature and grace. This distinction leads to seeing the world as divided into two spheres, for example: those who are religious and those who are not; those who have revelation and those who do not; those who live in contact with the sacred and those who live in contact with the profane. Newman often sets problems in terms of these opposites, describes the religious life in light of them, and uses language that echoes them.

Newman sometimes, however, uses three instead of two categories. Rather than speaking of a distinction between nature and grace, he speaks of natural religiosity, natural religiosity's deformation, and natural religiosity's fulfillment. This triadic form casts a different light on Newman's work. Moreover, it shows how he might respond to questions that press on us but that he saw only vaguely. Viewing Newman through this triadic form reveals a motif in him, sheds new light on his works, and provides us with a clearer view of his relationship to our questions.

Two Models of Religiosity

Problems that reside in the traditional Christian model of nature and grace are another reason to complement it with the triadic model. In specific instances, even the distinction's better Scholastic exponents develop the nature/grace model in a manner that places a great strain on its meaning. For example, consider Aquinas's formula that grace does not destroy but presupposes and perfects nature when it is applied to faith or charity. Similarly, modern theological analyses effectively destroy any clear application of the distinction's meaning. For example, consider the questions raised by the idea of a human being's natural desire for the vision of God. More important for this work, however, is the inability of the traditional model to analyze productively the notion of humanity's general religiosity. The nature/grace distinction was originally drawn largely to explicate the relation between "pagan" ideas, particularly Aristotelian ideas, and Christian ideas. In this and certain other contexts, careful explication may produce interesting results. Indeed, aspects of Newman's view of authoritative religion are best posed in terms of the traditional model. But its usefulness in other areas, particularly those relating to ideas of humanity's general religiosity, is at best limited and at worst positively misleading.[1]

Newman's labels for the three terms of the triadic model are inadequate. He uses the labels "natural," "revealed," and "Liberal" religion. Liberal religion may not even qualify as a religion under Newman's criteria, but, more important here, the labels "natural" and "revealed" obscure Newman's meaning and cause confusion in his analysis. For example, in the *Grammar of Assent* he calls revelation a defining characteristic of natural religion and then later opposes natural to revealed religion on the grounds of revelation. This confusion arises because Newman uses a distinction common to the age, but he then so transforms the distinctions that its usual sense is destroyed. His new wine breaks old skins, although Newman seems never to grasp this fully—a striking example of those undrawn implications that often characterize his work.

The Idea of Natural Religion

The remarkable story surrounding the distinction between natural and revealed religion need occupy us only as that story helps to set a background for understanding Newman. The impetus to make the distinction arose, in the Enlightenment, from a desire to find a "true religion" that could be used either to replace or to purify Christianity. "Natural religion" referred to some temporal or philosophic origin of all religions, the distinction between historical and ontological primacy usually remaining unclear. That origin was humanity's natural religion. The scheme's flaws are numerous: the pallor of its abstractions; the conditioned state of the observer its abstractions show; the inability of any religious *a priori* to do justice to actual religion's content; the disregarding of the seriousness with which adherents take a religion's specific elements.

The notion of natural religion did carry, however, a productive germ: the idea that human beings have a religious potential which manifests itself in specifiable actions or attitudes. A defining human characteristic is a religious potential that will, like the corresponding potentials for thought or toolmaking, produce activities with similar characteristics. Emphasizing this potential, however, necessitates replacing the idea of distinct natural and revealed religious spheres with the idea of one religious sphere containing various distinctions.

The problem remains that the word "natural," when referring to humans, has at least two distinct meanings. "Natural" may mean—and often does in either an Enlightenment or a Scholastic context—that which occurs normally, without any special aid from another realm. "Natural" may also, however, refer to a potential of human nature which may or may not be fulfilled, depending on the response that is made to what arises from another realm. That potential's concrete actualizations may differ greatly.

This latter idea of natural religion underlies Newman's work, although he continues to use the misleading labels. (He occasionally recognizes the difficulties they present, as when he says that "from the abuse of the term 'Natural Religion,' many persons will not allow the use of it at all."[2]) The terminology of natural and revealed religion, then, not only causes confusion in Newman's analysis but also, at most points, fails to reflect the most interesting aspects of his work. Newman's terminology is best replaced by the idea of a human religious potential that expresses itself in certain characteristic ways and can, on certain grounds, be seen as completed in one kind of religion.

Newman and the Modern Comparative Study of Religion

The numerous works on Newman have approached him through a variety of perspectives, such as those of Scholasticism, Existentialism, and Empiricism. Each generates a distinctive view by furnishing a particular set of spectacles to wear, a specific kind of question and concern to pursue. Each also runs risks—the more acute, the more different the approach from those of Newman's own intellectual world. The Scholastic approach, for example, is valuable, but it tends to ask questions Newman never answered as well as to drain out the particular significance of his work.

Any perspective may raise questions Newman only touches on, create constructs when Newman only gives hints, stand back from subjects Newman did not avoid, and push his ideas in directions he might be uneasy with. Moreover, Newman is particularly vulnerable to either pseudo clarification or distortion because he is nonsystematic and occasionally contradictory. In addition, he almost always writes to particular situations, is ever a more tentative man in private papers than in public proclamation, and in large part can be defined by his attempt to live in the tensions created by straddling the traditional Christian and modern

Western intellectual worlds. Some interpretative perspective is, of course, necessary. The temptation, however, is merely to select from him what substantiates a particular view. Since we will approach Newman by means of information and methods drawn from the modern comparative study of religion, some comment is needed on Newman's relationship to that perspective.

Newman's Outlook Contrasted with the Modern Comparative Study of Religion. Newman is not a student of human religion in the modern academic sense. His approach, aims, and informational base all differ from those of such students. His investigations are severely limited by his lack of information about the variety of human religious life. His comments, though not uncharacteristic of the times, often sound strikingly provincial. For example, his statement that the West "has a claim to be considered as the representative Society and Civilization of the human race, as its perfect result and limit"; or his comment that the language of savages can hardly express ideas; or his reference to China as "a huge, stationary, unattractive, morose civilization."[3] His ignorance was particularly acute in respect to the high religions of South and East Asia—those religions that are most different from Christianity. Information on those religions became available, if in a somewhat peculiar form, in the last half of the century, but Newman paid no attention to it. He knew little of those religions that would have most seriously tested his own ideas.

He was, however, aware of non-Christian religions, especially classical Greek and Roman religions. He wrote an examination paper at Oxford about Cicero's *On the Nature of the Gods* and later pursued extensive studies in early Christianity. In less rhetorical moments he shows a firm grasp of the integral religious spirit and practice present outside Christianity. It is important to remember, however, that his understanding of non-Christian religious life usually rests on Western classical religions and on the Bible's depiction of those religions competing with Judaism. Such religions do reflect general religious practice, but they do not reflect the guiding insights or even questions of some high South and East Asian traditions.

Another significant difference in Newman's thinking is his explicit apologetic aim. His interpretation of natural religiosity is formed by a desire to validate Christianity and to invalidate Liberal religion. Some apologetic exists in almost any comparativist, but in Newman this emphasis is more basic than in most. At times his rhetoric is strident. He will assert, for instance, that all views of religion save one are wrong, or that one religion may in no fashion be called as good as another.[4] Such passages show an unusual assertiveness and lack of qualification. Normally, the apologetic is more subtle and more aware of the question's difficulties. But the apologetic aim always remains; Newman never simply investigates religion as a human activity, he always desires to lead people to affirm or reaffirm Christianity's truth. Few religious phenomena are studied without some notion that the study is relevant to the investigator's present concerns. If one set up a line with the "apologetic" at one end and the "scientific" at the other, few indeed would be on the scientific end. Newman, however, would be far closer to the apologetic end than would almost any modern scholar.

One way to put the apologetic problem is to ask whether judgments about truth intrude on the description of human activity. The modern phenomenological study of religion examines religion only as a human action, leaving the truth or falsity of its reference undiscussed. In van der Leeuw's classical formulation, "for Religion, then, God is the active Agent in relation to man, while the sciences in question [of religion] can concern themselves only with the activity of man in his relation to God; of the acts of God Himself they can give no account whatever."[5] Not truth but people's experience of truth is the phenomenon to be studied. The degree to which this approach actually works in practice, is desirable, or even must exist, is a vexing question.

Clearly, however, Newman's analysis of religious activity is always concerned with the action's truth. Newman's judgments often rest on moral not religious grounds, on the general principle that "no religion is from God which contradicts our sense of right and wrong." As he said: "I take our natural perception of right and wrong as the standard for determining the characteristics of Natural Religion, and I use the religious rites and traditions which are actually found in the world, only so far as they agree with our moral sense."[6] Nevertheless, he does judge the validity of religious practices and ideas, and he does label some abnormal or untrue in a way phenomenologists never explicitly would. The apologetic aim does differentiate Newman from modern objective studies of religion. That does not mean, however, that we separate him from such studies, but rather that we carefully analyze him.

Similarities between the Phenomenological Approach of Newman and That of the Modern Comparative Study of Religion.   Newman's phenomenological approach resembles that of much modern comparative study of religion. The modern phenomenology of religion is a descriptive analysis of what occurs or, more precisely, impresses itself on the observer. The description makes no attempt to explain why the phenomenon occurs or whether it is true. Phenomenology attempts to strike a middle ground between "scientific reductionism" (for instance, a specific kind of worship refers to society not deity) and theological explication (for instance, a specific kind of worship reveals a true relation to deity). Inquiry focuses simply on what appears. In leaving unasked the question of causes, phenomenology differs from the explanatory approaches of, for instance, psychology, philosophy, or history.

Phenomenologists of religion use typologies to organize their raw perception of phenomena into intelligible forms. Such ordering of perceptions is, they stress, a normal mental activity. Specific experiences naturally connect to wider fields of experience through relations such as contrast, similarity, and affinity. These connections are neither factual nor causal, but they do facilitate understanding by organizing and therefore illuminating experience.[7]

Typological structures in religions sometimes concern whole religions—for example, religions of struggle and repose, religions of the father and the mother. More often, such structures are specific categories that cut across various traditions—for example, enthusiasm, prophecy, mysticism, reform, meditation. A brief example helps to clarify the idea. Van der Leeuw establishes a general type, sacred personhood, defined as an individual affected by sacral power. This type is then broken down into two representations of power. In one, the self remains intact, but it is sanctified for a particular office as in the sacral king or priest; in the other, the self and sacral power are unified as in the saint, possessed human, or founder. From this point even further types may be formed. Whether a person is a teacher, a prophet, a reformer, or an example depends on whether the message is inseparable from or conjoined with the person, or on what kind of effect is obtained or sought. Through such typological breakdowns, experiences are ordered and productive questions arise. For example: What type of representation do St. Francis, St. Paul, and Martin Luther personify? How do they stand in relation to Confucius or Mohammed? Typologies organize phenomena in a way that generates understanding. Descriptive analysis through typological structures characterizes, then, the phenomenological study of religion.

Others have pointed to Newman's phenomenological method in philosophy. They see Newman as steering between Empiricism and Idealism toward a method of investigation that gives a descriptive analysis of a subject's experience of concrete particulars. The *Grammar of Assent,* for instance, might be retitled the "Phenomenology of Assent" because Newman tries to articulate the rules, the grammar, underlying the phenomenon of human assent.[8] In similar fashion, Newman often just organizes and describes religious phenomena; he does not simply judge their value. He sees religious life as furnishing information that can be placed in descriptive categories which delineate the various aspects of the phenomenon of human religiosity. Such an effort is possi-

ble because there is an "objective matter of Religion . . . [with a] legitimate position and exercise of the intellect relatively toward it. Religion
has, as such, certain definite belongings and surroundings."⁹ For Newman, unlike many men of his time, religion exists as a fact of human
life with discernible characteristics. Religion is not reduced to an early
form of scientific explanation, or made a function of humanity's primitive mentality, or seen as a peculiar qualification of humanity's moral
life, or treated as an unanalyzable emotional state. Rather religion is
viewed as a phenomenon that, while presenting particular problems for
analysis, has definite and definable attributes. Viewing Newman as a
phenomenologist emphasizes, then, how Newman starts from certain
given circumstances and proceeds to description and analysis—if always
with the aim of reaching a truth that will compel people.

Newman's approach to religion is also illuminated by Sillem's sug-
gestion that Newman's phenomenological method in philosophy is constituted by two parts: one part negative and preparatory, the other part
positive and constructive.¹⁰ The negative tries to remove all the subjective cloudings that interfere with perceiving the concrete. The positive
tries to unify the knowing person and the object known so he may fully
know it. Making the one qualification that only untrue cloudings are to
be removed, as Newman believed first principles always affected perception, this perspective illuminates Newman's approach to human religiosity. Indeed, religion's distinctive character makes the two steps Sillem describes particularly important. The negative step of removing
the subconscious interference of *a priori* factors is important because
Newman thinks the current cultural milieu generates "a-" or "anti-"
religious first principles. These principles blind observers to the real
outlines and meaning of the religious phenomenon. Liberals, for instance, are blocked from seeing what traditional religious ideas and
practices are because they have unconscious ideas about what they must
be or ought to be.

The positive step is important because knowing religious phenomena involves more than just looking at or thinking about them. One
must also recognize their spiritual power, understand their revelation
of the sacred. Newman usually deals with such "religious realization" in
pastoral situations. He emphasizes that Christian ideas must not just be
thought about but must also be realized in the self, realization being a
knowledge that forms the person by uncovering an unknown aspect of
the self or causing a change in character. This point can be extended
beyond its pastoral context, although Newman would probably distinguish a realized religious perception that led to commitment from one
that did not. In any study of religion, the observer's spiritual state and
his union with the object are important. Indeed, an adequate percep-

tion may involve a new understanding of the self, a point made rhetorically in the dictum that to understand a religion one must be tempted by it. Newman's realization resembles Ricoeur's "hermeneutic circle." Ricoeur says, "You must understand in order to believe, but you must believe in order to understand [because] . . . no interpreter in fact will ever come close to what [is said] . . . if he does not live in the *aura* of the meaning that is sought."[11] Newman's approach to religion thus shows, at least at times, the phenomenological characteristics also evident in his approach to philosophy.

The other critical aspect of the phenomenological study of religion—the notion of types or categories—is also evident in Newman. Types are the mechanisms by which he orders concrete facts. Newman's overall explication of "types" is usually set in an Aristotelian framework. Like Aristotle, he argues that in viewing human affairs (ethics or politics in Aristotle's case, religion here) one works in a mutable realm where things can be other than they are. Therefore, rather than functioning by means of logical judgments, one must observe what actually occurs and then structure those occurrences in an illuminating way. Aristotle's division of governments into such classes as oligarchies and democracies exemplifies this approach. The structuring types never reflect the full complexity of concrete life. Moreover, critics can argue about the judgments that form the categories and place particulars within them. Those judgments remain a function of the observer's state of being—in ethics, the perceiver's goodness; in religion, the perceiver's religious sensitivity. Indeed, typological judgments exemplify the personal mode of illative action. They are part of that mysterious process of personal perception where judgments are so delicate that explanation, defense, or proof—either to another or to oneself—is difficult. The general difficulties in illative judgments are particularly acute in religion. Religious types often look like their opposites as, for example, in the relation between magic and sacramental action, superstition and faith, zeal and fanaticism, and speculation and fancifulness. Such explanatory categories are not compelling proofs; they represent only one individual's perception of man's behavior. Nevertheless, they are crucial to understanding life's actual occurrences.

Newman's mind seems naturally to work typologically; his work on religion abounds in typological distinctions. *The Idea of a University,* for example, speaks of the religions of warlike and of pastoral people, and of the religions of enthusiasm or of statecraft. A similar example is Newman's general contrast between barbaric and civilized religion, with the former based on imagination and the latter on sense. These two form distinct typological complexes that influence all aspects of religion. The barbaric is congenial to notions of divine mission, to images that excite the emotions, and to the flow of nature. The civilized is congenial to notions such as secular interest, country, and the legal protection of person and property.[12]

Another example is Newman's evocation of some principles of Christianity in the *Development of Doctrine*.[13] Although presented in a theological manner, these principles can be seen to specify the general types of religion evident in Christianity. For example, the dogmatic type concerns religious truths irrevocably committed to human language; the sacramental type deals with the conveyance of divine gifts in a material medium; the ascetic type concerns the attainment of religious fulfillment by means of the mortification of one's lower nature; the sanctification type emphasizes the possible sacred actualization of man's matter and mind. Such a typological analysis leads not only to a fruitful organization of Christianity's experience but also to the formulation of many productive questions. Questions arise about the relation of the sacramental type to the practice of relic worship; or about the relation of the types of asceticism and sanctification; or about a comparison of, say, Theravada Buddhism and medieval Christianity by means of the types asceticism and dogmatism.

A typological analysis grows naturally out of Newman's general approach, though he neither develops nor systematically applies a typological theory exactly akin to that of the phenomenologists of religion. His study of human religiosity bears an affinity to the phenomenological study of religion. Significant differences exist between the respective positions, especially in the informational base but also in the aims of their studies. The differences must be recognized, but the modern phenomenological study of religion can illuminate Newman.

Newman's View of Conscience

The Two Elements in Conscience.   Our study of the background for Newman's depiction of human religiosity is completed by analyzing his examination of conscience. Conscience is basic to Newman's perspective. Moreover, his examination of it is often astute. The examination exhibits a delicate dissection of different mental states and a persuasive explication of their implications. As is only to be expected, however, given the topic's subtlety and the difference between Newman's age and our own, there are serious questions about the viability of his account.

Conscience, for Newman, is the great internal teacher of religion. Indeed, conscience is nothing less than "a connecting principle between the creature and his Creator." Conscience communicates "to each separately . . . that knowledge which is most momentous to him individually . . . . [It] teaches us, not only that God is, but what He is; it provides for the mind a real image of Him, as a medium of worship; it gives us a rule of right and wrong, as being His rule, and a code of moral duties." Newman's work often focuses on conscience because "if there is a way of finding religious truth, it lies, not in exercises of the intellect, but close on the side of duty, of conscience."[14] For instance, his chosen "proof" for the existence of God is to analyze conscience, his manner of exhibiting the personal characteristics of deity is to examine conscience, his arguments against religious foes is often to criticize their proposed substitutes for conscience, and his setting of religious authority's limits is to probe the implications of conscience.

Indeed, the range of meanings he associates with conscience makes understanding his ideas a challenge. For Newman, conscience is more than a simple moral organ that either speaks intermittently about particular actions or underlies the moral deliberative process. Conscience is rather that knowledge of self which enables man to know God and thus the self's relation to God. Newman's view is best understood, not in relationship to recent centuries' ruminations on ethical theory, but in relationship to either the Augustinian tradition's views about possible ways of knowing God or its analogues in the modern comparative study of religion.[15] Newman probes conscience to discover what religious knowledge it implies or generates. In this wider sense, conscience reflects both the existence of a transcendent sacred object and the human desire for it. Conscience, in Newman's view, is thus the crucial element in the dialectic tension defining the human condition. It shows that a person has no single will but stands divided, with normal wishes and religious needs often in basic conflict. The self stands divided against itself, caught in a struggle that can make or destroy it. People become what they make of their consciences, or, more precisely, allow their consciences to make of them.[16] Conscience, according to Newman then, provides the avenue by which a person knows God, recognizes the need for God, and finds the battleground that truly defines the human condition.

Newman's more specific analysis rests on a distinction between two elements within conscience. Conscience's judgment of acts, declaring some worthy of blame and others of praise, contains two elements: the sense of transgressing a law and the sense of the law having a content; a feeling of being judged and a feeling that a particular action is rightly judged. Conscience, that "certain keen sensibility, pleasant or painful,—self-approval and hope, or compunction and fear,—attendant on certain of our actions, . . . is twofold:—it is a moral sense, and a sense of duty; a judgment of the reason and a magisterial dictate." The distinction points to the difference between the content of conscience's particular judgment—I must not *do that*—and a general sense of obligation—*I must not* do that. In typical fashion, Newman uses a variety of terms or phrases to specify the two parts: moral sense/sense of duty; judgment of reason/magisterial dictate; moral sense/commanding dictate; shame/fear; precept/injunction; critical/judicial; testimony of right and wrong/sanction; remaining within oneself/being carried beyond oneself to another person. However specified, though, the moral sense refers to a specific judgment about what must be done or avoided in particular circumstances.

In contrast, the sense of duty refers both to the general demand that good be sought and evil avoided and to the idea that present and future sanctions reinforce that demand. The former is a particular judgment on a particular act—for instance, the idea that *x* is wrong. The latter is the overall sense of wrong and right—the idea that whether *x* is really wrong or right, some idea of wrong and right remains. However particular judgments change, the general sense of sanction, of some right and wrong, is constant. Indeed, changes in the content of judgments are based in the ongoing sense of sanction. As Newman says, "If I practise deceit, or am grossly intemperate, or commit some very selfish act, I have a double feeling—first that I am transgressing a law, secondly that the law says this or that. This latter conviction I may change and yet the former ≤notion≥ will remain. If in any particular my conscience is false, and I come to see it, then I review my judgment in the *particular* case about what is right or wrong, but I do not thereby at all weaken . . . <my> sense of a law and consequent obligation."[17]

The distinction is important, but it must not overshadow Newman's affirmation that conscience is a unity where each element informs the other. Conscience's significance rests not just on the power to command but also on the goodness of the command. The command of conscience is adhered to, in part, because it reflects "the image of One who is good, inasmuch as enjoining and enforcing what is right and good."[18] The experience engenders not only hope of reward and fear of punishment but also gratitude and love. Conscience is followed not merely because it demands obedience and will bring misery if disobeyed but also because its commands are right and obedience will bring the goal a good God desires. It is not only that "you must do *x*, because I, whom you ought to obey, speak" but also that "you ought to do *x*, because I who speak am good and acting in your best interest." Conscience generates not merely injunctions but correct injunctions; its authority rests on both its power and its goodness.

Recognizing conscience's unity is especially important when analyzing Newman because he often divides the two aspects of conscience for explanatory or polemical purposes. He says, for example, that the magisterial aspect leads to God, the moral aspect to ethics, with real religion resting on the former and Liberal religion on the latter. If the obligatory aspect is emphasized, this division often gives his analysis a one-sided look: fear; the weight of sheer obligation; the foreign, judging presence of God all loom overly large. The distinction between conscience's two parts is crucial to Newman's analysis, but the essential unity of conscience must be remembered.

Three Questions about Newman's View of Conscience.   Newman's view raises three questions that need brief investigation. Is his notion of moral absolutes defensible? Does the obvious frailty of conscience undermine the significance he sees there? Does a modern social scientific perspective destroy his attempt to see absolute obligation and thus God in conscience? Newman does not explicitly confront these questions, but possible answers can be extrapolated. In fact, these questions must be faced if this critical aspect of his thought is not to appear hopelessly inadequate.[19]

The difficulties inherent in any notion of knowable moral absolutes are too clear to need much reiteration here. Both the objective facts of human life (the bewildering variety of apparently acceptable ethical stances) and the subjective witness of each man (the difficulty of knowing and applying ethical rules) seem to militate against the idea of knowable moral absolutes. Newman characteristically meets the question of the existence of moral absolutes by interrogating his own experience. He argues that conscience generates a self-validating perception of absolute moral values. Men have an "instinctive recognition of the immutable difference in the moral quality of acts, as elicited in us by one instance of them. Even one act of cruelty, ingratitude, generosity, or justice reveals to us at once *intensivè* the immutable distinction between these qualities and their contraries; that is, in that particular instance and *pro hac vice.*"[20] Newman is aware such recognitions can be dim, but he still argues there remain "notions which we may trust *without* blame; viz. such as come to us by way of our Conscience . . . I mean our certainty that there is a right and a wrong, that some things ought to be done and other things not done."[21] A person perceives a rightness and wrongness in certain acts by means of conscience just as other faculties perceive other opposites, the true and false, the ugly and beautiful. As those other perceptions ground a person's judgments on truth or beauty, so perceptions arising from conscience ground a person's moral behavior. The position is a version of the Thomistic argument that people know certain acts to be wrong or right by a connatural inclination of their own natures. Such self-validating reactions undergird moral theory and action. For example, the observation of the exploiting of people or of the taking of innocent life without reason brings responses that lead to action and the affirmation of certain absolutes.

Even granting this, the problem remains of how to apply such principles to concrete situations. Newman's answer, again like that of the Aristotelian tradition, is to emphasize the role of practical wisdom. Such wisdom forms particular moral action by recognizing general principles, correctly modifying them to fit concrete situations, and then commanding the specific proper act. It is a "capacity sufficient for the occasion, of deciding what ought to be done here and now, by this given person, under these given circumstances."[22] The general outline of Newman's answer is that a person spontaneously knows certain acts to be right or wrong because an affinity or repulsion is felt on seeing or imagining them. Intellectual reflection upon these spontaneous reactions leads to the formulation of certain general principles, such as that the willful destruction of innocent life is wrong. These principles are applied to specific problems by the use of practical wisdom. This model is cogent and can meet, in at least some fashion, the questions addressed to it.

The second question is whether conscience is not an entity too error-ridden and changeable to have the significance Newman gives it. All people see both in themselves and in others the mistakes conscience makes. It often commands an action later seen to be wrong or commands on one day what it opposes on another. The problem is particularly clear in the human maturation process. The movement from the scruples of childhood to a more flexible maturity illustrates how conscience's commands are often, in reality, the overscrupulous application of social or parental desires. Obedience to conscience in such instances may actually impede personal growth. But if conscience can be wrong and must grow, how can any of its commands be respected?

Newman recognizes that both aspects of conscience are frail and liable to misinterpretation or even destruction. The moral sense (in his phrase, the highest but least luminous of instructors) is most vulnerable to corruption. Its specific intimations, "instead of being obtruded upon our notice, so that we cannot possibly overlook them . . . are faint shadows and tracings, certain indeed, but delicate, fragile, and almost evanescent, which the mind recognizes at one time, not at another . . . [has] when it is calm, loses when it is in agitations."[23] The sense of obligation is hardier but still even it can be silenced. People can destroy their sense of obligation, with its given relationship to God, because

> whether it grows brighter and stronger, or, on the other hand, is
> dimmed, distorted, or obliterated, depends on each of us indi-

vidually, and on his circumstances. . . . [From] neglect, from the temptations of life, from bad companions, or from the urgency of secular occupations, the light . . . will fade away and die out. . . . Men transgress their sense of duty, and gradually lose those sentiments of shame and fear. . . . [A] genuine apprehension of Him, could [never be utterly lost,] . . . yet that apprehension may become almost undistinguishable from an inferential acceptance of the great truth, or may dwindle into a mere notion of their [men's] intellect.[24]

These statements reflect a tension between structure and growth, between given characteristics and their need to develop, that Newman sees in all human affairs. Conscience is a given potential, but it must either develop or decay. Here as elsewhere the general principle of development holds: to live is to change and to be perfect is to have changed often.

Though man cannot change what he is born with, he is a being of progress with relation to his perfection and characteristic good . . . man begins with nothing realized . . . and he has to make capital for himself by the exercise of those faculties which are his natural inheritance. Thus he gradually advances to the fullness of his original destiny. Nor is this progress mechanical, nor is it of necessity; it is committed to the personal efforts of each individual of the species; each of us has the prerogative of completing his inchoate and rudimental nature, and of developing his own perfection out of the living elements with which his mind began to be. It is his gift to be the creator of his own sufficiency; and to be emphatically self-made. This is the law of his being, which he cannot escape.[25]

Newman's answer, then, is that obligation and the first principles of the moral sense remain constant, but that the prudential moral sense develops to see its principles more clearly and to apply them more sensitively. The scruples of immaturity are lost, for instance, as prudential understanding sees that certain acts were falsely judged to be wrong. Such an abstract construct does answer some questions, but it barely meets other problems such as the possible loss of both senses or the practical uselessness of a constancy in first principles. Moreover, conscience is immobilized in abstract categories. It becomes a "pure something," unchangeable in itself and only vaguely related to a variety of lesser impulses. The inadequacy of this abstract resolution leaves Newman with only that "answer" pointed to by the general tension between structure and growth. Like all else human, conscience is frail yet reflects something constant and real; like all else human, it manifests a given structure yet must change.

Newman's final "answer," in effect, is to point up the dilemma and then rest his case on a practical imperative rather than on a theoretic resolution. He just argues that a person must be obedient to conscience as such obedience will, in time, reveal the answer. As he says, conscience "is so constituted that, if obeyed, it becomes clearer in its injunctions, and wider in their range, and corrects and completes the accidental feebleness of its initial teachings."[26] Such a statement does not answer the theoretic question posed by conscience's errors and growth processes. When combined, however, with a "true" experience of conscience and the general abstract explanation, it may (and surely did for Newman) provide a practical base for religious growth and moral judgment.

The third problem is the authority of conscience's voice. Admitting that conscience contains a voice, even an apparently authoritative one, the question remains as to whose voice it is. May not conscience, for instance, be the internalized voice of one's culture or parents and so be explainable in a way that reduces it to societal factors? How would Newman respond to a perspective that emphasizes the effect of social circumstances on all aspects of man's perception, thought, and action? Of the three questions addressed to conscience, this one is both the most modern and the most critical to religion. The beginnings of "social scientific" analysis lie in the nineteenth century, but the perspective they represent began to be felt, and then but crudely, only late in Newman's life. Questions generated by the "Freudian revolution" were unknown to Newman, as is shown by his straightforward description, in the *Grammar*'s section on conscience and God, of a child encountering within himself a being with qualities like those of his parents. Newman's was an age when, to refer to a famous anecdote, even a freethinker like George Eliot could believe God and immortality indefensible notions but still find duty inviolate. Today almost a century of clinical evidence and theoretic inquiry have raised important questions about the origin of any obligatory notions.

Indeed, the explanation of phenomena by analysis of their origins is one of the most distinctive motifs of modern intellectual inquiry. At its worst (and religious phenomena have often suffered such clumsy treatment) the attempt can rightly be labeled reductionistic. A crude attempt is made to explain any symptom in terms of its simplest causes—e.g., religious ideas of immortality arise solely because of people's fear of destruction. At a more refined level the confusion of principles with origins can still be possible. The attempt can be made to explain something by noting the occasion of its arising. That x occurred in situation y does not, however, necessarily mean y explains x. Principle x may merely be manifested in situation y rather than explained by it. Primitive worship may arise in conjunction with the planting of seeds, but the desire for a full crop need not necessarily explain worship. The principle of worship may just find a fitting expression there. Nevertheless, the probing of origins raises significant questions about the meaning of a phenomenon like conscience.

Investigating conscience's origin raises the vexing question of the conditions for an adequate explanation of one of humanity's most complex activities, but the issue can be presented briefly. Someone could argue that the judging presence in conscience arises from society. Conscience responds to the anticipated demands of other people upon one. Conscience's content reflects the approvals and disapprovals of a social group. Its obligatory force reflects the anticipated possibility of exclusion from the human community—the feeling of being outside those communal processes that generate identity, meaning, and forgiveness. Changes in conscience's content are explained by the self's life in many different communities—e.g., the family, the state, one's profession, one's religion. The particular demands of one group become prominent at one time but recede before the demands of a different group at another time. The apparent disinterestedness of conscience's commands, their distinction from the concrete desires of the self, occurs because the self and the group to which it belongs have different ideas. In this view, both the particular judgments of conscience and its general sense of obligation are relativized to the particular social contexts in which a person lives. Whatever constancy or reality conscience possesses is just that of a given social group. Conscience does nothing more than reflect social mores and enforce them by a real or implied threat of exclusion. Arising from one's social situation, conscience has no reference beyond the social matrix.

The conflict between this view and Newman's exemplifies what Newman calls a clash in first principles. The common "fact" of conscience's judging, authoritative voice is interpreted by means of different first principles. Newman argues such clashes are unresolvable because the differing first principles are not themselves debatable. The perceptions that might change the first principles are themselves formed by what the principles will and will not admit as either possible or real.

Nevertheless, some points about conscience are open to discussion. Newman, for instance, does recognize that societal influences not only inform but also can even dominate conscience. He knew nothing about either the clinical evidence that shows the power of attitudes received in childhood or about those sophisticated analyses that show how society forms behavior. But he is aware that societal influences can inform or even dominate conscience, as his analysis of notional assents shows.[27] Nevertheless, he continues to believe that an analysis of the content and obligatory force of some judgments of conscience points to absolutes.

The perception that persons are valuable, for instance, cannot be explained solely in terms of a society's attitude. The universal and intensive character of that judgment shows more than a social base. Social relations furnish the occasion where the value is revealed, but an adequate explanation demands more than a combination of social factors.

Moreover, those critical situations where people act against societal mores are important. A person's action against general social norms may arise from membership in a smaller group whose demands take precedence. For example, participation in a pacifist group may cause someone to oppose a society's war. This explanation is obvious in some cases and possible in all cases, but questions do remain. For instance, why did the small group's values take precedence? What are people's own explanations of their actions? These and other issues may be unsolvable, but Newman's position, if extensively reformulated, can at least arrive at a standoff with an alternative view.

Of importance here, as with the other two problems, is the ability of Newman's analysis to formulate cogent answers to these major criticisms. Newman's emphasis on the personal element in conscience gives his views a kind of "unassailability," unless there are obvious problems. Newman attempts to explicate his own experience and then to extend that explication to others' experience. His analysis, if reasonably coherent, will necessarily have a certain invulnerability—if also, perhaps, a certain unfalsifiability. Such an approach can never generate a publicly demonstrable conclusion, but it can present a picture of conscience that may adequately explain some people's experience. This is the strength of Newman's exposition of conscience. Recognizing this strength is important for understanding the view of religion that flows from it.

The Three Forms of Religious Expression

With the preceding analysis as background, we can now focus directly on Newman's depiction of human religiosity. We begin with Newman's idea that human religious activity expresses itself in three forms: thought, action, and community. Newman's view of the general forms of man's religious activity is clearest when we examine his treatment of the Church's three offices, in the preface to the 1877 edition of the *Via Media,* through the frame presented by Joachim Wach, one of this century's leading students of religion. Wach argues that a "comparative study of the *forms* of the expression of religious experience, the world over, shows an amazing similarity in structure. . . . All expression of religious experience falls under the three headings of *theoretical expression, practical expression,* and *sociological expression.* Everywhere and at all times man has felt the need to articulate his religious experience in three ways: conceptually; by action, or practically; and in covenanting, or sociologically."[28] In theoretical religious expression, ideas are formulated. In practical religious expression—worship and ethics—actions flowing from religious experience are manifested. In sociological religious expression, specific social forms and relationships are created and sustained. Wach's outline highlights the wider implications of Newman's portrait of the Roman Catholic Church's three offices.

Newman says the Church's offices reflect those of Christ's sacral mediation: Prophet, Priest, and King.

> After His pattern, and in human measure, Holy Church has . . . three offices, which are indivisible, though diverse, viz. teaching, rule, and sacred ministry. . . . Christianity, then, is at once a philosophy, a political power, and a religious rite: as a religion, it is Holy; as a philosophy, it is Apostolic; as a political power, it is imperial, that is One and Catholic. As a religion, its special seat is pastor and flock; as a philosophy, the Schools; as a rule, the Papacy and its Curia. . . . Truth is the guiding principle of theology and theological inquiries; devotion and edification, of worship; and expedience of government. The instrument of theology is reasoning; of worship, our emotional nature; of rule, command and coercion. Further, reasoning tends to rationalism, devotion to superstition and enthusiasm, and power to ambition and tyranny. . . . Each of the three has its separate scope and direction; each has its own interest to promote and further; each has to find room for the claims of the other two; and each will find its own line of action influenced and modified by the others.[29]

In this passage, Newman not only describes the Church's ideal constitution but also draws out a general notion of religious expression. A view emerges, resembling Wach's, about how the basic divisions of human activity are reflected and consummated in religion. A human being has three aspects: a mind, specifically religious "emotions" leading to worship and distinctive actions, and a desire to live in society. A human being is definable as *homo sapiens, homo religiosus,* and *homo politicus.* All three interact, but each element is distinct. Moreover, each element aims to a particular consummation and is liable, or even tends, to a particular degeneration. Reason aims at truth, at an inquiry leading to rational understanding. But reason also tends to rationalism, to measuring all by what can be clearly understood, to believing only what can be proved. Religious emotions aim at worship, at those signs and actions that express people's felt relation to the sacred, and the emotions extend themselves through pastoral care. The degenerative form here is enthusiasm and superstition—the unchecked, primitive response of the emotions. The human desire to live with other people aims at the perfection of just government. This desire makes use of rules and commands in contrast to pastoral care. It will employ coercion, though a coercion based on a notion of what will best actualize human relations. This ambition to command can, however, lead to the corruption of tyranny, to that misuse of power which imposes rigid, destructive forms on man's communal life.

These three basic expressions of human beings are all manifest in religion; in religion, in fact, they ought to be both in perfect form and in proper equilibrium. The search for rational understanding is exemplified in the careful theological explication of revealed truth and in the inspiration of prophecy, with its intuitive recognition and application of sacred demands. Indeed, humanity's restless intellectual quest reaches its zenith in seeking to understand and to convey religious truth. In like manner, the religious emotions are perfected in the religious community, in those actions that manifest sacrality and that generate a reconciliation among human beings and between a human being and God. Finally, humanity's social desires are consummated in a society of believers. This spiritual community is bound by religious laws and is organized as a hierarchy, a hierarchy being for Newman the supreme exemplification of proper spiritual and social order. Each of the three aspects aims at a particular perfection, although their actual forms will always be mixtures of consummation and degeneration: reason liable to either skepticism or the creation of idols, worship liable to superstition, community liable to institutional rigidity and tyrannical abuse. Because the community must relate directly to the outside world; maintain an institutional form; and work, at times, by expedience, its ideal form is most liable to contain degenerative elements. Newman's portrait is theological; he depicts the Catholic Church's ideal form in order to criticize its current abuses. But that portrait also reflects a vision of both the expression and perfection of religious activity. Like Wach's, it sees religion as finding expression in theoretical, practical, and social forms.

The Two Sources of Religion

Estrangement and Reconciliation.   Newman thinks that one source of religion is the human sense of estrangement from the world, the self, and the sacred. The other source is the answer to estrangement that is contained in the ideas, rites, and forms of religions. These two sources interact but they are separate, and both are necessary if religion is to exist.

Examining the sources of religion here and religion's defining marks in the following section leads us into that part of the *Grammar of Assent* entitled "Natural Religion." That part is brief and cryptic, but it is also very rich. Newman applies the theoretic conclusions of the *Grammar*'s second part to the subject of religion in order to show that humanity is inherently religious. Moreover, he attempts to show that Christianity completes "natural religion"; a section that takes up about a fifth of the *Grammar* explicitly argues this point. Finally, he attempts, if covertly, to show that Liberal religion stunts humanity's basic religiousness.

Newman analyzes the implications of his own experience, particularly his conscience, and then correlates those results with the actual facts of religious life. He then postulates two sources for religion: a need to overcome the pain and apparent futility of human life and an answer to that need in the ideas, rites, and forms of religion. Put in terms of conscience, where the need element predominates, the two sources are the existence of a sacred realm and of humanity's estrangement from it. Put in terms of lived religions, where the answer predominates, the two sources are the existence of divisions in human life and of means for overcoming them. The two sources constantly interact, but we will first examine the estrangement element and then proceed to its overcoming, seen as a possibility in conscience and as a reality in religion.

Each part of conscience exhibits one aspect of the divine's relation to people. The moral sense shows that the divine is the foundation of our sense of right and wrong, while the sense of obligation shows that deity is a judging person. God must be personal because the emotions that characterize conscience arise only in personal relations. Conscience exhibits, then, a moral, personal God to whom humanity is related, from whom humanity is estranged, and before whom humanity is judged responsible for that separation. Conscience's insight is verified and expanded by the religious activities arising from conscience. Religion's "many varieties all proclaim or imply that man is in a degraded, servile condition, and requires expiation, reconciliation, and some great change of nature." Indeed, this idea underlies Newman's general definitions of religion: the knowledge of God, of his will and of our duties toward him, or in the words of an earlier, more general statement, "the system of relations existing between us and a Supreme Power, claiming our habitual obedience."[30]

Newman usually notates humanity's servile condition by the word "sin," but I shall substitute "estrangement" for "sin." "Estrangement" lacks the overtones of personal responsibility before a transcendent judge, but "sin" has peculiar colorings today. More important, "estrangement" reflects that perception of human beings as strangers in the world that Newman thinks undergirds religion. Religiosity arises from a negative theophany, a dark revelation of feeling out of place, of desiring a more hospitable world but being unable to discover or live in it.

Schematically, estrangement has three aspects: estrangement from the world, from the self, and from the sacred. The first, a persistent motif in Newman, sees the world as a "heart-piercing, reason-bewildering fact . . . [as] a vision to dizzy and appal," as a seemingly chaotic panorama of disorder, pain, and defeat. If one simply looks at the world, "it is a silence that speaks. It is as if others had got possession of His work." Considered in length and breadth, the world shows

> the progress of things, as if from unreasoning elements, not towards final causes, the greatness and littleness of man, his far-reaching aims, his short duration, the curtain hung over his futurity, the disappointments of life, the defeat of good, the success of evil, physical pain, mental anguish . . . the many races of man, their starts, their fortunes, their mutual alienation, their conflicts; and then their ways, habits, governments, forms of worship; their enterprises, their aimless courses, their random achievements and acquirements.[31]

The world appears made to a measure other than humanity's; it either is without concern for humanity or is destructive of humanity's best efforts.

This terrible vision of people's estrangement from the world is intensified by conscience's testimony that people are also estranged from their better selves. People see that a gulf separates what the moral sense proclaims and what people do, what people desire to be and what people actually are. As Newman's preaching constantly reiterates, people are divided against themselves. People, at best, are able to make only humiliating compromises between the better self's demands and the normal self's needs. Even more frightening, however, is conscience's proclamation that people are estranged from a personal judging God. That proclamation reveals estrangement to be a fault that God will judge. Religion rests on these recognitions of a world apparently without meaning, a self divided against itself, and a personhood opposed to Deity. These combine with the crushing realization that God will judge people because people are responsible for that situation's existence. Divided against themselves, separated from a hostile world, judged by God, people find in this negative theophany one firm base of religion.

Religion's other base, however, is the hope for a reconciliation that overcomes estrangement. Although lived religious life especially reflects this hope, it is also evident in conscience. The basic dialectic of both religion and conscience is estrangement and a hope of reconciliation. Conscience pronounces both "that God exists [and] . . . that I am alienated from Him . . . that our iniquities have divided . . . us and our God."[32] This testimony terrifies by showing the possibility of just judgment. But it also heartens by testifying that a personal God exists and that his absence from the world arises from human not divine action. The external world testifies only either that no Creator exists or that he is uninterested in his creatures. Conscience, however, testifies that God exists and that his absence is explainable by human actions. Hope remains because a will other than God's has affected the world. Hope remains because there exists a powerful, personal being who is neither touched by nor responsible for the present estrangement and yet is unhappy with it. The two sides of conscience testify to the two parts of religion—a good, caring God yet one who judges; an awesome fear and a bright hope.

Humanity's possible freedom from estrangement is clearest in actual religious actions. Conscience testifies only that relief is possible, that a Power exists who could bring relief. Humanity's actual religious life, however, shows that the Power has given relief. The exact characteristics of this relief will be examined later, but Newman thinks that the wellspring of religious actions is hope. The sense of things received and to be received, the touch of reconciliation and the movement toward it, underlie religion. Although hope looks to the future's final alleviation of estrangement, it also rests on received benefits. Newman admits religion answers questions, overcomes difficulties, and solaces humanity. But, for him, this admission does not compromise religion's reality, it merely reflects religion's power. Religion lives because it gives life. Religion's existence is based on what it can and has given, all "religion . . . is a blessing."[33] Hope undergirds religion, even if hope always exists together with religion's severe aspect. Both aspects are needed for true religion to exist, but hope is the defining characteristic of religion. Hope makes religion religion.

Newman and Two Contemporary Theorists.   The implications of Newman's account of religion's two bases can be clarified by briefly relating it to the work of two theorists of religion—van der Leeuw and Eliade. The two pair nicely with Newman because van der Leeuw tends to emphasize the need and Eliade the gift. Moreover, Newman influenced van der Leeuw, while Eliade shares a similar concern about modern people's life in a desacralized cosmos. Van der Leeuw also sees two underlying elements to religion, calling them the given and the possible. As he puts it:

> Man . . . does not simply accept the world in which he lives: he also feels apprehensive about it; or expressed in religious terms, this means that the world *appears alien or strange* to him and

alarms him. . . . Man . . . does not . . . find himself at home therein: he experiences a foreignness that can all too readily deepen into dread or even into despair. He does not resignedly assent to the world given to him, but again and again says to it: "No!" This saying "No!" is indeed the very basis of his humanity; it proves that he has spirit: "Spirit is life which itself cutteth into life." In life, then, man sees far more than givenness: he perceives possibility also. But this possibility demands his activity. . . . His behavior, in other words, must accord with the Powerful which reveals itself to him.

Religion rests on humanity's unwillingness to accept the life given to it, on humanity always seeking new possibility and new power. Human beings can never rest with the given; they must always seek the possible.

The limit of human powerfulness . . . and the commencement of the divine, together constitute the goal which has been sought and found in the religion of all time;—*salvation* . . . religion is always directed towards salvation, never towards life itself as it is given; and in this respect all religion, with no exception, is the religion of deliverance.[34]

Eliade's two bases of religion are the sacred and the profane. He emphasizes that sacred power breaks into the ordinary world in hierophanies, kratophanies, and epiphanies. In these breakthroughs we are confronted by the same mysterious act: the manifestation of a wholly different order of existence in objects that remain part of our normal profane world. Such breakthroughs establish the sacred and the profane as "two modes of being in the world, two existential situations assumed by man in the course of history." "The *sacred* is equivalent to a *power,* and, in the last analysis, to *reality.*" Because the sacred, saturated with being, reveals an enduring, efficacious reality, the polarity of sacred and profane "is often expressed as an opposition between *real* and *unreal* or pseudoreal." The principal function of religion then is

that of maintaining an "opening" toward a world which is superhuman, the world of axiomatic spiritual values. These values are "transcendent" in the sense that they are revealed by divine beings or mythical ancestors. They therefore constitute absolute values, paradigms for all human activity. The function of religion is to awaken and sustain the consciousness of another world, of a "beyond." . . . This other world represents a superhuman "transcendent" plane, that of absolute realities. It is this experience of the sacred, that is, the meeting with a transhuman reality, that generates the idea of something which *really* exists and, in consequence, the notion that there are absolute, intangible values which confer a meaning upon human existence.[35]

Eliade emphasizes that gift of meaning which both establishes the shortcomings of normal life and furnishes the answer for them.

Both men see religion as constituted by two elements, the given and the possible, the sacred and the profane, or, in Newman's language, the severe and the hopeful. The former ideas are the base of religion, but the latter ideas generate the salvation that defines religion. The two sides are closely related, however; they are separated only for purposes of analysis. The severe and the relieving aspects always exist together; one exhibits the need for religion, the other offers the solace of religion. Recognizing this unity is especially important because Newman often stresses religion's dark side in order to exhibit the shortcoming of Liberal religion. Despite this emphasis, however, his full view shows the two sources as interdependent parts of the single whole that is religion.

The Five Characteristics of Religion

Providence.   We may now turn to Newman's examination of humanity's actual religious life, as it provides concrete manifestations of religion's relieving aspect.[36] Newman sees five attributes of such religious activity. He entitles them the principles—in phenomenological language, the types—of human religiosity. These five types specify hope's content by marking off religion's particular traits. (Newman actually calls hope a mark of religion, thereby expanding the list of marks from five to six. To clarify his account, I call it a source, as hope is more general than the other five marks.) Newman's explication of each type is brief, almost telegraphic, and the relations among them are left unclear. Nonetheless, through close attention to the text, reference to the rest of his work, and the utilization of contemporary comparativists' ideas, a most interesting scheme emerges.

The first type, providence, signifies the divine presence in the world. It is concretely specified by the second and third: prayer from the side of humanity, revelation from the side of God. These in turn lead to the two crucial if mysterious characteristics of religion—sacrifice and the mediating power of the holy person. Providence is that "interpretation to the course of things, by which every event or occurrence in its order becomes providential" through its manifestation of an unseen hand. In an earlier sermon, Newman says that before becoming religious, people "took things as they came, and thought no more of one thing than of another. But now every event has a meaning; they form their own estimate of whatever occurs; they recollect times and seasons; and the world, instead of being like the stream which the countryman gazed on, ever in motion and never in progress, is a various and complicated drama, with parts and with an object."[37] The providential view sees all particular events—whether personal, physical, political, religious, or social—as illustrations of divine governance.

Newman notes various kinds of providential activity, though he fails to separate them explicitly. The constant in these activities is the Divine presence, the variable is the specificity of divine actions. One kind encompasses the specific providential actions of a personal God or gods, actions such as causing miracles or effecting the rise and fall of kingdoms. Another kind sees providence as the divine structuring of things. The divine structuring, for instance, gives people natures that will bring happiness if the nature is followed and unhappiness if it is not followed. Since all people seek happiness, this divine structure affects how people will act. A final kind of providence refers to the divine's general presence, to the possibility of seeing the sacred in all things: "the successive passages of life, social or political, are [seen as] so many miracles, if that is to be accounted miraculous which brings before . . . [one] the immediate Divine Presence."[38]

The type providence contains certain ideas: the willed, particular actions of a personal Deity; a structure that brings destruction if flouted and fulfillment if followed; and a general presence of the divine. These distinctions help to clarify various types of religions or various movements inside a single religious tradition. For example, pre-Han Chinese religion moves from an emphasis on a willed providence (*T'ien ming*) to, on the one hand, a notion of a moral order that brings destruction if violated, and, on the other hand, a general sense of a divine presence that is either evident everywhere or particularly evident in certain rites. More generally, Newman's triadic breakdown can be directly correlated to van der Leeuw's notion of how Power's presence defines religion and how its different specifications—such as Form, Will, and Person—establish the basic types of religions.[39]

These variations within providence are important, but Newman's major point is that some sense of the divine presence is basic to the religious outlook. In the vocabulary of Rudolf Otto, a vocabulary often surprisingly close to Newman's, religion is defined by the presence of the Numinous—the mysterious, overwhelming, yet fascinating presence of the Holy. Indeed, Otto even argues, as Newman implies, that predestination exemplifies the Holy's presence by crystallizing the presence's main elements. Whether in Christianity, Islam, or forms of Buddhism and Hinduism, predestination preeminently manifests the sense of being acted upon rather than acting.[40] Religious people's concrete life, then, testifies that the sacred's continuing presence defines the religious perspective.

Prayer and Revelation.   The next two characteristics arise from the general divine presence that is providence: in prayer humanity speaks to the sacred; in revelation the sacred speaks to humanity. Newman uses "prayer" in the same general sense Heiler's *Prayer* does; that is, he includes under it, for instance, rite, sacred dance, and even worldly action.[41] Prayer, or perhaps more accurately worship, manifests the distinctive religious belief that relationships between humanity and divine power can exist. It relates directly to hope and providence: to providence because the sense of a divine presence underlies it, to hope because prayer testifies to either the possibility or the actuality of solace. Prayer or worship, then, stands for any human attempt to reach or recognize the divine presence. This attempt testifies to the belief that a fuller relationship with the divine is possible, that means exist by which interaction can occur so that relief can be mediated. Newman often speaks of prayer as the exercise of humanity's citizenship in a sphere beyond the disorder of this world. This citizenship at once constitutes the very pulse of the spiritual life and defines the new possibilities that religion generates.

The importance of worship in Newman's own understanding of religion can hardly be overestimated. His Anglican life is filled with attempts to elevate others' sense of sacramental action, and his Catholic writings often reflect an appreciation of what he saw as the extraordinary gifts the sacraments offered. Personal propensities and the study of religious phenomena both led to his affirming the centrality of worship in religion. The *Via Media* preface, for instance, makes theology the regulator of worship, the "act of our devotional nature," but it also emphasizes that "theology did not create it, but found it in our heart and used it."[42] Indeed, as we saw in examining religion's three expressions, worship is the particular expression of humanity's religiosity.

Such an emphasis harmonizes with modern views on the centrality of worship in religion. The attempt through worship to structure space and time, to give certain objects sacral significance, to surrender to or to receive power, to move into harmony with the ultimate, to use symbol, gesture, and sound to mirror or effect the sacred's presence—all are central to the lived reality of religion. Whatever worship's particular content, the activity itself usually represents that complex mixture of attitudes—adoration, fear, hope, celebration—that defines humanity's relation to the sacred. As Wach says, cult is important because it may be "defined as a *reaction* to the experience of Ultimate or Supreme Reality . . . [in which] a relationship or communion . . . is established by and through performance of the religious act."[43] Moreover, worship preeminently shows that embodiment of the sacred which is particularly important to Newman with his emphasis on the "real." Only such embodiments make possible relationships in which people's thinking, feeling, seeing, and acting can come together.

Revelation, the third type, presents a set of particularly complex ideas to which the later discussions of Liberal religion will return. Here we will note only: the definition's generality; revelation's defining "gift character"; its manifestation in real rather than notional objects; and its relation to mystery. All four aspects illustrate that this analysis arises from the phenomenological perspective of the receiving subject rather than from the philosophic or theological perspective of the divine who reveals. Newman's definition includes any idea, image, institution, or action that people recognize as coming from a source beyond themselves. Revelation is that "something" which people realize their own resources cannot generate. Revelation is exemplified not only in religious rites or sacred writings but also in, say, civil order or the wisdom of ancestors.[44] People's ascription of their civil polity to minor deities rather than to plebiscites and their subsequent attempt to protect the state by oracles reflect, for example, how the state is seen as a product of revelation. Similarly, traditional wisdom, with Confucianism as perhaps the clearest example, is a revelation, if its authoritative statements of truth are seen as undiscoverable by normal people. Revelation's key characteristic is that certain things are seen not as deductions of reason but as gifts received from a sacred source. Revelation and so religion has a gift character; it comes from without. Revelation grasps and makes a person rather than a person grasping or making it; understanding revelation is a meditation on the passive voice.

An obvious alternative to Newman's explanation of revelation is worth noting because it illustrates his phenomenological approach. This alternative argues that people projected to another realm ideas and actions which were in fact human creations. Such a hypothesis can devour almost any criticism because it articulates what must be, by its own standard, religious action's real meaning and motives. Newman, in contrast, just describes the fact that people have believed the only adequate descriptions of certain ideas was to call them revealed. In van der Leeuw's phrase, people believed "something has been done, or something has happened on the part" of the religious Object.[45] Newman's willingness just to describe people's testimony about revelation's gift character is set in stark relief by how this alternative explains revelation by calling it a human projection.

Another important point about revelation is that revelation produces traditions, rites, and persons, not propositional truths. The particular and the singular, not the abstract and the general, constitute revelation. "Revelation meets us with simple and distinct *facts* and *actions*"; all "revelation . . . relate[s] some course of action, some conduct."

Revelation exists in real objects; the notional arises only from reflection on the real. Revelation's basis in real objects leads directly to our final point, the interrelation of revelation and mystery. Revelation and mystery are complementary not contradictory ideas. In fact, one implies the other:

> No revelation can be complete and systematic, from the weakness of the human intellect; *so far as* it is not such, it is mysterious. When nothing is revealed, nothing is known, and there is nothing to contemplate or marvel at; but when something is revealed, and only something, for all cannot be, there are forthwith difficulties and perplexities. A Revelation is a religious doctrine viewed on its illuminated side, a Mystery is the selfsame doctrine viewed on the side unilluminated. Thus Religious Truth is neither light nor darkness, but both together; it is like the dim view of a country seen in the twilight, with forms half extricated from the darkness, with broken lines, and isolated masses . . . this way of considering it, is not a revealed *system,* but consists of a number of detached and incomplete truths belonging to a vast system unrevealed.[46]

Religious truth is "neither light nor darkness but both together," is "detached and incomplete," is based in an unknown matrix. All revelation's aspects—idea, rite, and community—are mysterious, though conversely all those mysteries contain some clarity. The known and the unknown are always intermingled in revelation.

Mystery's presence in revelation does not distress Newman because he believes anything that refers to the divine must necessarily contain mysteries if it is to manifest the divine truly. The "outward exhibition of infinitude is mystery . . . nothing else than the mode in which His infinitude encounters us and is brought home to our minds." In fact, if revelation is too clear, the divine is improperly mediated; "if there be mysteriousness in her [religion's] teaching, this does but show that she proceeds from Him, who is Himself Mystery."[47] Newman emphasizes that humanity is without clear religious knowledge. The battle for religious understanding is best imagined as a night battle. Rather than a clash at midday on a flat plain where the landscape is clear and the enemy evident, this battle is fought at night on a slippery hillside where footing is difficult and the darkness makes difficult the distinguishing of friend from foe. Revelation is a great aid, but humanity can have little clear knowledge of the divine. Newman's emphasis on revelation's "gift character," its real not notional nature, and its tie to mystery all show a noteworthy closeness to modern analyses of the category.

Sacrifice and the Mediatorial Power of Holy Persons.   Newman's fourth type is sacrifice, for him the most general and notable of those observances that arise from revelation and prayer. As a theological issue in Christianity sacrifice has caused much debate, but more important here, it is one of the most studied and least understood of all general religious phenomena.[48] Newman's idea of sacrifice is best understood by examining his belief that sacrifice concretely manifests the essential religious principle of mediation. Mediation is that action whereby warring or unrelated elements are reconciled through an intermediary. In the religious arena, sacrificial actions can mediate because certain sacrifices are ordained worthy, despite human frailty, by a higher and perhaps offended party. Indeed, the very ability to sacrifice represents the divine's mediating presence. Sacrifice is a divine manifestation of the means by which reconciliation can take place. As "a," perhaps "the," basic mediatorial relationship between the divine and humanity, sacrifice exemplifies the religious recognition that estrangement can be overcome.

Newman thinks religious sacrifice just exemplifies the basic law that guides all human relationships. Sacrifice rests on what Butler, whom Newman follows as "the great master of this doctrine," calls the principle of atonement. Social life rests on sacrifice. Bearing one another's burdens is the basic law of human relationship; making vicarious satisfaction and reparation is built into the fabric of all relationships. For example, mothers bear pain for their children or soldiers endure deprivation or death for their country. On the more specifically religious level, the divine either sacrifices itself or institutes forms of sacrifice that both ameliorate and explain all human suffering. The principle of mediation, the accepting of suffering and punishment for others, is the great alleviating principle that makes life both possible and valuable. Mediation's highest expression exists in religious sacrifice, where an object or the self is offered in a way that, having been proclaimed acceptable, brings reconciliation. Newman does not employ a simple "I give that thou may give" idea of sacrifice. Rather he employs a framework similar to van der Leeuw's. Humanity participates in a sacred cycle of giving and receiving that empowers a sacrificial community's reconciling relation to the sacred.[49]

Sacrifice attains its highest form when the sacrificial offering is rare and unblemished. That fact points to natural religion's last principle, the mediatorial power or meritorious intercession of the holy person. The perplexing ideas either that the sacrifice of the innocent for the guilty is appropriate or that only the purest sacrifice is worthy enough to effect the needed reconciliation appears in myriad contexts, ranging from the Bodhisattva's forgoing salvation to save others to the *Epistle to the Hebrews* describing salvation in the terminology of the high priest's sacrifice. Many kinds of holiness seem to demand a sacrifice of the self for the sake of the estranged; in fact, holiness often seems to include a drive to sacrifice. Holy people recognize the matrix of sacrifice by which humanity lives, and they place themselves completely within it by offering themselves for others.

This drive to sacrifice underlies the holy person's mediatorial power. These people function as signs of the divine's possible reconciliation with humanity. Normal people are drawn to a holy person's concrete representation of reconciliation. Holy people witness to what humanity can and ought to be, both as teachers giving verbal guidance and as examples drawing others by their power. Making concrete the essential hope that underlies religion, holy people mediate to others a vision of both the character and possibility of salvation. Such holy people also act, if in a less explicable manner, as direct intercessors; they "have influence with Him and extend a shelter and gain blessings for those who become their clients."[50] Their spiritual powers and their recognition of people's special needs allow them to serve as vehicles for the beneficent reconciliation.

In many ways, the mediatorial power of holy people sums up in personal form the various types of religion. They stand as concrete manifestations of religion's basic hope by embodying the divine power to reconcile. Moreover, their existence illustrates the divine's movement in the world, thereby reflecting providence and revelation. Finally, their action shows the power of prayer and the importance of sacrifice. The holiness and power present in the personal life of holy people is the summation and ultimate manifestations of religion's marks.

The centrality of the holy person to Newman's idea of religion is not unexpected, as his work resounds with an appreciation of the power of both the concrete and the personal. For example, his emphasis on the real as the wellspring of religion, his argument about the importance of the personal attributes of the divine, his recurrence to the Incarnation to focus Christianity's message, his stress on personal influence's role in propagating the truth. Other comparativists echo this emphasis on the role of personified holiness in religion. Jaspers argues for the centrality of what he calls the "paradigmatic individual," and even a work on the cult of the Jain religion declares that "experience tells us that nothing kindles the zeal of the faithful quite as much as the example of a great one . . . who serves as a paradigm for his endeavors . . . whom he venerates as master, and to whom he is dedicated with all the ardor of his heart."[51] The idea's importance is also exemplified by the previously mentioned description of the type "sacred personhood" that van der Leeuw develops. Indeed, van der Leeuw's analysis of the type "founder" casts a striking light on Newman. Van der Leeuw sees religion as consummated in that mediator "whose whole being is mediation, and who surrenders his own life as the 'means' for Power."⁵² Religions without an emphasis on holy people do exist. For example, some sophisticated forms of Buddhism consider any personification an impediment. Generally, however, concrete embodiments of mediation are central to religions and they function in something like the manner Newman describes. Their expression of a specific experience of Power, in van der Leeuw's phrase, or manifestation of the numinous, in Otto's phrase, or bearing of religious authority, in Wach's phrase, is critical.

The hope especially defining religion is, then, concretely specified in the five types that characterize natural religion. The first type, which is basic to the rest, is some more or less specific sense of the divine's presence. The next two manifest that presence particularly. Prayer shows humanity's relation to the divine; revelation shows the divine's gift of various aids to humanity. The last two manifest the special matrix of mediation that undergirds religion. All of sacrifice's various modes reflect mediation, but the highest exemplification is that intercession of holy people whose continuing sacrifice gives guidance, hope, and power to others. The types proceed from the abstract to the specific, from general ideas or attitudes to concrete particulars. On the most general level, providence's reference to the divine presence in the world specifies religion's basic mediation and hope. More particularly, prayer and revelation delineate that presence's two specific sides, while sacrifice and the intercession of holy people are the clearest manifestation of the concrete matrix of salvation. Together the five manifest concretely the available relief that characterizes actual religious life.

The five types specify the reconciliation that can overcome estrangement. Estrangement and reconciliation are religion's two sources. Estrangement is particularly evident in conscience. Here Newman's analysis, whatever its problems, can explain some people's experience of judgment and direction. Reconciliation is particularly evident in lived religious life. Newman thinks that all religions manifest themselves in specifiable ways. To reach this conclusion, he employs a phenomenological approach, describing what occurs and organizing his raw perceptions into intelligible forms by means of types. This approach is similar to that of the modern comparative study of religion, although Newman has both a greater apologetic aim and a more limited informational base than does that modern approach. For Newman, then, humans have a natural religious potential that can be either fulfilled or deformed. This idea sheds on his work a light different from that light provided by the traditional Christian idea of nature and grace. Examining the possible deformation or fulfillment of this potential is the subject of the following chapters.

2

Christianity: The Fulfillment Model

The Idea of Economy

Newman's view of Christianity's relationship to human religiosity—to natural religion, in his language—rests on his idea of how the divine makes itself present in the world. Divine action accommodates itself to the particular circumstances in which people exist and thereby takes different forms at different places and times. In developing this image, Newman employs the idea of economy, an idea developed by the Patristics to describe the manner of God's governance. Economy arises from the notion of "economic" political administration, governance that prudentially executes a plan intended to bring proper goods to the state's subjects. A ruler's economic actions prudentially accommodate an abstract plan to the recipient's concrete situation. Using this notion of economical rule to explain God's action can, for example, help explain the existence of human pain (the ruler must sometimes be severe in helping his people reach their ultimate good) or the apparent absence of clear-cut directives (the ruler must never infringe on his subject's free choice by making the correct path too evident).[1]

Especially important here, economical actions help explain the relations among religions. The Patristic period resembles the nineteenth century insofar as for both eras an important issue is the relation of Christianity to positions that resemble natural and Liberal religion. As with some Patristics, Newman argues both that any revelation is economic and that all religions reflect a general economic revelation. Divine revelation's mode is economic and universal. Such an analysis moves us into theological areas because Newman focuses on divine activity. In our previous discussion he focused on human religious activity, and his method was phenomenological not theological.

Newman often expresses the economic character of revelation by pointing to how ideas are communicated, especially when teaching the young:

Children . . . are taught, by an accommodation, on the part of their teachers, to their immature faculties and their scanty vocabulary. To answer their questions in the language which we should use towards grown men, would be simply to mislead them, if they could construe it at all. We must dispense and "divide" the word of truth, if we would not have it changed, as far as they are concerned, into a word of falsehood; for what is short of truth in the letter may be to them the most perfect truth, that is, the nearest approach to truth, compatible with their condition.

The need for economic representation is particularly clear in this example. But any communication of significant ideas has a similar character because the "cognitive method . . . of one man is notoriously very different from that of another . . . [as] abstractions, generalizations, definitions, propositions, all are framed on distinct standards." Economies are necessary bridges because people "seem ever to be dodging each other, and need a common measure or economy to mediate between them." Communication can occur only if some "common measure or economy" mediates between people's different principles, cognitive methods, and vocabularies. Economy exemplifies, then, a normal element in human understanding: "the receiving of the truth only in as full a measure as our minds can admit it." We always see "the truth . . . under the conditions of thought which human feebleness imposes," and we are "obliged to receive information needful to us, through the medium of our existing ideas, and consequently with but a vague apprehension of its subject-matter."[2]

This idea finds a religious exemplification in the *disciplina arcani* or secret teaching. The phrase arose in the seventeenth century, but it refers to the Patristic way of teaching Christianity to nonbelievers or initiates. Christian ideas were formed so as to accord with the listeners' perspective; if necessary, ideas that were bound to be misunderstood were even concealed. Kingsley cites the *disciplina arcani* as evidence for the duplicity of Newman and all Roman clergy. Newman responds that the idea merely reflects how any communication must be conditioned by the situation of the recipient. Newman argues that any sensitive teacher must, however unconsciously, adjust the message to the resources and abilities of the listeners. The teacher must take those images and ideas that are most suitable and employ a "cautious dispensation of the truth, after the manner of a discrete and vigilant steward."[3] A good teacher, for example, always uses examples familiar to the listeners to communicate the meaning. The secret teaching, then, just reflects an accommodation to the general ideas, feelings, and prejudices of the hearers in order to facilitate their understanding of novel ideas. Newman's acceptance of this accommodation has wide implications; it influenced, for instance, the mode of many of his later writings. Most important here, however, is Newman's argument that the secret teaching reflects the character of all revelation.

The secret teaching works only because revelation is universal. The normal teacher can work from the student's experience because it contains, however inchoately, analogues of what is to be conveyed. Similarly, the secret teaching works because the recipient's religious experience contains, however inchoately, analogues to what Christianity conveys. Precisely because a general revelation exists, the secret teaching can function. As Newman says, "the elementary information given to the heathen or catechumen was *in no sense undone* by the subsequent secret teaching, which was in fact but the *filling up of a bare but correct outline*."[4]

The secret teaching's effectiveness relies on the non-Christian standing within a general economy of revelation. Generally put, there were

> various Economies of Dispensations of the Eternal. . . . Nature was a parable: Scripture was an allegory: pagan literature, philosophy, and mythology, properly understood, were but a preparation for the Gospel. The Greek poets and sages were in a certain sense prophets; for "thoughts beyond their thoughts to those high bards were given." There had been a directly divine dispensation granted to the Jews; but there had been in some sense a dispensation carried on in favor of the Gentiles. . . . In the fulness of time both Judaism and Paganism had come to nought; the outward framework, which concealed yet suggested the Living Truth, had never been intended to last, and it was dissolving under the beams of the Sun of Justice which shone behind it and through it. The process of change had been slow . . . till the whole evangelical doctrine was brought into full manifestation.[5]

The fulfillment of these various economies in Christianity is the subject of this and the following chapters, but for now the point to be made is that a general revelation exists.

Newman often calls this general revelation the "divinity of Traditionary Religions" or the "dispensation of paganism." "All knowledge of religion is from Him, and not only that which the Bible has transmitted to us. There never was a time when God had not spoken to man, and told him to a certain extent his duty. . . . It would seem, then, that there is something true and divinely revealed, in every religion all over the earth . . . [so] Revelation, properly speaking, is an universal, not a local gift." This dispensation arises in part from reflection on conscience, but something beyond conscience is also evident. For example, all people "have more or less the guidance of Tradition, in addition to those internal notions of right and wrong which the Spirit has put into the heart of each individual"; all general truths "have been secretly re-animated and enforced by new communications from the unseen world." All these various religions stand within a general economic revelation. Therefore, "there may have been heathen poets and sages, or sibyls again, in a certain extent divinely illuminated, . . . [who existed as the] organs through whom religious and moral truth was conveyed to their countrymen"; indeed "the Sacrifice, which is the hope of Christians, has its power and its success wherever men seek God with their whole heart."[6]

The generality of revelation means pagans have a revelation; indeed, "pagans may have, heretics cannot have, the same principles as Catholics."

> The prerogative of Christians consists in the possession, not of exclusive knowledge and spiritual aid, but of gifts high and peculiar; and though the manifestation of the Divine character in the Incarnation is a singular and inestimable benefit, yet its absence is supplied in a degree . . . with more or less strength, as the case may be, in those various traditions concerning Divine Providences and Dispensations which are scattered through the heathen mythologies.

Christianity is "recovering and purifying, rather than reversing the essential principles of their belief . . . [for their] infidelity is a positive, not a negative state." Newman even goes so far as to say that pagans are to be seen "not as men in a state of actual perdition, but as being in imminent danger of 'the wrath to come,' because they are in bondage and ignorance, and probably under God's displeasure, that is, the vast majority of them are so in fact; but not necessarily so, from the very circumstance of their being heathen."[7] The notion of economic communication, as that is applied to revelation and leads to an idea of universal revelation, undergirds Newman's views on how Christianity completes natural religion.

Newman's notion of economic preparation and fulfillment contains both a "chronological" and a "phenomenological" aspect, although he never clearly distinguishes them.[8] Chronological preparation focuses on the historical evolution of religious beliefs. For example, certain religious practices first occurring in 1000 B.C. find their fulfillment in other religious practices introduced in A.D. 40. This view contains both historical and theological elements: historically one needs to show causal connections between the early manifestations and their later fulfillment; theologically, one must show God as a teacher slowly giving human beings ideas fitted to their maturity until he finally presents them with the full truth. A teaching that starts with accommodations ends by presenting "what is, as it is."

This chronological view stands or falls on the cogency of its exhibition of historical relations and the adequacy of its theological idea that God's message is clear now that economic accommodations are no longer in effect. By granting the theological idea and tracing out the developments of certain religions in the Ancient Near East, a case can be made for a chronological, preparatory process that culminates in Christianity. But the position's problems are significant: Is it theologically cogent to speak of a "noneconomic" revelation? Can one trace, much less prove, the needed historical connections? Is not the whole idea restricted to religion's having causal connections?

When working from this chronological view, Newman either crashes on the above rocks or, at best, flounders in the turbulent waters they create. Newman, for example, sees all revelation as economic, as always involving some accommodation to circumstances. Moreover, while he gives a subtle account of how, in the abstract, historical connections may be shown, the application of that account is often less than satisfactory, as the *Grammar*'s treatment of fulfillment shows. Finally, the restriction of fulfillment to religions that are causally connected generates serious problems, even if one overlooks all those religions Newman leaves out. Ancient Judaism and its direct competitors present no problems, but Islam and even Greek, Roman, or other "pagan" religions present almost insuperable difficulties. They either postdate Christianity or have little contact with it.

The idea of "phenomenological preparation" does not have these problems. It depends only on the idea that certain general religious phenomena can be viewed as having been fulfilled in other religious phenomena, whatever their historical connections may be. The meaning or aim of certain religious ideas may be said to find phenomenological fulfillment in another religion's ideas whether the first phenomenon comes before or after the second or is ever even in contact with it. For example, a religion may focus on the sacrificial intercession of a holy person. If no historical connection to Christianity exists, chronological fulfillment is impossible, but phenomenological fulfillment can be argued for.

Newman fails to distinguish the two perspectives because of the intellectual climate in which he lived. Moreover, he worked with Ancient Near Eastern and Hellenistic religions where the two perspectives may easily be muddled. The perspectives are separated in this book, however. Phenomenological preparation is concentrated on, as it is both considerably less fragile and considerably more interesting than chronological preparation. In focusing this way our analysis moves from the study of the relationship of a theology and a history (Christian theology and Western history) to the study of a theology, Christian theology, and the comparative study of religion.

The Models of Christianity's Relationship to Natural Religion

The basic models of the relation between natural religion and Christianity that arise from the idea of phenomenological preparation are the "fulfillment model" and the "authority model." The fulfillment model stresses that Christianity perfects all aspects of natural religiosity; the authority model stresses that the new kind of authority evident in Christianity is fulfillment's most distinctive mark. The authority model represents, of course, a specific kind of fulfillment, but utilizing two models clarifies the analysis. Moreover, the two models represent distinct strands in Newman's thought. The fulfillment model is flexible, subject-centered, and irenic. The authority model is formal, object-centered, and divisive. The remainder of this chapter analyzes the fulfillment model while the next chapter analyzes the authority model. First, however, we will look at some other models of the relation between natural religion and Christianity, both for the sake of completeness and for the reason that Newman or his interpreters often give them a prominent place.

The other models may be dealt with briefly, as they are based on terminological ambiguities, are criticized by Newman himself, or have their integral aspects developed by our primary models. These models usually arise from Newman's loose, often polemical, use of the word "natural." This use clouds the distinction between natural and Liberal religion. In one model the relation between natural and revealed religion focuses on natural religion's worthlessness. For example, sermon notes from 1859 speak of natural religion's basis in sight and reason and revealed religion's basis in faith. In like manner, if now in full polemical garb, a sermon declares "the religion of the natural man in every age and place—often very beautiful on the surface but worthless in God's sight; good as far as it goes, but worthless and hopeless because it does not go farther, because it is based on self-sufficiency and results in self-satisfaction."[9] The model is clearly inadequate in light both of Newman's mature work on religion and of his early work on the divine witness of conscience and the dispensation of paganism.

Another model draws the distinction between natural and revealed religion in terms of the difference between a personal and an impersonal deity. As an early *Oxford University Sermon* says, natural religion gives no information about God's personality. Based only in abstract ideas, it relates humanity to a divine principle not a divine agent and so contains no true picture either of deity or of the power of revealed religion.[10] A later edition of the *Sermons* corrects this idea, declaring it too strong and noting it is inconsistent both with the later ideas of the *Grammar* and even with the sixth of the *Oxford Sermons.* The correction was generated by Newman's realization that natural religion's basis in conscience meant divine personhood must be evident, but another reason for the change is his analysis of religious types such as providence and a personal mediator. Here again the problem is Newman's failure to distinguish natural and Liberal religion. The personal/impersonal dichotomy is important for the relation of Liberal and revealed religion. Although Newman rejects this model, the tendency to link natural and Liberal religion together by saying both have an impersonal deity will appear in his later works, if in muted form.

A final model is stated most concisely in the *Grammar,* where Newman says that "Revelation begins where Natural Religion fails . . . Natural Religion is based upon the sense of sin; it recognizes the disease, but it cannot find, it does but look out for the remedy. That remedy, both for guilt and for moral impotence, is found in the central doctrine of Revelation, the Mediation of Christ."[11] The oversimplicity of this statement makes it inadequate. By saying natural religion consists solely in people's recognition of their estrangement, this model touches only one of natural religion's two foundations. It leaves out both the hope and the actual alleviation that is mediated. Natural religion does more than just "look out for the remedy"; it contains a remedy—a remedy that some may have found sufficient. Indeed, religion to be religion must not only contain a recognition of the disease but also an offer of the cure. Here, as with the other two models, Newman relates natural and revealed religions by means of the idea of absence and possession rather than by means of the more subtle idea of partial and complete possession. Interestingly enough, this model occurs in that section in the *Grammar* which undercuts its overly simple view. This is striking evidence of Newman's occasional failure to grasp or at least follow out the implications of his own thought.

The simple disjunction emphasized in these models is replaced in the fulfillment model by an emphasis on how Christian revelation completes all the aspects of natural religiosity. In a particularly evocative presentation of that idea Newman writes, "the life of Christ brings together and concentrates truths concerning the chief good and the laws of our being, which wander idle and forlorn over the surface of the moral world, and often appear to diverge from each other. It collects the scattered rays of light, which, in the first days of creation, were poured over the whole face of nature, into certain intelligible centres, in the firmament of the heaven."[12] The controlling ideas in the fulfillment model are completion, collection, fullness, and actualization. Rather than validating Christianity by contrasting it with the worthlessness of natural religion, the model achieves the validation by recognizing natural religion's worth but emphasizing Christianity's still higher actualization.

The Fulfillment of Natural Religion's Characteristics

We will begin our analysis of the fulfillment model with a brief examination of how Newman's analysis of natural religiosity can be seen as fulfilled in Christianity. Then we will relate the model to the general framework of the *Development of Doctrine,* particularly its notion of assimilation. Finally, we will examine three specific examples of completion: the reference of everything to a single transcendent center; the unification of the divisions of the notional and the real made possible by the Incarnation; and the addition of a new sacral power.[13]

Christianity's fulfillment of natural religion can be illustrated by examining how Christianity can be said to fulfill each of natural religion's five characteristics of providence, prayer, revelation, sacrifice, and the mediatorial power of the holy person. To highlight the fulfillment, we will also briefly note how Liberal religion can be said to distort natural religiosity. Each category of natural religion, in Newman's view, starts from a natural phenomenon and rises to more and more profound religious exemplifications. This progress illustrates how religion originates in normal life and finds fulfillment in Christianity.

The hope of benefits, one source of religion, starts from those normal goods, like earthly beauty, that alleviate human misery. When seen from a religious perspective, however, an act such as the appreciation of natural beauty acquires greater significance as that beauty is thought to reflect deity's beauty and beneficence. Religious rites focus such religious perceptions of natural goods. For instance, food's nourishing power and water's cleansing ability acquire a fuller meaning in the Christian rituals of the Eucharist and Baptism. Nourishing and cleansing are now seen as done by higher forces.

Finally, however, religious hope relies not on those alleviations brought by natural goods but on a reconciliation with that Power who can alleviate human distress completely. Providence, sacrifice, and revelation express a greater hope than any natural goods can offer. Indeed, religious hope may even demand the rejection of natural goods, as when food or family are surrendered in fasting or celibacy. Religion introduces both a deepened appreciation of natural goods and reasons to reject them.

Christianity, for Newman, most clearly manifests the relationship of natural and religious hope. The notions of a creator God and of an Incarnate Lord show how Christianity both fulfills natural hope and yet points beyond it. The creator God made the world yet stands distinct from it, while the Incarnate Lord took up earthly values and yet died to a new life. Liberal religion, on the other hand, only recognizes natural goods and fails to infuse them with religious meaning. More significantly, it fails to see that only the divine can finally sustain hope.

Providence, the first specific mark of natural religion, also exhibits this hierarchy that starts from natural phenomena and rises to higher religious exemplifications. It starts by perceiving a moral order which brings happiness if followed, then moves to seeing a general divine presence in the world, and ends by recognizing a divine will active in particular situations. Christianity, in Newman's eyes, places all these elements in the appropriate hierarchy. Christianity views general order, especially its moral aspect, as arising from God; it maintains, particularly through its sacramental theory, a sense of the divine presence in the world; and finally it recognizes the specific will of God. Liberal religion, on the other hand, fails to reflect even providence's moral aspect. Its morality rests on the self rather than on a divinely grounded moral order. Moreover, its notion of a distant, impersonal deity allows for only a faint divine presence, opposing completely any idea of particular, willed actions of deity. The hierarchy within providence finds in Christianity an exemplification as clear as the deformation it finds in Liberal religion.

Prayer's natural characteristics are evident in those supplications, invocations, and thanksgivings that inchoately arise in human beings. Normal life manifests people's sense of inadequacy and their need to invoke or thank powers beyond themselves. The levels of prayer are fixed by the object's value (e.g., the difference between deity and the state) and the response's selflessness (e.g., the difference between "I want" and "what you will is what I want"). Prayer's character depends on what is aimed toward. Petition to or adoration of a friend, the community, or a limited deity is partial when compared with the worship aimed toward a transcendent Creator. The object's status also affects the prayer's form. Prayer to the Creator, for example, ought to be adoration not petition, given the Creator's knowledge and power. Prayer is perfected, then, when people relate not to lesser arbiters but to the final transcendent Arbiter. Liberal religion accepts prayer in its lowest form, the petition of or thanks to people or community. But it totally opposes the higher forms, saying that people ought to shun prayer and take control of their own lives. For Liberal religion, prayer denies people's ability to help themselves and leads to superstition. Christianity, however, not only validates the spontaneous impulse underlying prayer but also perfects it by revealing the character and receptivity of prayer's highest goal. Moreover, the Christian worshiping community, both alive and dead, widens the matrix in which prayer moves.

The third mark, revelation, also grows from a natural base. At the lowest level, it refers to any idea or action that so exceeds human abilities as to need explanation as a gift. At this level it covers, for example, an inspired artistic production or a remarkably workable political constitution. From here the hierarchy rises to those ideas and actions that mediate a reconciliation beyond that contained in a political constitution or the insights of a work of art. For Newman the final consummation is Christian revelation, whose content both makes its gift character explicit and exhibits a comprehensive reconciliation. Liberal religion rejects the notion of gifts to humanity. Cultic activity, for instance, is seen as a questionable focus of human energy at best and as a debilitating superstition at worst.

The fourth mark, sacrifice, has a clear natural base—man's suffering for man undergirds all social life. This base attains higher forms in the sacrificial rites found in all religions, but it reaches perfection in the sacrifice of Christ that is theoretically expressed in the Atonement and ritually expressed in the Mass. A continuity exists between soldiers who sacrifice themselves for some people and Christ who sacrifices himself for all people, but Christianity completes the notion of sacrificial intercession by widening its scope to include the living and the dead as well as the divine and the human. Christ's sacrifice is manifested in a variety of ways: the deed itself, the words of Scripture, the ritual of the Mass, and the spirit-imbued actions of individual Christians. The sacrifice's scope and direct relationship with deity make it the highest sign of that hope, that calming and alleviation of conscience, which religion effects. Liberal religion, on the other hand, fails even to recognize that society is built on self-sacrifice. Unable to affirm even the natural quality of sacrifice, it also lacks the notions of a personal deity or of a revealed means of reconciliation. For Liberal religion, sacrifice is a meaningless or superstitious act.

The natural basis of the mediating power of holy people is evident in the ability of human beings to affect other people's ideas, attitudes, and actions more effectively than do abstract ideas. People mediate to other people a reconciliation with themselves and their worlds that ideas alone cannot generate. Religion too must be mediated by people because only people can make evident religion's full power and mystery. Liberal religion, however, replaces personal influence with abstract ideas; it denies the essential role personal mediation plays in religion. It thereby overlooks the personal force that alone can motivate humanity and thus mediate salvation. It thereby also denies the mysterious element in religious manifestations; although a person's existence is always cloaked in mystery, ideas must be clear to be effective. Finally, it thereby rejects the possibility of a particular revelation, which revelation by a person must always be, favoring instead conclusions that are binding because they are general. Christianity, however, affirms and completes the centrality of personal mediation. For Newman, then, each aspect of natural religion can be seen as fulfilled in Christianity and deformed by Liberal religion.

The Fulfillment Model as Seen through the Framework of the Development of Doctrine

Another way to look at Newman's fulfillment model is through the general framework provided by the *Development of Doctrine*. One of that book's central ideas, assimilation, illustrates how Christianity relates to the various elements of other religions. By examining assimilation we can see how the fulfillment model works. Such an analysis poses questions that the *Development* itself does not directly answer and thereby saves us from entering the maelstrom enveloping the interpretation of that work. Nevertheless, we must briefly note the work's overall purpose.

The *Development* is a historical investigation that attempts to prove a theological point. The investigation starts from the idea that Christianity has existed long enough to be dealt with as a historical fact having definite characteristics. Examination of Christianity, Newman thinks, shows that developments, which are to be expected, do occur; that an infallible authority able to distinguish developments from corruptions, which is to be expected, does arise; and that criteria for distinguishing genuine developments and thus validating authority's judgments are identifiable. In the *Development,* Newman writes not only as a historian but also as a theologian and as an apologist. He wants to show that Christianity has undergone changes that are neither corruptions of its original essence nor evidence that no such essence exists.

This position is one of several options operative in Newman's time. The "orthodox Protestant" position argues Christianity's basic revelation has been corrupted by pagan or man-made additions, such as Purgatory, the cult of Mary, and the five extra sacraments. The "orthodox Catholic" position works from the premise that the existence of real change validates the Protestant positions. This position, therefore, sees changes only as part of a logical process that makes explicit the implicit. The "Liberal Protestant" position takes two forms. The less viable of these two is akin to its orthodox heritage in seeing later additions as corruptions. If focuses, however, on Christ as simply a teacher. In Harnack's phrase, it distinguishes (in an indefensible way) between what Christ said—e.g., the Sermon on the Mount—and what was said about Him—e.g., "He was resurrected." The second form, clearly the most significant alternative to Newman, argues that revelation is an ambiguous event which each age interprets in terms of its own ideas. In Coleridge's phrase, Christianity is whatever any age sees as the ideal of the human soul. No substantive center exists; each age just turns to the event of revelation and interprets it by means of the current intellectual framework. For example, one age thinks in terms of incarnate gods, another in terms of the legal relations of propitiation, still another in terms of teachings. Arguing against all these positions, arguing that Christianity has an essence yet one which has developed, is the task of the *Development*.[14]

Such is Newman's overall problem. Our specific concern is with but one small aspect of it: the fact that Christianity at least reflects and perhaps incorporates aspects of natural religion. A variety of ideas and actions—such as mediator deities, celibacy, sacerdotal orders, and ritual worship—appear in other religions, often before they appear in Christianity. Such parallels bring up the question of the relationship between the two religions, and Newman's answers show certain of his ideas about the overall relationship of Christianity to natural religion. We must, however, emphasize that the *Development* focuses mainly on the "chronological" question, while we will focus on the "phenomenological" question.

One possible answer is that Christianity has been "substantially modified and changed, that is, corrupted, from the first, by the numberless influences to which it has been exposed."[15] Newman calls this the Protestant view and makes it his specific target in the *Development*. This view argues that the original revelation has been distorted by additions from paganism, so that recovering true Christianity involves stripping away its false additions. The Christian revelation is unique, nothing even harmonious with it exists elsewhere. If a practice or idea is found in paganism, its revelatory character is precluded. This perspective's major premise is that natural and revealed religion are so fundamentally distinct that any mixing can lead only to the corruption of the higher religion. Revelation cannot complete, it rather must destroy natural religion.

Two other positions both deny the fundamental difference between natural and revealed religion, arguing that the two mix because they are without distinguishing characteristics. The two positions differ only on whether such a mixture is caused by deity or is the result of human skill. Newman saw these two positions manifested in early movements in the Church (in what he called the Eclectic sect and the heresy of Neologism), but he believed they represented enduring movements that had modern counterparts like Liberal Christianity.[16] Newman recognizes this perspective is an attractive, viable way to view Christianity. Indeed, any religion may be seen as a combination of various elements from different traditions.

Newman's own view tries to steer between the Scylla of a totally distinctive Christian revelation and the Charybdis of a single, general revelation. He tries to hold a middle course between affirming either an absolute difference between or a complete similarity of "natural" and "revealed" religion by arguing that Christian revelation is distinctive and at the same time "various, complex, progressive, and supplemental of itself."[17] His answer is organized around the notion of assimilation or unitive power.

Assimilation refers to the incorporation or absorption of external elements. It can connote processes ranging from the physiological absorption of food to the sociological adaptation of various cultural traits into a new environment. Newman focuses on assimilation as the ability to receive, purify, and incorporate disparate elements around a new center, as the ability to meet apparently foreign objects and transform them into harmonious additions. As a growing power, assimilation relates to chronic vigor, another mark of development. Chronic vigor is the life force that moves into, lives from, and grows out of apparently hostile situations. Chronic vigor highlights assimilation's ability to bring together apparently disparate or contradictory elements. For instance, Christianity's ability to bear "principles or doctrines, which in other systems of religion quickly degenerate into fanaticism or infidelity."[18]

Assimilation refers then to that growing power which composes divergent elements around a new center. It is exemplified in proper human maturation where self-expansion incorporates new attributes in a way that does not derange the self but rather builds a stronger, more variegated self. Conversely, that process's failure, immaturity, is the inability either to expand the self or to do so without dislocation. Immaturity is the inability to both grow and stay one. Immature people must safeguard themselves from new influences and thereby risk narrowness and inflexibility. Human development exemplifies that general process whereby a vital center can incorporate distinct but potentially harmonious elements, rejecting only what is absolutely incompatible.

The analogy with personal assimilation is helpful but it falters if pushed too far because Christianity's center is more stable than any individual's center. This problem reflects one pitfall inherent in reading the *Development* solely in terms of Newman's psychological work. Newman does argue, as when he discusses the indefectibility of certitude, that continuities underlie the apparent changes in men, but clearly a person's vital center can change in a way Christianity's center cannot.[19]

The ideas of "type" and the "classical" are especially important to Newman's argument here. "Type" is employed to distinguish apparent from real failures of assimilation. Assimilation does fail when a type is destroyed by what is incorporated, but enormous changes may occur that only modify the type. Assimilation must be judged, then, by whether the type is preserved. That judgment is a difficult one, given how types may endure through significant changes, but the comparativist's notion of the "classical" helps.

In studying various religions, the comparativist attempts to articulate those essential characteristics that define a religion's historical existence. They say, for example, that early Theravada Buddhism is this, medieval Catholicism that, pre-Han Confucianism this. The modes of identification can differ; for example, the religion's single generating principle or its answer to the question of the *telos* of existence. The most enlightening, however, is Wach's notion of the "classical." He defines it as "paradoxically, a *relative norm* which does not need to do violence to heterogeneous phenomena from a preconceived point of view."[20] The classical conveys something more than an individual instance. It focuses on something that is especially illuminating or paradigmatic, though always seeing that something as a heuristic concept open to correction in time. This identification of some critical, stable elements in the diversity and flux of a religion makes possible an appraisal of that religion's similarities with, and differences from, other religions. From this perspective, Newman attempts to articulate the classical elements in Christianity. He tries to show how certain elements have endured through apparent changes and then to exhibit how they relate to the classical elements of other religions. His desire to validate the truth of "classic" Christianity does differentiate him from the comparativist's approach, of course.

The ideas of assimilation, chronic vigor, preserved type, and the classical combine with ideas on the divine economy and on natural religion, to allow Newman to see Christianity as incorporating various elements of natural religion around its center. Against the Protestant's disjunction of the Christian revelation from natural religion, he argues for a fulfillment that maintains and even aids Christianity, while purifying natural religion. Against the syncretists, he argues that an enduring center exists in Christianity, around which divergent elements are organized. Foreign ideas and practices can then be accepted through an assimilative process that transforms them by organizing them around a new center. Indeed, even alien elements can be so transformed. For example, the notion of demonic creator gods cannot coalesce with the Christian idea of an omnipotent deity, but it can be assimilated into a lower world. That shift preserves those gods but transforms their status and meaning. Assimilative incorporation illustrates, then, how Christianity accepts and completes natural religion.

Three Examples of Fulfillment

The Reference to a Single Source.   Having considered the general meaning of assimilation, we can now turn to three examples that exhibit Christianity's fulfillment of natural religion. In the first, the fulfillment takes place because everything is referred to a single center, God. In the second, the Incarnation, as a concrete focus, generates a unity that completes natural religion's divisions, particularly the division between the notional and the real. In the third, the completion comes through the addition of a new divine power. (Though overly speculative analogies can be misleading rather than helpful, those three examples do mirror the Trinity. The first focuses on God, the second on the Son, and the third on the Holy Spirit, though all finally refer to one unified entity.)

The first example argues that though God has never been without witness, God now fulfills previous witness by referring "all truth and revelation to one source, and that the Supreme and Only God." The various ideas, actions, and institutions of paganism are completed by relating them to their one ultimate source. Christianity's organization of everything around the notion of a transcendent, creator God "succeeded in thus rejecting evil without sacrificing the good, and in holding together in one things which in all other schools are incompatible."[21] Christian fullness consists in accepting various pagan ideas, while its uniqueness consists in relating all of them to a new center. The idea is put in various ways by Newman, but let us begin our analysis by examining the idea of a deity who is both transcendent and a creator, and then we can turn to some examples.

The notion of a transcendent, creator God attempts to harmonize the apparently disparate ideas of divine immanence and divine transcendence. Using classical religion as his reference point, Newman thinks natural religion emphasizes either a plurality of immanent deities or a transcendent but disinterested or at least unreachable deity.

Christianity, however, offers a deity who is both transcendent and immanent, indeed one who can be fully immanent because he is so transcendent. In Scholastic terminology, God gives himself his own existence and thereby transcends all else which receives its existence from him. Yet God must also be immanent in the created world as without his presence the world would cease to exist. Deity is totally distinct from and transcendent to the world, yet also the immanent creator and support of it. In the terminology of Eric Voegelin, Christianity fulfills classical religion by overcoming a cosmological mode of experience and symbolization. The sacrality of order symbolized by classical religion's intra-cosmic gods is fulfilled by the Gospel's Unknown God, who is transcendent to all yet immanent in the "in between" of existence. This shift charges history and human consciousness with a new meaning as well as causing them to point beyond themselves.[22]

This abstract idea has specific consequences that can be seen as concrete illustrations of Christianity's fulfillment. For example, political or agricultural deities are recognized, but they are no longer seen as completely independent entities demanding special honors and propitiations. These deities now only reflect the power and purposes of a higher deity. Divergent sources of power remain, but their status is altered by their new position beneath a transcendent, omnipotent deity. The mysterious, forceful presence of the state, for instance, is still recognized, but it now is seen as only a limited reality. The recognition that superhuman "principalities and powers" work through life remains, but that recognition is transformed by the relation of everything to a single source.

Another example is the view of the natural world. The malignancy of the natural world and the need to escape from it are widespread notions in some classical religions; indeed, they are prominent motifs in many other religions. Viewing the human body as a prison for the human spirit means that the spirit is freed only by harsh ascetical practices that destroy urges for such things as food, sex, and physical comfort. Christianity recognizes the truth in such a view. Spiritual and material needs may often conflict. Physical pain or fatigue, for instance, may impede the desire or ability to pray, contemplate, or love. But the original idea is transformed by the affirmation that the material world is created by deity and therefore is fundamentally good. The attitude toward the body, for instance, changes; it is now also seen as a good given by God. Ascetic discipline remains, but the body's essential goodness is also upheld. The need to discipline the body is upheld because of God's transcendence, the need to value it because of God's immanence. This complex Christian attitude to the body is exemplified in Newman's seeing both asceticism and the sanctification of matter as

Christian principles. That attitude fulfills natural religion. Indeed, by harmonizing both acceptance and rejection, it fulfills both the "ascetic" and the "hedonistic" sides of natural religion—the "under" and "over" valuing of the body.

The list of particular instances of fulfillment could be extended to great length, but only two more particularly illuminating examples will be noted. Various personal mediators are important to natural religion as they are the accessible manifestations of divine reconciliation. These various mediators are assimilated by means of the idea of a communion of saints that surrounds deity. Particular personal intercessors remain, but their function and force are transformed because they now refer to and receive power from a single source. In similar fashion, the various rites of natural religion are assimilated into Christian ritual life, yet they are changed by being referred to a single mediator deity. For example, entrance into and departure from the religious community are purified and unified by being referred to a single deity. The distinct truths and actions of natural religion find their completion by being organized around the new focus of a single ultimate source.

The Unification of Natural Religion's Division between the Notional and the Real.   The second example of the fulfillment rests on Christianity's possession of a concrete focus that can harmonize conflicting elements in natural religion. We have already seen how certain apparently contrary ideas—e.g., honoring yet disciplining the body—may be unified by relating everything to an ultimate source. Here, however, Newman focuses on the basic polarity of the notional and the real, arguing that they can be harmonized only by the Incarnation. The issue is clearly set in an early Oxford sermon, "The Influence of Natural and Revealed Religion Respectively." This sermon tests the practical efficacy of the two religions in the laboratory of classical history. Newman affirms the saving knowledge found in the dispensation of paganism. He even says:

> it may be even questioned whether there be any essential character of Scripture doctrine which is without its place in this moral revelation. For here is the belief in a principle exterior to the mind to which it is instinctively drawn, infinitely exalted, perfect, incomprehensible; here is the surmise of a judgment to come; the knowledge of unbounded benevolence, wisdom, and power, as traced in the visible creation, and of moral laws unlimited in their operation; further, there is even something of hope respecting the availableness of repentance, so far (that is) as suffices for religious support; lastly, there is an insight into the rule of duty, increasing with the earnestness with which obedience to the rule is cultivated.

The problem in such religion is not content but efficacy. Determining efficacy involves answering some complex factual and philosophic questions. For example, did Christianity effect certain changes, and why are these changes seen as advancements? Did it, for instance, actually generate improvement in society, and by what criteria does one label certain changes as improvements? Newman does not fully face these questions, but he does say natural religion lacks efficacy because it lacks a tangible history of deity, "that most efficient incentive to all action, a starting or rallying point,—an object on which the affections could be placed, and the energies concentrated."[23] Religiosity, for Newman, is generated only by real events, by concrete occurrences which stir, guide, and hold people's imagination. The point, however, does not affect religion where such concrete images do exist, and Newman seems to recognize that he is confusing Liberal and natural religion. He queries himself as to whether natural religion has not really solved this problem. His reply, though fragmentary, is highly suggestive.

Natural religion, he says, did try to specify God concretely, but in so doing it degraded "His invisible majesty by unworthy, multiplied and inconsistent images." The concrete images of pagan religion—its gods, heroes, myths, and rites—were too diverse, impure, and limited to manifest deity adequately. Although these bases did furnish the animating power for actual religious life, their inadequacies were so clear that the more sophisticated adherents recognized the necessity for an intellectual reformulation. Their reformulation, however, created a philosophy which was either unrelated to or in basic conflict with people's actual, lived religions. This result left classical religion with two partial and discordant systems, the one arising from sophisticated religious reflection and the other from religious sentiment. Neither by itself was efficacious: "The God of philosophy was infinitely great, but an abstraction; the God of paganism was intelligible, but degraded by human conceptions. Science and nature could produce no joint-work; it was left for an express Revelation to propose the Object in which they should both be reconciled, and to satisfy the desires of both in a real and manifested incarnation of the Deity."[24] Natural religion could be fulfilled only when the notional and the real, religious sentiment and intelligent reflection, were brought together. That union could occur only through an incarnation of deity.

Newman's emphasis on the need for both the real and the notional requires a brief explication. As is shown by the preface to the 1877 edition of the *Via Media,* Newman thought religion begins with the real and finds real expression in action and community, but that it also needs for completion the notional, theoretical expression. Religion's source must always remain the real, as deductions have no power of persuasion. The heart is commonly reached, not through the reason, but through the imagination, by means of direct impressions, by the testimony of facts and events, by history, by description. Persons influence us, voices melt us, looks subdue us, deeds inflame us. Many a man will live and die upon a dogma: no man will be a martyr for a conclusion. . . . No one, I say, will die for his own calculations: he dies for realities. . . . After all, man is *not* a reasoning animal; he is a seeing, feeling, contemplating, acting animal. He is influenced by what is direct and precise.[25]

Religion basically deals with the real, with those images of reality which stimulate devotion.

Theology or theoretic expression, on the other hand, "deals with notional apprehension[; it works] . . . when the proposition is apprehended for the purposes of proof, analysis, comparison, and the like intellectual exercises . . . [when it] is used as the expression of a notion." The notional and the real differ, but there is no "contrariety and antagonism between a dogmatic creed and vital religion." The real is the true source of religious action, but the notional is important "as ascertaining and making clear for us the truths on which the religious imagination has to rest. Knowledge must ever precede the exercise of the affections. We feel gratitude and love, we feel indignation and dislike, when we have the informations actually put before us which are to kindle those several emotions . . . we must know concerning God, before we can ·feel love, fear, hope, or trust towards Him." The religious imagination and affections must always "be under control of reason . . . because religion cannot maintain its ground at all without theology. Sentiment, whether imaginative or emotional, falls back upon the intellect for its stay, when sense cannot be called into exercise." Notional reflection is important because it generates clear formulation that can guide people. Moreover, the notional's critical function is also crucial, as it shows the limits of all formulations. By exhibiting the frailty of intellectual processes, notional reflection constantly confronts people with the mystery they face and the need to believe. A complete religion, then, must harmonize the notional and the real because

each . . . has its own excellence and serviceableness, and each has its own imperfection. To apprehend notionally is to have breadth of mind, but to be shallow; to apprehend really is to be deep, but to be narrow-minded. The latter is the conservative principle of knowledge, and the former the principle of its advancement. Without the apprehension of notions, we should for ever pace round one small circle of knowledge; without a firm hold upon things, we shall waste ourselves in vague speculations.

The real may have a kind of precedence as "the scope and end and the test of the notional," but a proper harmony of both is necessary. Indeed, Newman approves of Clement's idea that philosophy is God's special dispensation to the Greeks.[26] The constructive and critical activity of philosophy is a divine gift that deity wanted joined with those real religious objects that arise from the Judaic tradition. The philosophy arising from the Greek dispensation gives birth both to dogmas, by showing reason's power, and to the sense of dogma's limitations, by showing reason's shortcomings. For religion to be complete, the two must be in harmony as in Catholic Christianity, not in contradiction as in paganism.

This harmonious combination cannot be produced, however, by any human attempt to reconcile the two. Paganism's failure shows that such a combination can occur only with a real yet manifested incarnation of deity: a concrete, real image of the divine that also carries the message that it images a higher being. A single image must be able both to manifest deity as nothing else can and to proclaim that it is but a manifestation of the sacred object itself. There must be an incarnation where "in His life we are allowed to discern the attributes of the Invisible God, drawn out into action in accommodation to our weakness."[27] The incarnate being is the most complete manifestation possible, yet one that remains the sort of limited manifestation able to affect human beings.

This incarnation's "realness" generates religious devotion and action, while its reference beyond itself generates a rational reflection that rises beyond the particular image. The real apprehension guides the religious life. The notional reflection on it guards against any undue attachment to the particularities of the manifestation, though one recognizes it is the fullest possible incarnation of deity. The image, then, must at once be real and yet point beyond itself. Only such an incarnation contains the concrete form of a described life and yet opens out beyond itself toward the higher mystery of its source. Christianity completes natural religion through a harmonization of the notional and real that arises from a real yet manifested incarnation of deity.

In a different and more speculative statement, Christianity completes natural religion by the establishment of that one idol by which all other idols can be destroyed—including any parts of itself that can become idolatrous. Newman thinks the problem of idolatry is acute in religion. If concrete representations must exist for religion to be effective, such representations are prone to become idols, prone to be seen as adequate images of higher reality. Indeed, Newman thinks idolatry is perhaps the most normal of all religious perversion; as he commented, the "primary object of Revelation was to recall men from idolizing the creature."[28] People need real objects, but final religious fulfillment involves honoring not those real objects but the transcendent, mysterious God. Only a full but economic incarnation, a unification of finite and infinite, can provide both the concrete object and the clear reference beyond itself. This alone can preserve both the purifying processes of notional abstractions and the deep movements arising from real objects. Christianity's fulfillment of natural religion rests on this union, in the Incarnation, of the two essential poles of religion, the real and the notional.

The Addition of New Sacral Power.   Fulfillment also occurs through the transmuting force of Christianity's new power. "Christianity differs from other religions and philosophies, in what is superadded to earth from heaven; not in kind, but in origin; . . . being informed and quickened by what is more than intellect, by a divine spirit"; so that "the great characteristic of Revelation is addition, substitution. Things look the same as before, though not [sic: now] an invisible power has taken hold upon them." There is a "truth, a certain virtue or grace in the Gospel which changes the quality of doctrines, opinions, usages, actions, and personal character when incorporated with it."[29] Our examination relates this idea only to some general notions of sacred power's role in religion and then examines how that new power fulfills natural religion's ritual and gives a new salvatory power to the individual.

Various people have emphasized the importance of Power in religion. Van der Leeuw argues that the various permutations of the triad Power, Will, and Form define, almost exhaustively, the object of religion. He even says that Power experienced as God is a definition of salvation. Others put forward similar views, as in Otto's use of Power as the basis for a description of religion; Streng's emphasis on the structural processes of ultimate transformation; or Wach's criteria for the religiosity of certain experiences. Such approaches illuminate Newman, who views all religion as a kratophany that Christianity completes by releasing ultimate sacral power, showing its form is personal and good, and revealing its will as particular and ever-active. Natural religion's Power is broken into various centers, its personality and goodness are sometimes denied, and its sacred actions are seen as sporadic. A Power which is single, good, personal, and ever-active fulfills it. The "active interposition of that Omnipotence"[30] which started Christianity and continues today is, then, a significant example of the fulfilling process.

An example of this fulfillment is the way natural religious rites are fulfilled by the new sacramental power that Christianity brings. A relatively early work makes the point eloquently, if in a fashion that too severely limits the meaning of pagan rites:

What is prior to Him is dark, but all that comes after Him is illuminated. The Church, before His manifestation, offered to Him material elements "which perish with the using"; but now He has sent His spirit to fill such elements with Himself, and to make them living and availing sacrifices to the Father. Figures have become means of grace, shadows are substances, types are Sacraments in Him. What before were decent ordinances and pious observances, have now not only a meaning but a virtue. Water could but wash the Body in the way of nature; but now it acts towards the cleansing of the soul. "Wine which maketh glad the heart of man," and "bread which strengthens man's heart," nay, the "oil which maketh him a cheerful countenance," henceforth are more than means of animal life, and savour of Him. Hands raised in blessing, the accents of the voice of man, which before could but symbolize the yearnings of human nature, or avail for lower benefits, have now become the "unutterable intercessions" of the Spirit, and the touch and breath of the Incarnate Son.

Newman often highlights the new strength of sacramental power by drawing natural religion's worship as "rites, which are but worthless in themselves," or as ceremonies which result from human attempts to control deity.[31] His more balanced view does not, however, denigrate the rites of natural religion in order to highlight Christianity's new sacramental power. Moreover, his basic point is that Christianity transforms these rites by means of its new sacramental power.

As we have seen, Newman thinks ritual is a crucial part of religion. Prayer and sacrifice are two types defining human religiosity and ritual itself is that one of religion's three expressions which most directly corresponds to man's religious potential. Christianity fulfills natural religion's rituals both by adding a new power and by clarifying the power's character. The power's goodness defines what sacrifices are appropriate, while the power's form defines the sacrifice's efficacy. Ritual attains a new ability to reveal and effect a reconciliation with sacral power.

Another example views Christianity's fulfillment in how it divinizes people. The theme of deification has been prominent in parts of the Christian tradition. Evident in both the Patristics and the Scholastics, the theme appears in a few moderns with quite the same prominence it does in Newman. A brief description, using his own words, shows both the form and the prominence of the motif in him. To be saved, he says, is "to receive the Divine Presence within us, and to be made a Temple of the Holy Ghost." People do not die as they were born, being changed only on death; rather they are divinized here on earth. People "are new-created, transformed, spiritualized, glorified in the Divine Nature ... we receive ... the true Presence of God within ... us." Christ is the channel for such a Presence; "there is ... the actual entrance of Himself, soul and body, and divinity, into the soul and body of every worshipper who comes to Him for the gift, a privilege more intimate than if we lived with Him during His long-past sojourn upon earth." The "communication is made to us of His new nature, which sanctifies the soul, and makes the body immortal." The attributes which belong to the Divine world by nature are given by grace to man; man receives a gift which "exalts him inconceivably on the scale of being." Indeed, the sanctified Christian now surpasses the normal man as that man does lower orders, so much "more sacred is the indwelling of God in the hearts of His elect people ... that compared with it, He may well be said not to inhabit other men at all." "A brute differs less from a man, than does man, left to himself with his natural corruption allowed to run its course, differ from man fully formed and perfected by the habitual indwelling of the Holy Spirit."[32]

This divinization is a sacred empowerment that remakes people and thereby fulfills natural religion. The idea and its importance to Newman are clear. But the idea's rationale and the evidence to support it are unclear, particularly when Newman argues that the transcendent source of the sacred presence makes impossible any empirical identification. Newman appears merely to assert that such a distinctive fulfilling power exists in Christianity. Two arguments can, however, be extrapolated from his works. One, based on subjective evidence, is very ambivalent; the other, like many theological arguments, is only as compelling as its premises. Given the centrality to Newman of the idea of a new sacral presence, both arguments need to be examined.

The first argument rests on the religious person's own sense of why change occurs and of what characterizes the forces of change.

> A religious person ... [becomes] different from what he was, his tastes, his views, his judgments are different. You will say that time changes a man as a matter of course; advancing age, outward circumstances, trials, experience of life. It is true; and yet I think a religious man would feel it little less than sacrilege, and almost blasphemy, to impute the improvement in his heart and conduct, in his moral being, with which he has been favored in a certain sufficient period, to outward or merely natural causes ... he has a conviction ... that God has been with him ... that God is present with him to an extent, with a fulness, in a depth, which he knows not.

Newman recognizes, at least at times, the frailty of this solution. On the one hand, he will say we know "we cannot change ourselves ... God alone can change us; God alone can give us the desires, affections, principles, views, and tastes which a change implies." But on the other hand, he also says that when we find ourselves "much more able to obey God in certain respects than heretofore . . . [our] minds are so strangely constituted, [that] it is impossible to say whether it is from the growth of habit suddenly showing itself, or from an unusual gift of Divine grace poured into our hearts."[33]

This problem arises from Newman's acceptance of the Aristotelian idea that habits give people a second nature which makes easy actions that were almost impossible before. But divine power also gives people a second nature which makes easy actions that were almost impossible before. If a habit is a permanent power which prompts a person to act in a particular way, without rational reflection and self-discipline, the distinction between acts arising from natural habits and those arising from the divine presence is extremely difficult to draw. Though the intricacy of this problem may not have been fully recognized by Newman, clearly another ground for affirming a divine presence must have existed for him.

That ground exists in a classic kind of theological argument that Newman uses but never fully develops. Newman says, for example, that deification is necessary if salvation is to occur because of "the great and general truths . . . that nature cannot see God, and that grace is the sole means of seeing Him." He also argues that the divine presence is our title to Heaven, is what will be accepted at the last day, and is what may give us confidence at the day of judgment.[34]

The argument extrapolates certain necessary consequences from the affirmation that one is or could be saved; Athanasius, whom Newman revered, is perhaps its classic exponent. The argument is that for salvation to be complete certain needs must be met; specifically, people must be able to live after death, to meet judgment, and to contemplate a reality higher than they normally can. Any salvation that fails to meet these needs is an incomplete salvation. As only divinization meets these needs, if people are saved they must also be deified. The basic premises, components, and theoretic movements of the argument are clear. Challenging questions, of course, lurk in the premises. For example, are the outlined needs the most basic human needs? Liberal religion will say no. Has salvation, whatever the needs, occurred? Skeptics will say no. Is the contemplation of deity either a need or a possible aspect of salvation? Some Protestants will say no. Whatever the truth of the premises, however, Newman did accept them, and he thought theoretic reflection on them inexorably led to the idea of deification. However difficult an empirical identification of the exact marks of the divine presence, such a presence must exist if salvation was to be complete.

This argument, then, provides the central reason for Newman's emphasis on deification. It also tells us why the notion of a sacred presence within man is one of the key ways in which Christianity fulfills natural religion.

Newman's fulfillment model stresses Christianity's completion and perfection of all aspects of natural religiosity. The model rests on the premise that revelation is universal and economic, present everywhere but always fitted to the recipient's situation. Examining how Christianity fulfills each of natural religion's characteristics illustrates how a specific characteristic, such as sacrifice, finds its actualization in the acts of Christ, the ritual of the Mass, and the actions of individual Christians. Focused more generally, the notion of assimilation, in the *Development of Doctrine,* illustrates how Christianity relates itself to the various elements of other religions without losing its identity. Christianity can incorporate various elements of natural religion around its center. This general notion is illustrated more concretely in three examples of Christianity's fulfillment of natural religion. In one example, the fulfillment takes place by referring everything to God as a single center and source. In another, the Incarnation provides the concrete center that completes natural religion's division between the notional and the real. In a final example, completion comes through the addition of a new divine power. For Newman, Christianity fulfills natural religion.

3

Christianity: The Authority Model

The idea of authority was a crucial element in Newman's conversion, religious life, and general reflections on religion. More important here, the general notion of fulfillment acquires a distinctive form when authority is the focus. For instance, the authoritative model, especially in its dogmatic mode, contains Newman's most uncompromising assertions about how religious strivings find specific fulfillment in Roman Catholicism. Many of Newman's contemporaries found his ideas on authority perplexing. Most today share that perception.

The topic is complicated for a variety of reasons. It leads to many difficult philosophic questions such as the peculiar characteristics of religious language. Furthermore, reflections on religious authority often exemplify how religiously important ideas are upheld despite their incoherence or unclarity. Moreover, it is impossible to know exactly how much Newman modulated his ideas on authority in response to the circumstances he faced. Finally, significant aspects of Newman's ambivalence about authority are explainable only in the terms of an as yet unwritten psychohistory of him. His intellectual conundrums or religious battles cannot simply be reduced to nonintellectual or nonreligious factors, but his personality was both very receptive to and very hesitant about authority. Recognizing these problems, we will examine the topic by outlining the abstract argument that underlies his position and note the particular problem it creates. Then we will analyze his mature ideas on the constitution of the final authoritative religion as those ideas appear in four late works. Finally, we will investigate Newman's views on dogma, a subject that exemplifies both the character of and the problems in his vision of an authoritative religion.[1]

We also need, however, to examine briefly the effect of the cultural situation on Newman's mature reflections. The historical context in which Newman discussed authority is very different from our own. Feeling itself attacked from all sides, the official Roman Catholic Church constructed battlements, assumed a siege mentality, and shelled rather than negotiated with those who would approach. For example, the *Syllabus of Errors,* issued in 1864, declared that the Church was not to align or even sympathize with the main currents of modern thought and condemned an almost exhaustive cross section of progressive ideas. Severe limitations were placed on responsible inquiry, and dissident opinion generally was silenced rather than discussed. The repression is exemplified by the Munich Brief, the official reaction to a congress of liberalizing theologians held in Munich in 1863. In the name of doctrinal conformity, it asks for strict limitations on investigation and publication.

The situation was, Newman felt, a new and grave one. "This age of the Church is peculiar,—in former times, primitive or medieval, there was not the extreme centralization which now is in use. . . . There was true private judgment in the primitive and medieval schools,—there are no schools now, no private judgment (in the religious sense of the phrase), no freedom, that is, of opinion. That is, no exercise of the intellect. No, the system goes on by the tradition of the intellect of former times." Some might desire, with Faber, to be a "cadaver in the Superior's hands," but Newman thought that the Church was "sinking into a sort of Novatianism." Instead of "aiming at being a world-wide power, we are . . . narrowing the lines of communion, trembling at freedom of thought, and using the language of dismay and despair at the prospect before us, instead of, with the high spirit of the warrior, going out conquering and to conquer."[2] The Church's actions seemed to validate the idea that an authoritative religion was bound to enforce uniformity, to stifle free expression, to repress personal growth, to meet a changing world only as a hostile enemy, and even to claim inordinate temporal power.

Newman's intellectual response to this situation was to describe how an authoritative religion ought to function, to show what it must be if humanity's natural religious impulses were to be fulfilled. The circumstances stimulated Newman to develop an image of an authoritative religion's true form. But the same circumstances also necessitated an often indirect and always fragmentary presentation. Moreover, Newman's sensitive personality, strong feelings about the need for obedience, and peculiar position as not only a convert but also a convert whose ideas were questioned, heightened his indirectness and reticence. Finally, Newman's ideas about economy and the *disciplina arcani* enforced the need for forming statements to fit particular times and places. To Newman's mind, "veracity, like other virtues, lies in a mean. Truth indeed, but not necessarily the whole truth, is the rule," because "not all knowledge is suited to all minds; a proposition may be ever so true, yet at a particular time and place may be temerarious, offensive to pious ears, and scandalous, though not 'heretical' nor 'erroneous.' It must be recollected what very strong warnings we have from our Lord and St. Paul against scandalizing the weak and unintellectual."[3] The historical content influenced the form and, to a degree, the substance of Newman's work on authority. His response to the stultifying climate of the times is to portray an ideal authoritative religion, but he did so only when specifically called to and then usually either in subdued tones or by indirect means.

The Abstract Argument for an Authoritative Religion and the Quandary It Produces

Newman's argument for an authoritative religion is coherent, but its accentuation of supernatural intervention leaves Newman with the problem that natural processes, such as normal reasoning, seem to be superseded. Such processes can no longer measure authority in any effective way. We can best approach Newman's abstract argument for authoritative religion's fulfillment of natural religion by reconstructing the steps in his thought processes. The stage for that analysis is best set by noting two summations of his general argument. The first, from the *Norfolk Letter,* is posed in terms of infallibility:

> [To] determine therefore what is meant by the infallibility of the Pope we must turn first to consider the infallibility of the Church. And again, to determine the character of the Church's infallibility, we must consider what is the characteristic of Christianity, considered as a revelation of God's will.
>
> Our Divine Master might have communicated to us heavenly truths without telling us that they came from Him, as it is commonly thought he had done in the case of heathen nations; but He willed the Gospel to be a revelation acknowledged and authenticated, to be public, fixed, and permanent; and accordingly, as Catholics hold, He framed a Society of men to be its home, its instrument, and its guarantee. The rulers of that Association are the legal trustees, so to say, of the sacred truths which He spoke to the Apostles by word of mouth. As He was leaving them, He gave them their great commission, and bade them "teach" their converts all over the earth, "to observe all things whatever He had commanded them"; and then He added, "Lo, I am with you always, even to the end of the world."

The second summation, from the *Apology,* deserves mention because it emphasizes that authoritative religion fulfills a need nothing else can:

> Considering the faculty of reason actually and historically; . . . its tendency is towards a simple unbelief in matters of religion. No

truth, however sacred, can stand against it, in the long run. . . .
Experience proves surely that the Bible does not answer a purpose for which it was never intended . . . a book, after all, cannot
make a stand against the wild living intellect of man. . . . Suppos-
ing then it to be the Will of the Creator to interfere in human
affairs, and to make provisions for retaining in the world a
knowledge of Himself, so definite and distinct as to be proof
against the energy of human scepticism, in such a case . . . there
is nothing to surprise the mind, if He should think fit to introduce a power into the world, invested with the prerogatives of
infallibility in religious matters. Such a provision would be a
direct, immediate, active, and prompt means of withstanding the
difficulty; it would be an instrument suited to the need. . . . And
thus I am brought to speak of the Church's infallibility, as a
provision, adapted by the mercy of the Creator, to preserve religion in the world, and to restrain that freedom of thought,
which of course in itself is one of the greatest of our natural
gifts, and to rescue it from its own suicidal excesses. . . . A
power, possessed of infallibility in religious teaching, is happily
adapted to be a working instrument, in the course of human
affairs, for smiting hard and throwing back the immense energy
of the aggressive, capricious, untrustworthy intellect.[4]

Such is Newman's argument in outline. Tracing out the steps leading to
these conclusions opens up his argument.

The authority model starts from the simple notion that revelation
distinguishes natural religion and Christianity. This simple distinction
collapses, however, as natural religion also contains revelation. The
next step differentiates Christian revelation by showing its singularly
authoritative character. One attempt to show this singularity argues as
follows:

The distinction between natural religion and revealed lies in this,
that the one has a subjective authority, and the other an objective. Revelation consists in the manifestation of the Invisible Divine Power, or in the substitution of the voice of a Lawgiver for
the voice of conscience. The supremacy of conscience is the essence of natural religion [sic]; the supremacy of Apostle, or Pope
or Church or Bishop, is the essence of revealed. . . . Thus, what
conscience is in the system of nature, such is the voice of Scripture, or of the Church or of the Holy See, as we may determine
it, in the system of Revelation.

This argument fails, however, because natural religion contains the authority of both conscience and objective revelation. It leads, however, to the more subtle idea that both Christianity and the preceding Judaic tradition have a more authoritative revelation because they have distinctive credentials.

> There are various revelations all over the earth which do not carry with them the evidence of their divinity. Such are the inward suggestions and secret illuminations granted to so many individuals; such are the traditionary doctrines which are found among the heathen. . . . There is nothing impossible in the notion of a revelation occurring without evidences that it is a revelation. . . . But Christianity is not of this nature: it is a revelation which comes to us as a revelation, as a whole, objectively, and with a profession of infallibility. . . . Christianity, unlike other revelations of God's will, except the Jewish of which it is a continuation, is an objective religion, or a revelation with credentials.[5]

Newman points here to Christianity's challenging proclamation that it is ultimately valid and authoritative. This aspect of Christianity led Newman to say that were it not the true revelation, none had been given. As no other religion makes a similar claim, either Christianity is true or no final revelation has come. Although religion always involves revelation and thus authority, some revelations may not assert that they are final. For example, Hinduism, when interpreted by some modern adherents, contains a revelation and yet is open to additions from other revelations. Confucianism and Taoism, in like manner, have often been seen by adherents as revealed and yet as open to supplements. A distinctive fact about traditional Christianity is the proclamation that its revelation is final. Whether this is or must be a unique fact about Christianity if Newman's argument is to be viable is discussed in the last chapter of this book, but the claim to finality does allow Newman to argue that it completes revelations not claiming such authority.

If an authoritative revelation is accepted, the next task is to ascertain its character. Newman usually assumes that sacred writings—rather than, say, rites or orally preserved myths—contain the revelation. But he also argues that the authoritative finality of the written revelation demands an authoritative teaching body to know, protect, and live from those writings. If authoritative religion is to be complete, both sacred writings and an infallible authority to interpret them must exist. In Newman's own terminology, the Church working in and from Scripture, rather than Scripture alone, must be that final authority which completes other, less authoritative revelations.

Newman's position rests on the premise that a written revelation is insufficient.[6] Sacred writings demand interpretation, must be applied to new situations, and contain implicit insights that become clear only over a period of time. Therefore, some organ must judge the validity of variant interpretations, different applications, and newly explicit ideas. The general principle underlying Newman's position is his idea that the human mind never simply receives any object "as it is." The mind always interprets the object in the light of personal concerns, given social circumstances, and the object's relation to other objects. Moreover, as all meaningful objects are complex rather than simple, a full understanding involves seeing all possible aspects of the object.

These general problems of understanding are made even more acute by the particular character of the Christian Scripture. It has "a structure so unsystematic and various, and a style so figurative and indirect, that no one would be sure at first to say what is in it and what is not." Key statements like "the Word became flesh" demand interpretation: for instance, what does "flesh" mean, what is the exact sense of "became," how is the idea of the "Word" to be understood? Furthermore, many essential questions that Scripture raises are left either without answers or with only inadequate answers: for example, the state between death and resurrection. Finally, incompleteness must exist, since Scripture's subject is divine action and no assignable number of books "comprises a delineation of all possible forms which a divine message will assume when submitted to a multitude of minds."[7] Sacred writings heighten all the general problems about an adequate understanding of significant facts.

Given such problems, some agent must exist who is able to decide between interpretations. Revelation's fulfilling cannot simply rest in sacred writings. It must rest in an agent that interprets these writings, an agent that has the infallible authority to determine the correct interpretation, application, and development of the authoritative revelation. Indeed, an authoritative revelation necessitates such an authoritative body, because "a revelation is not given, if there be no authority to decide what it is that is given."[8] This need is particularly acute if the revelation is to be universal. If the revelation is not protected, the movement through different situations and times could lead to significant changes through ignorance, malice, and shifts of perspective. If God is to give a final revelation he must preserve it, just as anyone who creates something, such as a parent, sees preserving it as an adjunct to the creation itself.

Newman's argument relies on the normal expectation that things of worth are cared for when they are created. The argument's underlying premise is an extraordinary one, however. The gift of a final authoritative revelation is not a normal expectation. Newman uses this premise to meet the criticism that normal experience leads one to anticipate an authority whose power is limited because it will mix truth and falsehood. Newman argues that using normal processes to judge is improper. Such normal processes would never lead to any expectation of revelation at all. The analogy between the normal and religious sphere "is in some sort violated by the fact of a revelation."[9] One cannot accept the violation of natural order evident in revelation and then use a naturalistic criterion to criticize infallibility.

The overall argument is, then, clear in outline. A revelation with credentials, with the claim of final authority, is present. Although sacred writings are revelation's most obvious form, they demand interpretations and applications. This need calls for a body able to judge on correct and incorrect use. Without such a body revelation's message is bound to be erroneously interpreted, and a final revelation would not be given and then left open to misinterpretation. To argue that such a revelation's meaning is not final is to overlook Christianity's own claim. To argue that its meaning is plain is to overlook both the historical fact of differing interpretations and the philosophic reasons explaining these differences. To argue that all human authorities are flawed is to overlook the fact that a final revelation, which is by definition abnormal, has been given. If certain premises and Newman's mode of argumentation (from such bases as presumption and antecedent probability) are accepted, the argument's strengths are obvious.

The major question for our analysis, however, is whether this authority model so accentuates supernatural intervention that it destroys the natural component. The fulfillment model emphasizes that the sacred does not destroy but presupposes and perfects the natural materials it works on. But the authority of revelation and of its ongoing interpretative body breaks so completely with life's normal processes that people apparently cannot even measure it by natural means. The general question has long been central in Christianity. Does accepting a transcendent God's interruption of normal processes in a final revelation mean that all normal processes are now inadequate? Put in terms of the nature/grace model, the question is whether the natural order is presupposed and perfected by God or whether it is overturned and made totally new.

Much of Newman's intellectual work and personal struggle as a Catholic was concerned with answering this question. Is infallible authority too divine a gift to measure, form, or judge by normal means? Newman faces various problems, among them the relation of individual conscience to papal authority and the tension between religion's authoritative demand and secular education's concerns. All can be seen as attempts to analyze whether religious authority is distinct from or continuous with normal human functions. His early Catholic works often emphasize how revealed authority's sacred distinctiveness breaks

with nature. It led him, for example, to state that the Irish university
plan must succeed because the Pope had commanded it. But his later
years, filled with frustration and a growing disquiet with the official
Church, show his attempt to see how religious authority can be a miraculous gift and yet still be continuous with the complex, fallible functionings of normal life.

The Ideal Form of Authoritative Religion as Seen in Four Works

There emerges in Newman's later writings a portrait not of the existing
authoritative Church but of that model of authoritative religion which
ought to exist if natural religion is to be completed. His work can
almost be seen as the construction of an ideal type; "almost" because
Newman believed the type could exist, or perhaps even had existed.
This raises the question of whether Newman's portrait of Roman Catholicism's authoritative aspects is not open to the same charge he made
about his portrait of Anglicanism as a middle way. Is it only, in his
phrase, a "paper religion," an intellectual idea that never has existed,
and perhaps never could? As Karl Barth rhetorically puts a similar
point, "no protest in *principle* can be raised on our part either against
the summation of the apostolate in Peter, nor yet against the possibility
of a primacy in the Church, which in that case might very well be that
of the Roman community. . . . [But] I cannot hear the voice of the
Good Shepherd from this 'Chair of Peter.' "[10] Arguing for the historical existence of this perfect, authoritative type would be very difficult,
though Newman may have believed it possible. His main concern, however, is the need for its existence in the future just as our main concern
is its abstract character.

Newman attempts to resolve the fundamental tensions in any authoritative religion: the tension between fallible people and a sacred
truth that meets them; the tension between a timeless revelation and
recipients always bound to a particular time; the tension between the
need to respond to authoritative commands and the need to maintain
personal integrity. All these tensions take their most troublesome form
when focused in dogma, the authoritative definition of revelation's
truth in binding intellectual expressions. This problem especially
pressed on Newman because he lived in the cauldron set boiling by the
promulgation of the dogmas of the Immaculate Conception and Papal
Infallibility. Nevertheless, dogmatic definition represents the single
most acute issue that the authoritative model of religion presents. The
authority of sacred writings or rites, even the general authority of the

community, leave open a possible sphere of individual freedom that is apparently foreclosed by the authority of dogma. Newman's analysis often focuses on dogma, then, as it presents a crucial problem.

Analyzing the exact content of Newman's vision of authoritative religion must take into account Newman's predilection to write only when called and then only to the specific question that called him, as well as the repressive character of the times, his own exposed position, his honoring of authorities, and his belief in economic presentation. These factors lead to the idea of authority being treated in an often fragmentary and usually subdued manner. Although the subject is occasionally treated at length, no systematic examination exists, and the intellectual climate, sometimes clearly but always forcibly, affects what is written. Given these factors, general observations ought to arise only from a careful consideration of specific works both in chronological order and in their historical settings. Such an approach allows us to see the outlines of Newman's own development of his distinct theoretic patterns and concerns. The first work we will treat, *On Consulting the Faithful in Matters of Doctrine,* examines the laity as an aspect of Church authority. The next two, the *Apologia pro Vita Sua* and the *Norfolk Letter (A Letter Addressed to His Grace the Duke of Norfolk on Occasion of Mr. Gladstone's Expostulation),* are Newman's personal answer to two direct attacks arguing that religious authority necessarily leads to duplicity and depersonalization. Typically for Newman, these two responses contain the most complete examination of his position, more speculatively in the *Apology,* more concretely in the *Norfolk Letter.* Finally, the Preface to the 1877 edition of *The Via Media of the Anglican Church* presents Newman's last and most sweeping treatment of authoritative religion. An outline of that ideal form of authoritative religion which completes humanity's natural religious impulses emerges from these works.

On Consulting the Faithful in Matters of Doctrine.   *On Consulting the Faithful in Matters of Doctrine* first appeared as an article in the July 1858 edition of *The Rambler. The Rambler,* a Catholic periodical of small circulation but considerable influence, was founded in 1848 as a vehicle for educated Catholic scholarship and criticism. Such aims made conflict with the authorities almost inevitable. When the situation became critical, Newman was asked to become editor, as he alone seemed able to pilot the periodical through the storm. Believing *The Rambler*'s service to the educated laity was very important, he accepted. His navigational efforts were unsuccessful, however, in large part because of the general issue of the laity's role in the Church. His editorship ended with the issue in which *On Consulting* appears. The article is a scholarly piece concerned with those historical situations when the laity rather than the priesthood preserved orthodoxy. It was probably also intended, however, to serve as a general validation of the laity's integral role in the Church. The piece generated a momentous reaction including a formal accusation of heresy from the Bishop of Newport, a fierce controversy in Great Britain, and a clouding of Newman's name in Rome. The furor was such, the aspersions so bitter, the suspicions so deep, that Newman seems to have been permanently marked. From that time on he wrote less than he had, and he remained constantly on his guard. The dispute made painfully clear that attempts to move certain issues to an intellectual level of discussion were bound to be met only by repressive means.

Newman argues that because authority resides in the Church's members, they must be "consulted" before a doctrine is defined. Their belief is important because "the body of the faithful is one of the witnesses to the fact of the tradition of revealed doctrine, and because their *consensus* through Christendom is the voice of the Infallible Church." This does not mean "that infallibility is *in* the 'consensus fidelium,' but that that 'consensus' is an *indicium* or *instrumentum* to us of the judgment of that Church which *is* infallible." The faithful's belief is an aspect of infallibility for various reasons, such as that it is directed by the Holy Ghost and that it stands as an answer to prayers. The most important reason, however, is that such belief is "a sort of instinct or *phronema,* deep in the bosom of the mystical body of Christ . . . [having] a jealousy of error, which it at once feels as a scandal."[11] Newman introduces here, in a religious context, a motif common in all his writings: the idea that ordinary people usually judge well on significant matters with which they are familiar, even if they cannot express their reasons clearly. However flawed their explicit justifications, their conclusions are excellent. This soundness of judgment is particularly evident when they meet objections or attitudes inconsistent with their own vision. As Newman says in the *Grammar,* the mark of common belief is its spontaneous rejection of some objections. For example, the argument that innocent life may be taken without reason is spontaneously rejected by a normal person.

In both religious and nonreligious areas, this ability to judge well is more likely to protect from error than to generate a full account. As Newman, quoting from an earlier work to clarify his point, writes:

> We know that it is the property of life to be impatient of any foreign substance in the body to which it belongs. It will be sovereign in its own domain, and it conflicts with what it cannot assimilate into itself, and *is irritated and disordered* till it has expelled it. Such expulsion, then, is emphatically a test of uncongeniality, for it shows that the substance ejected, not only is not one

with the body that rejects it, but cannot be made one with it; that its introduction is not only useless, or superfluous, or adventitious, but that it is intolerable. . . . The religious life of a people is of a certain quality and direction, and these are tested by the mode in which it encounters the various opinions, customs, and institutions which are submitted to it. Drive a stake into a river's bed, and you will at once ascertain which way it is running, and at what speed; throw up even a straw upon the air, and you will see which way the wind blows; submit your heretical and Catholic principle to the action of the multitude, and you will be able to pronounce at once whether it is imbued with Catholic truth or with heretical falsehood.

The natural ability to make wise practical decisions and to use the illative sense finds in the *phronema* a religious counterpart that is even more sure because it is inspired. Authority must include this element as "each constituent portion of the Church has its proper function, and no portion can be safely neglected. . . . There is something in the *'pastorum et fidelium conspiratio,'* which is not in the pastors alone."[12] The judgment of the laity is significant. Authority resides within the whole, even if it finds propositional voice only in one part.

Apologia pro Vita Sua.   The work we now know as the *Apologia pro Vita Sua* was instigated by a passing remark in an anonymous book review in *Macmillan's Magazine:* "Truth for its own sake, has never been a virtue with the Roman clergy. Father Newman informs us that it need not, and on the whole ought not to be; that cunning is the weapon which heaven has given to the Saints wherewith to withstand the brute male force of the wicked world."[13] Newman was inclined to let the remark pass until he discovered its author was Charles Kingsley, tutor to the Prince of Wales, chaplain to the Queen, and Professor of Modern History at Cambridge. As a private correspondence brought no satisfaction, the correspondence was published, Kingsley answered with a pamphlet, and Newman produced the *Apology* as a reply. The background is significant. Those parts of the work of special interest to us were intended to answer the integral thrust of Kingsley's basic question about Newman and Roman Catholicism: Must not a religion based on an infallible authority demand an obedience that would violate conscience and free inquiry? Must not an authoritative religious system destroy a person's integrity?

Much of the book recounts Newman's own movement toward Catholicism in a way that shows his integral if painful growth. This autobiographical account illustrates how, in at least Newman's own life, authority perfected rather than destroyed his personhood. The work's last section fills out this concrete account with the abstract argument that a religion of authority can perfect rather than destroy the personhood of its adherents. This last section constructs a defense against Kingsley, but it also erects an ideal model of how an authoritative religion ought to operate. When Newman paints a portrait of that ideal authoritative religion to which he converted, his defense of the Church before Kingsley also becomes a criticism of the official Church's current actions. His defense is also a prescription. Newman's letters from this time, as well as the occurrences of the time, make clear the difference between his picture and the actual reality. To accept Newman's defense—and thus the reasons for his conversion—is to subscribe to his ideal and thus to criticize the Church's actual operation.

For our purposes the key aspect of this section of the book is Newman's answer to the charge:

> That I, as a Catholic, not only make profession to hold doctrines which I cannot possibly believe in my heart, but that I also believe in the existence of a power on earth, which at its own will imposes upon men any new set of *credenda,* when it pleases, by a claim to infallibility; in consequence, that my own thoughts are not my own property; that I cannot tell that tomorrow I may not have to give up what I hold to-day, and that the necessary effect of such a condition of mind must be a degrading bondage.

The question is whether "the assumption of infallibility by the proper authority is adapted to make me a hypocrite . . . [or], whether authority has so acted upon the reason of individuals, that they can have no opinion of their own."[14]

The outline of his abstract defense of the need for authority we examined earlier. His personal response is put in the following simple reminder to non-Catholics: "We priests need not be hypocrites, though we be called upon to believe in the Immaculate Conception [dogmatically defined in 1854] . . . indeed, it is a simple fact to say, that Catholics have not come to believe it because it is defined, but that it was defined because they believed it."[15] His overall defense, however, goes beyond either an abstract argument or a personal statement; it describes how an authority may protect and perfect rather than destroy personhood. This description is especially important when it examines authority's relation to cultural pluralism, to the belief of the uneducated, and to the questions of the educated.

Newman argues that authority must represent and protect the multitude of cultural traditions within the Church.[16] Emphasizing how authority must do more than merely apply the attitudes of one nationality is a criticism of a hierarchy that was Italian in tone, but a more general point is also being made. A truly universal, authoritative religion must honor cultural pluralism, the diversity of attitudes, actions, and perspectives that are represented in various cultures. Newman's sensitivity to the distinctions among cultures is acute; he once illustrated the unconscious significance of first principles with the example of the strange dislocation a person feels in a foreign country. He recognizes that different cultures act on their religious beliefs in different ways. As he later said, "I prefer English habits of belief and devotion to foreign, from the same causes, and by the same right, which justifies foreigners in preferring their own."[17] He argues, for instance, against transplanting certain European religious practices to England on the ground that they would become either superstitions or false, flamboyant shows of piety in the context of English culture. Authority must never stifle different cultural religious expressions for the sake of uniformity, particularly as any uniformity was liable to be no more than the distinctive ethos of a particular culture. The implications of this view are wider than probably even Newman himself realized. For example, does not the variety of cultures imply a variety of ways of formulating doctrines, acting out rituals, and forming communities? These questions are examined in the last chapter, but here we just note that Newman emphasizes that an authoritative religion must value the variety of ways in which religion can be expressed.

Another issue that concerns Newman is the exercise of authority toward the uneducated. He emphasizes the need to protect simple people from ideas that might destroy their belief because they are untrained to deal with them. If unguided, uneducated people are liable to be led to a "bottomless liberalism of thought" unless they are protected. Even the implicit power to discriminate pointed to in *On Consulting* will be unable to survive certain assaults. Newman's analysis is a classic example of a cogent argument for censorship. The argument rests on a sense of the intellect's frailty, particularly in the uneducated; on the need for the trained to care paternally for the untrained; and on the possibility of leaders prudentially exercising a censoring authority. Such an argument is as difficult to refute as to affirm, standing as it does on two experiential judgments: that authorities can act wisely and that people without intellectual training may lose integral beliefs because of intellectual challenges that can be met, but only by sophisticated minds.

A final issue Newman confronts is authority's actions toward the educated, toward those able to formulate new modes of religious thought and action. In this area the Church is to act slowly and carefully, originating nothing and serving only as a brake on the development of dogma. Here particularly, Newman's portrait of authority is both a defense and a prescription. His portrait contrasts almost completely with his descriptions, in letters, of the Church's actual actions.

His description of authoritative action in the past—which is best seen as an "ideal type"—contrasts sharply with the actual practice of his times and sets a goal for the future:

> All through Church history from the first, how slow is authority in interfering! Perhaps a local teacher, or a doctor in some local school, hazards a proposition, and a controversy ensues. It smoulders or burns in one place, no one interposing; Rome simply lets it alone. Then it comes before a Bishop; or some priest, or some professor in some other seat of learning takes it up; and then there is a second stage of it. Then it comes before a University, and it may be condemned by the theological faculty. So the controversy proceeds year after year, and Rome is still silent. An appeal is next made to a seat of authority inferior to Rome; and then at last after a long while it comes before the Supreme Power. Meanwhile, the question has been ventilated and turned over and over again, and viewed on every side of it, and authority is called upon to pronounce a decision, which has already been arrived at by reason. But even then, perhaps the supreme authority hesitates to do so, and nothing is determined on the point for years; or so generally and vaguely, that the whole controversy has to be gone through again, before it is ultimately determined. It is manifest how a mode of proceeding, such as this, tends not only to the liberty, but to the courage, of the individual theologian or controversialist.

Of crucial importance is how such a use of authority not only leads to the truth but also helps rather than hinders the development of an individual's ideas. "Many a man has ideas, which he hopes are true, and useful for his day, but he is not confident of them, and wishes to have them discussed. He is willing, or rather would be thankful, to give them up, if they can be proved to be erroneous or dangerous, and by means of controversy he obtains this end. . . . He would not dare to do this, if he knew an authority, which was supreme and final, was watching every word he said, and made signs of assent or dissent to each sentence, as he uttered it."[18] Just as instantly applied authoritative judgment hinders free expression, so also does the absence of any mechanism by which others may judge a person's thoughts.

Newman's ideal is that of a slowly developing discussion of significant issues in the Church. By means of the interaction of mind upon mind, of one part of the Church upon another, this process leads finally to a new, clearer vision. This form of authority does not constrain free inquiry but opens, develops, and forms it. Authority does not "command people about like so many soldiers or pieces of wood . . . [rather it lets providence] gently . . . work out separation . . . as fruit ripens on the tree and falls." This organic ideal actually frees the intellect and helps it move toward understanding. The overall vision is well articulated in the following passage:

It will at first sight be said that [by authority] the restless intellect of our common humanity is utterly weighed down, to the repression of all independent effort and action whatever, so that, if this is to be the mode of bringing it into order, it is brought into order only to be destroyed. But this is far from the result, far from what I conceive to be the intention of that high Providence who has provided a great remedy for a great evil [the unhindered reason's corrosive effect on religion],—far from borne out by the history of the conflict between Infallibility and Reason in the past, and the prospect of it in the future. The energy of the human intellect "does from opposition grow"; it thrives and is joyous, with a tough elastic strength, under the terrible blows of the divinely-fashioned weapon, and is never so much itself as when it has lately been overthrown. It is the custom with Protestant writers to consider that, whereas there are two great principles in action in the history of religion, Authority and Private Judgment, they have all the Private Judgment to themselves, and we have the full inheritance and the superincumbent oppression of Authority. But this is not so; it is the vast Catholic body itself, and it only, which affords an arena for both combatants in that aweful never-dying duel. It is necessary for the very life of religion, viewed in its large operations and its history, that the warfare should be incessantly carried on. Every exercise of Infallibility is brought out into act by an intense and varied operation of the Reason, both as its ally and as its opponent, and provokes again, when it has done its work, a re-action of Reason against it; and, as in a civil polity the State exists and endures by means of the rivalry and collision, the encroachments and defeats of its constituent parts, so in like manner Catholic Christendom is no simple exhibition of religious absolutism, but presents a continuous picture of Authority and Private Judgment alternately advancing and retreating as the ebb and flow of the tide;—it is a vast assemblage of human beings with willful intellects and wild passions, brought together into one by the beauty and the Majesty of a Superhuman Power,—into what may be called a large reformatory or training-school, not as if into a hospital or into a prison, not in order to be sent to bed, not to be buried alive, but (if I may change my metaphor) brought together as if into some moral factory, for the melting, refining, and moulding, by an incessant, noisy process, of the raw material of human nature, so excellent, so dangerous, so capable of divine purposes. . . . [The] Infallibility of the Church . . . is a supply for a need, and it does not go beyond that need. Its object is, and its effect also, not to enfeeble the freedom or vigour of human thought in religious speculation, but to resist and control its extravagance.[19]

A premise of all Newman's work is that truth can never really conflict with truth. He realized both that truths appeared to conflict and that reason alone could easily lead to skepticism, but he thought the answer to that problem was further inquiry within a community. The whole Church talking with itself, being asked only "to pronounce a decision, which has already been arrived at by reason,"[20] can harmonize the demands of inquiry and belief. In that process the Church grows to a fuller vision of itself, its mission, and its world. An authoritative religion will protect religion's revelation, lead to its own growth, and allow the full exercise of its member's independent minds.

The Norfolk Letter.   A Letter Addressed to His Grace the Duke of Norfolk on Occasion of Mr. Gladstone's Recent Expostulation, published in 1875, was a response to a pamphlet of Gladstone's entitled *The Vatican Decrees in the bearing on Civil Allegiance.* Gladstone, recently forced to resign as Prime Minister when a bill was defeated, attributed the defeat to the influence of Irish bishops on the Catholic members of Parliament. He concluded that Catholics, after the First Vatican Council's definition of infallibility, could no longer be loyal citizens. The pamphlet covers a variety of papal actions including the *Syllabus of Errors.* But its major question, as Newman saw it, is "can Catholics be trustworthy subjects of the State? has not a foreign Power a hold over their consciences such, that it may at any time be used to the serious perplexity and injury of the civil government under which they live?"[21] Gladstone's charge was similar to Kingsley's, though the form was more civilized and cogent: the teaching authority characterizing Roman Catholicism necessarily leads a Catholic to blind obedience and a duplicitous division of self. Here again, Newman claims that religious authority does not violate natural realities but presupposes and perfects them. He argues that only an authoritative Church divided from the state allows for the realization of both people's religious and political nature. Moreover, as in the *Apology,* he argues that only an authoritative community allows truth to be preserved and proper free inquiry to be stimulated. Although the topic is similar to that of the *Apology's* last section, the *Norfolk Letter* is important because the treatment is more extended, the adversary more worthy, and the issues much clearer, the Vatican Council having defined infallibility.

Newman's portrait never denies the fallibility of Rome, its human, or perhaps more than human, frailty. As he said, "the Rock of St. Peter on its summit enjoys a pure and serene atmosphere, but there is a great deal of Roman *malaria* at the foot of it."[22] His main concern remains the ideal form of an authoritative religion. Of special importance to us is his vision of how that authoritative teaching operates in the areas both of general guidance and of infallible definition. The analysis of general guidance is striking; it is the final fruit of reflections on the relation of church and state that reach back to the Tractarian period. Laski called it among "the profoundest discussions of the nature of obedience and of sovereignty to be found in the English language."[23] The subtleties of Newman's distinctions among degrees of allegiances and sovereignties are not central to our inquiry, but we do need to look briefly at the two major grounds for possible resistance to general Papal guidance: the generality of rules and the primacy of conscience.

Rules can never guide behavior completely because rules are general, but their application is in particular situations. Although obeying the Pope and the Queen are rules, "there is no rule in this world without exceptions . . . [so] I give an absolute obedience to neither." A remarkable passage makes the point in a general fashion:

> It is a great mistake to suppose our state in the Catholic Church is so entirely subjected to rule and system, that we are never thrown upon what is called by divines, "the Providence of God." The teaching and assistance of the Church does not supply all conceivable needs, but those which are ordinary; thus, for instance, the sacraments are necessary for dying in the grace of God and hope of heaven, yet, when they cannot be got, acts of faith, hope, and contrition, with the desire for those aids which the dying man has not, will convey in substance what those aids ordinarily convey.

Newman carefully hedges the position, saying private judgment is not, as for Protestants, the "*ordinary* guide in religious matters . . . I use it . . . in very extraordinary and rare, nay, impossible emergencies."[24] Nevertheless, the principle remains that infallible authority can never shelter people either from life's problematics or God's particular call. (He even says the substance of the sacraments, a clear manifestation of the Church's distinctive authoritative power, can be obtained without the Church's direct action.) In general, one is to be obedient to the authoritative body, but its "rule or system" may fail to meet life's concrete problems or a person's specific needs.

Few such boundaries exist for conscience, as Newman unhesitatingly affirms its primacy. Manifesting the natural law implanted by God in man, conscience rightfully commands obedience. Indeed, "conscience is ever to be obeyed whether it tells truly or erroneously, and that, whether the error is the fault of the person thus erring or not. . . .

Of course, if a man is culpable in being in error, which he might have escaped, had he been more in earnest, for that error he is answerable to God, but still he must act according to that error, while he is in it, because he in full sincerity thinks the error to be truth."[25] Newman stresses that conflicts will not arise. Conscience and the Pope have the same authoritative base, and infallibility gives general commands while conscience gives particular commands. Moreover, his analysis is studded with phrases about "impossible cases" (the Pope ordering all Catholics to avoid service in a war which Newman believed just) and about "being obedient if called to" (he even affirmed his willingness to submit to the *Syllabus of Errors* had it been officially promulgated by the Pope).[26] These statements must not be discarded; they are not the mere rhetorical garb of economic presentation. Nevertheless, the point remains that finally people are bound to make their own decisions. They must assent or rebel depending on what, if after arduous examination, they think is true. To overstate the case a little, Newman denies the need to be obedient at exactly the point where it is most needed. Newman's emphasis on the generality of rules and the responsibility to follow conscience stresses the need for either the personal application of or the possible resistance to the commands of authoritative religion.

The arena for free action appears to be more constricted with the Church's infallible definitions, with those statements that "become *de fide,* that is, a truth necessary to be believed, as being included in the original divine revelation . . . [; the] terms, revelation, *depositum,* dogma, and *de fide* . . . [being] correlatives." Newman agreed with Vatican I's definition of papal infallibility, though he thought the definition's timing and background were inappropriate. As he said, "there are two sides of ecclesiastical acts . . . right ends are often prosecuted by very unworthy means, and . . . in consequence those who, like myself, oppose a line of action, are not necessarily opposed to the issue for which it has been adopted." "For myself, ever since I was a Catholic, I have held the Pope's infallibility as a matter of theological opinion."[27]

The exact meaning of Newman's affirmation of an infallible teaching authority requires unpacking, however. His analysis is not only subtle, but it also often represents one of the few times he employs the mode of theology that makes precise verbal distinctions inside a systematic, technical framework. This kind of theological argument has remained, in modern times, a distinctively Catholic procedure, and Newman recognizes how strange the method appeared to most. He even states that many fail to grasp the Catholic position because they misunderstand the terminology and style of the theology.[28] He also thinks, however, that understanding authoritative pronouncements involves a series of technical problems that require this kind of close analysis. The simple notion that the Pope's "saying it" makes it true fails to penetrate the meaning of the promulgation and reception of authoritative pronouncements. The question can be divided into the following problem areas: *who* defines; exactly *what* is said infallibly; and *how* that definition is to be *interpreted*.

Newman says that the Pope explicitly defines, but, in so doing, that he speaks for the Church in order to manifest its belief. The Church has the office of teaching, the Pope just takes the "special form or posture" signified by the phrase *ex cathedra* when he vocalizes the communal mind and tradition. The implications of this point become clear when Newman explicates the major criteria for recognizing the conditions of infallibility. These criteria are the reference to Scripture, Tradition, or moral law; the unified judgment of the hierarchy; and the general acceptance of the definition by the whole Church not only now but in a future where what was accepted may be "explained" and "completed."[29] Rather than a single man authoritatively proclaiming a simple truth, the Church, seen as an ongoing body with different aspects, speaks.

Newman's idea that definitions are explained or completed leads to questions about exactly what is said and how those statements are to be interpreted. Newman treats the question of "what is said" as a technical problem and draws out few of the possible implications. He does emphasize, however, the limited range of dogmatic definitions. The Church is kept from errors only in a very narrow realm. "Since the process of defining truth is human, it is open to the chance of error; what Providence has guaranteed is only this, that there should be no error in the final step, in the resulting definition or dogma. . . . Accordingly, all that a Council, and all that the Pope, is infallible in, is the direct answer to the special question which he happens to be considering."[30] The discussions leading up to, surrounding, and coming from the definition, the implications that might be or have been drawn, are all liable to error. One is obligated to believe only the direct answer. Most important, that direct answer demands interpretation.

Newman believes that every statement, but particularly those referring to the sacred, requires interpretation. Scripture, for example, needs an authority able to judge its various possible interpretations. But that authority's statement would also seem to need interpretation. Indeed, Newman seems trapped by an infinite regress: each new authoritative interpretation demands still another interpretation, which in turn must be interpreted, and so on to infinity. In terms of the question of development, Newman appears ensnared by the position he fought. Christianity appears to possess no essence but to be whatever any particular age interprets it to be. Newman "solves" both problems by ar-

guing that particular infallible statements are understood by their continuing interpretation in the authoritative body that is the Church. The
matrix of authoritative interpretation provided by the Church is as
necessary for understanding infallible statements as it is for understanding Scripture.

This striking perspective on authoritative statements is exemplified
when Newman speaks of how a "wise and gentle *minimism*" is made
necessary by the fact that interpretative clarity grows over time. In both
channels of infallibility, "direct statements of truth, and . . . the condemnation of error," "instances frequently occur, when it is successfully
maintained by some new writer, that the Pope's act does not imply what
it seemed to imply, and questions which seemed to be closed, are after
a course of years re-opened." The necessity for and the "opportunity of
a legitimate minimizing lies in the intensely concrete character of the
matters condemned; [while] in his affirmative enunciations a like opportunity is afforded by their being more or less abstract."[31] Precisely
determining the import of condemnations is difficult. They usually
refer to a specific verbal formulation held by a particular person in a
distinct context. If a similar idea appears either in a different context
or with different intent, the condemnation may not apply.

The abstract character of positive pronouncements exhibits equivalent ambiguities. For example, how is one to understand the idea that
"out of the Church and out of the faith, is no salvation"? (As Newman
notes, the interpretation of this idea had changed recently.) Understanding hinges on penetrating the meaning of the words "faith,"
"Church," and "salvation," and the exact force of the phrase "out of."
Furthermore, these words must be understood not just in themselves
but also as they relate to each other. For instance, the word "Church"
acquires a distinct coloring if one speaks of man's salvation or damnation; the defining characteristics of membership in that context may
differ from those contexts where the reference is only to society, doctrine, or ritual. Moreover, new perspectives may involve reinterpre-
tations of certain ideas. "Church" and "salvation," for example, may
acquire different meanings when nonbelievers face situations where
Christianity is unknown or where the cultural setting makes Christianity an almost impossible choice for most people.

"Minimizing" contrasts with what Newman called that "fierce and
intolerant temper [now] abroad"[32] about the meaning of accepting authoritative pronouncements. To minimize is to accept infallible pronouncements both with a recognition of difficulty in interpretation
and, perhaps more important, with a recognition that new implications
may lead to a filling out of present understanding. Although faith
remains in the Church's ability to pronounce authoritatively, the actual

process of understanding those pronouncements is viewed as a continuing and fallible one.

The central figures in this crucial task of continuing interpretation are the theologians. The Church sets "her theologians to work to explain her meaning in the concrete, by strict interpretation of its wording, by the illustration of its circumstances, and by the recognition of exceptions."[33] Theologians mediate the mind of the Church to the Church, they focus the Church's self-understanding as that is constituted by its Scripture, general tradition, infallible pronouncements, and present situation. This crucial idea of theology as the regulative principle of the Church is just barely mentioned in the *Norfolk Letter*. It finds clear expression, however, in our last work, Newman's preface to the *Via Media*.

The Preface to the 1877 Edition of The Via Media of the Anglican Church.
The first volume of *The Via Media of the Anglican Church* contains Newman's 1877 reissue of the 1837 *Lectures on the Prophetical Office of the Church*. The reissue contains new explanatory footnotes and, most important here, an extensive preface. The original work centered on the distinction between the prophetic and episcopal traditions, the former giving life, the latter form to the Church. It viewed the Anglican Church as a middle way between the extremes of Protestantism and Roman Catholicism. The author of the new notes and preface attempts to answer the criticism of Catholicism made by the original book's author. Newman at seventy-six pits himself against the Newman of forty years earlier. The central question for our purposes is whether an authoritative religion is able to reform itself and to protect the freedom of men. Newman's answer to this question contains one notion of great importance for our analysis: the argument that theology must be the regulating principle of an authoritative religion.

Assuming the Church's three aspects—its communal, active, and intellectual expressions—Newman starts from the apparent differences between "its formal teaching and its popular political manifestations." The Church's three aspects appear to be separate rather than unified, indeed intellectual reflection often appears to be sacrificed to its two brothers. Seen at one level, he defends the Church from the charge that political considerations and superstitious worship always overrule its more sophisticated reflection. But seen at a more general level, he illuminates how an authoritative religion can maintain a harmonious balance among its three expressions. He recognizes the problem is a major one:

> Who, even with Divine aid, shall successfully administer offices so independent of each other, so divergent, and so conflicting? What line of conduct, except on the long, the very long run, is at

once edifying, expedient, and true? Is it not plain, that, if one determinate course is to be taken by the Church, acting at once in all three capacities, so opposed to each other in their idea, that course must, as I have said, be deflected from the line which would be traced out by any one of them, if viewed by itself, or else the requirements of one or two sacrificed to the interests of the third?[34]

Obviously, infallibility cannot meet this need. Its scope is too limited, its interpretation too complex, and its application too variable. The problem can be met only by theology:

I say, then, Theology is the fundamental and regulating principle of the whole Church system. It is commensurate with Revelation, and Revelation is the initial and essential idea of Christianity. It is the subject-matter, the formal cause, the expression, of the Prophetical Office, and, as being such, has created both the Regal Office and the Sacerdotal, and it has in a certain sense a power of jurisdiction over those offices, as being its own creations, theologians being ever in request and in employment in keeping within bounds both the political and popular elements in the Church's constitution,—elements which are . . . far more liable to excess and corruption, and are ever struggling to liberate themselves from those restraints which are in truth necessary for their well-being.[35]

Theology is crucial because it alone can deal with the problems presented both by interpreting scriptural and authoritative statements and by judging the new applications of revelation. Newman's view can be said to apply to the Church the Aristotelian notion that practical reason should guide human growth. For Aristotle, practical reason both understands general principles and applies them to the circumstances of life. Moreover, it harmonizes people's distinct parts by properly ordering their emotional life and guiding their social actions. Regulating but not dominating man's various aspects, practical reason guides people's personal growth. Aristotle himself applies this model to government, arguing that the proper ordering of the whole community should reflect reason's ordering of the individual person. The leader of a community, like practical reason in a person, recognizes general goals and then commands those actions that will help reach those goals. Similarly, theology seeks a true understanding, but it also prudentially adjusts itself to the demands of the diverse and largely uneducated Church. "Theology cannot always have its own way; it is too hard, too intellectual, too exact, to be always equitable, or to be always compassionate; and it sometimes has a conflict or overthrow, or has to consent to a truce or a compromise, in consequence of the rival force of religious sentiment or ecclesiastical interests; and that, sometimes in great matters, sometimes in unimportant."[36] Not surprisingly, the preface has an extended discussion of economy: of how the teacher says only what is needed, of how veracity lies in a mean, of how esoteric and exoteric doctrines are necessary, of how formal statements are to be delayed until the popular imagination is ready. Faith and the unity of the Church are not to be endangered for the sake of intellectual precision. Theology does regulate but like practical reason in the individual or a leader in the state, its reign is modified by the demands of circumstances and the needs of the whole.

The analogy with Aristotle is helpful, but it must not be applied too strictly because the bases of action differ in the two cases. The truth religion seeks to understand and apply is a sacred, mysterious one. Since it is mysterious, reason's pronouncements upon it will always be only approximations, only limited attempts to grasp what is largely ungraspable. Since it is sacred, the "pursuit of truth in the subject-matter of religion, if it be genuine, must always be accompanied by the fear of error, or error which may be sin." "An inquirer in the province of religion is under a responsibility for his reasons and for their issue." The peculiarities of the theological pursuit are well put in a notebook entry. Fitting the pursuit of truth into the tripartite constitution of the Church, the entry tries to answer the criticism that Catholics do not honestly seek the truth:

> This misapprehension [that truth is not honestly sought] arises from the fact that religion is not solely a *philosophy* <science>, but also a *devotion* <passion>, and a party adherence or ≤a≥ fellowship. Devotion brings in hope and fear—and fellowship brings in fear of scandal. In philosophy there is no fear or consideration of any thing but <<is this so or not>>? but devotion brings in the fear of error and its consequences, and fellowship introduces the necessities of all moving together—the duty of deference to superiors, and consulting for the interest of our neighbors.[37]

Religious truth reaches only an approximation, demands spiritual as well as intellectual abilities, induces a fear of error, and lives only within the context of a community. All these elements have analogies in Aristotle. For example, he states that the truths guiding particular judgments are difficult to understand; are recognizable only if one's character is good; and are pursued within the communal life of ethical men. But in Newman's account, the sacral mystery of the truth, the perfection of self needed to recognize it, and the nature of the community are all of a different, higher order.

The regulating principle of the authoritative religion, then, is the-

ology. People's reflective attempt, in community and through a relationship to a holy mystery, to understand and to apply the gifts given to
them is the final arbiter of revealed religion. At its highest point, theology's issue will be a binding infallible pronouncement, an explicit statement of right belief and action. But the interpretation and application
of those pronouncements, as well as the mass of problems they touch
on only tangentially, will also remain under the regulation of theology.

Conclusion Concerning the Ideal Form of Authoritative Religion.   By using
the four works we have examined, we can schematically draw out the
key elements that define an ideal authoritative religion. The whole
religious community is the authoritative agent. This point is made in
regard to normal members in *On Consulting* and to more sophisticated
or official members—past, present, and future—in the *Norfolk Letter*.
The insights and attitudes that define the religion exist in all of the
community's aspects, whether they explicitly pronounce, continuingly
interpret, or merely accept. This view of the spatial width, temporal
length, and varied functions of the religious community makes impossible any simple definition of the seat of authority.

Furthermore, an ideal authoritative religion must honor a considerable variety of cultural outlooks. Different modes of perception, expression, and action function in such a religion's past, present, and
future. Because any form authority takes will be culturally conditioned,
its judgments on different views must be made carefully and even
tentatively. The ideal authoritative religion will also honor a pluralism
of individuals. The variety of integral ways in which individuals can
formulate their ideas and make their decisions will be recognized. As
the *Apology* says, authority and private judgment will ever be in their
"aweful never-dying duel"; as the *Norfolk Letter* says, conscience's commands and the need to apply rules mean a sphere for free action will
continue to exist. Authority will recognize the distinctive integrity that
each individual possesses.

Moreover, as the *Apology* says, authority fosters appropriate intellectual development. Its paternal action protects the unsophisticated
from false arguments that could destroy their vulnerable belief. It also
furnishes a forum of discussion and review for the educated. This
forum aids both the individual and the community by freeing speculative vigor yet guarding against its extravagances. Authoritative religion
guards those who are unable to enter intellectual discussions fruitfully,
while it aids those who search for new modes of understanding. This
organism is complex but its various elements interact to protect the
integrity of each. Theology is its ultimate principle of regulation, as the
Norfolk Letter hints and the *Via Media* preface expressly states. Theology

interprets the various languages and actions of the community to the community and thereby helps identify the community's present character and future direction.

The authority model's most distinctive features are the incorporation of change and pluralism. The recognition that all changes and that variety exists is clear in our normal life. Incorporating both recognitions shows that an authoritative religion need not violate the normal processes of life. Such an incorporation, however, raises the question whether the natural elements are now so prominent that authority is destroyed. Newman thought authority remained, but the viability of his affirmation is questionable. Examining dogma probes this question, as dogma is the area where the synthesis Newman hopes to achieve is most difficult to effect.

Dogma

The Problem Dogma Presents and Newman's Apparent Ambivalence on the Subject.   The authoritative religion Newman describes could function without great difficulties in certain areas. For instance, its relationship to worship is easy to imagine. Worship "has many shapes and many objects, and, moreover, these are not altogether unlawful, though they be many."[38] Authoritative dogmas, however, appear to proclaim that a specific group of words is an adequate enough statement of truth that all who would belong to the community must affirm. Clearly the notions of pluralism and change appear to be severely strained or perhaps even destroyed by the idea of dogma. Dogma sets problems that worship does not and thereby focuses the critical question of how authoritative religion relates to normal forms of life.

Newman's recognition of this problem is reflected in his apparent ambivalence on dogma. His writings contain two contradictory streams; one stresses, the other minimizes dogma's importance. The more obvious strand stresses dogma's centrality. It is prominent when Catholicism is contrasted with either Liberalism or Protestantism. In a classic instance, Newman's *Apology* states that a principle he never deviated from "was the principle of dogma. . . . *From the age of fifteen, dogma has been the fundamental principle of my religion.*"[39] This same thread runs from early arguments in the *Arians of the Fourth Century* about the necessity of precise dogmatic language down through his last defenses of dogmatic authority. Indeed at times dogma seems almost to be a one-word slogan that defines true religion.

Newman also shows, however, an undogmatic temper, or more strongly put, a hesitancy about or even fear of dogma's role in religion.

As he says, "the greatest risk will result from attempting to be wiser than God has made us, and to outstep in the least degree the circle which is prescribed as the limit of our range." Speculation about religion can easily overlook God's majesty and forget the finitude and sin of the human condition. Newman's undogmatic temper is evident, for example, in his statement that "freedom from symbols and articles is abstractly the highest state of the Christian communion"; or in his delight in the "poetic not scientific" Benedictine, who contrasts with other orders, because the Benedictine "does not analyze, he marvels; his intellect attempts no comprehension of this multiform world, but on the contrary, it is hemmed in, and shut up within itself." This side of Newman is perhaps best exemplified by his great interest in the saint's life, "where dogma and proof are . . . at the same time hagiography,"[40] and individuality is mixed into writings that are personal or controversial rather than speculative. The rich terrain of a complex personal life has more appeal to him than the abstract intricacies of a speculative analysis.

This undogmatic temper arises from a distinct strand in Newman's thought, a strand that indicates his particular genius more clearly than does his emphasis on dogma. Briefly noting aspects of this strand, especially as they question dogma's importance, shows the tension in Newman's position. Newman gives great prominence to mystery in his account of religion. Religious realities are painted as mysterious, as inexpressible by human language. But how, given this, can one rather than another proposition describe the mystery more fully? Furthermore, Newman desires to limit reason's role in faith in order to highlight the place of love and the influence of the total personality. He emphasizes the critical role of spirituality, calling faith, for example, a spontaneous movement of the heart that tests a person's heart not intellect. In an especially clear example, Newman even uses love to distinguish faith from superstition, a distinction that is crucial to his analysis of faith.[41] But if the movements of will represented by love and by other, only partly rational, factors are crucial, how central can the objective propositions of dogma be?

Moreover, Newman emphasizes that revelation is not a gift of certain propositions but rests on ambiguous historical occurrences. "Revelation is not of *words*—from the derivation of the term it is addressed to the *sight*." There is "one principle object . . . of all revelation, so especially of the Christian; viz., to relate some course of action, some conduct, a life (to speak in human terms) of the One Supreme God." "Revelation meets us with simple and distinct *facts* and *actions*, . . . not with generalized laws or metaphysical conjectures"; thus "the Apostle's speeches in the Book of Acts and the primitive Creeds insist almost exclusively upon the history, not the doctrines, of Christianity."[42] Revelation consists not of dogmas but of necessarily ambiguous events. But how can particular statements exhaust all the conceivable meanings of the events?

Newman also emphasizes the problems inherent in an exhaustive interpretation of anything's meaning, given the great variety of possible points of view, imaginable connections, and conceivable meanings. Reliance on Scripture, for instance, is judged to be inadequate because the possible interpretations of its events are so numerous. Although less ambiguous than Scripture, dogmas both are open to interpretation and are incomplete renderings of the revelation they interpret. But if various interpretations are possible, what exactly can dogmas clearly convey?

Finally, Newman's thought stresses the distinction between the notional and the real. Real apprehension, the basis of vital religious life, deals with the concrete; notional apprehension, the basis of theology, deals with those more general ideas read from particulars. Although he emphasizes the necessity of both, he places a premium on personally apprehended, concrete religious facts. Here again one asks how this idea accords with an emphasis on dogma. These strands of Newman's thought constitute a major thrust in Newman's work; they do not clearly harmonize with his emphasis on dogma.

This tension creates difficulties that appear throughout Newman's writings. An excellent example is his idea of assimilation. Most dogmas rely on assimilated elements; indeed the idea of formulating dogmas and asking for obedience to them rests on a certain view of philosophy. The question, then, is whether an assimilated element, such as a particular Aristotelian formulation, is essential to or only a possible form of faith's expression. In thought about the Eucharist, for instance, are Aristotelian categories like substance absolutely necessary to a correct expression or are they just some among other possibilities? Assimilated elements are either necessary or are significant but unnecessary. If they are necessary, Christianity's meeting with a particular philosophy was crucial and foreordained; the use of Aristotelian formulations is revelatory and binding. If they are significant but unnecessary, then Christianity has a central event whose interpretation is not bound to any particular form of expression. The problem with this is how to decide the event's true character if no formulation is binding. But the alternative view, where a philosophy is ordained by God for an exact expression of revelation's truths, also has obvious problems. Both alternatives seem unacceptable and thereby reveal a dilemma that indicates a tension in Newman's attitude to dogma.[43]

Although dogma often seems to be a crucial element in Newman, it also appears to be ill-fitted with other basic aspects of his thought. Dogma appears to be unabsorbed into his general perspective. It is either a mysterious element that sits in judgment on the rest of his thought or one with less significance than it often appears to have. We can best approach these alternatives by examining dogma's various meanings in Newman's work and dogma's character as particular expression of religious thought.

Three Explications of Dogma.   Dogma has various meanings in Newman, but three are particularly important. Newman views dogma as an attitude that expresses more than a subjective judgment; as a practical expedient for contacting a preverbal master vision; and as a means by which a religious community regulates its life. In the first, dogma describes the attitude that believes something is important. Here dogma qualifies persons more than propositions; one is dogmatic when firmly holding to an idea. "Dogmatism is a religion's profession of its own reality as contrasted with other systems; . . . liberals . . . hold that one religion is as good as another." To be dogmatic is to believe that something is so real that it must be affirmed and other options rejected. For example, Newman opposes his statement that "dogma has been the fundamental principle of my religion" to an undogmatic position where religion is a mere sentiment. Similarly, his assertion that "many a man will live and die upon a dogma" is opposed to the idea that "no man will be a martyr for a conclusion . . . [no one] will die for his own calculations; he dies for realities."[44] Seriousness, personal commitment, a belief that an absolute truth has been touched are the keys here—an attitude toward reality is the basis of this usage.

Although working fundamentally with attitudes, Newman still desires to distinguish dogmatic attitudes from "sentiments or conclusions" that are recognized as reflecting only what a person subjectively affirms. A dogmatic attitude is believed to arise from contact with an external reality; it is distinguishable from an attitude felt to arise solely from within oneself and to imply nothing about a reality outside the self. The latter attitude is a simple private judgment that binds only the self and is open to change. A dogmatic attitude, however, is felt to be unchangeable and to imply that other positions are either wrong or incomplete. Implying more than mere subjective belief, it judges others and demands action. Newman's comment that "religion cannot but be dogmatic" means that religious attitudes always imply contact with a reality outside the self. Even when viewed subjectively, dogma shows religion is a reflection upon the passive voice, a recognition that something has been done to rather than by the self. The interrogation of experience shows two kinds of attitudes: private opinion implying nothing beyond the self and dogma implying contact with some exterior reality.

This view of dogma can also be approached through those philosophic perspectives that focus on the idea that language is to be understood in terms of its use. From this perspective, dogmatic statements are differentiated from other statements by the attitudes or actions they directly imply or indirectly generate. For example, one might judge contrary statements false, although one cannot clearly demonstrate that judgment. Here, then, dogma is seen in terms of a distinctive attitude.[45]

A second perspective arises from Newman's attempt to relate dogmas to their preverbal source and his subsequent characterization of them as an expedient for practical purposes. Dogma's basis is given various descriptions: an "impression on the Imagination"; "a sacred impression . . . which acts as a regulating principle"; "a definite, consistent, entire view." Newman insists that religion and its dogmas rest on a view that neither depends on nor consists in propositions. "Creeds and dogmas live in the one idea which they are designed to express, and which alone is substantive; and are necessary only because the human mind cannot reflect upon that idea, except piecemeal." The religious "view does not depend on such propositions: it does not consist in them; they are but specimens and indications of it." Dogmas are important but only as vehicles to help one maintain the image. They are to be used "just as if they were the realities which they represent," but with the recognition that they are "but an expedient for practical purposes, not a true analysis or adequate image."[46]

The believer recognizes the inadequacies of dogmas and yet continues to utilize them, if with caution, as an "expedient for practical purposes." The believer behaves "as if" reality is conveyed while recognizing that only a partial image of reality is given. Seeing dogma as a practical principle of guidance reflects Newman's idea of people's necessarily limited understanding. The limitation is religiously significant, not merely an inescapable fact, because it forces people to focus on God's providential care. As Newman says:

> Should any one fear lest thoughts such as these should tend to a dreary and hopeless scepticism, let him take into account the Being and Providence of God . . . and he will at once be relieved of his anxiety. . . . What is it to us whether the knowledge He gives us be greater or less, if it be He who gives it? What is it to us whether it be exact or vague, if He bids us trust it? What have we to care whether we are or are not given to divine substance from shadow, if He is training us heavenward by means of either?[47]

Newman focuses here both on the irreducible mystery of an economic revelation and on the centrality of a belief in God's providential care. Truly religious people do not seek total understanding. They embrace the commandment to have only one God and destroy even the idol of dogma. They commit themselves to the care of a guiding deity and accept whatever images are given to them. Rather than seeking clear formulations, people ought to ask for just enough clarity to move forward; they ought to desire only that minimal light which the present situation needs, can bear, and will find fruitful. Indeed, only in such circumstances are choice and growth possible. With either complete darkness or complete clarity people would need neither to develop themselves nor to make decisions. People must, then, stand to God as the catechumen to the practitioner of the *disciplina arcani*. They must trust that they are being led according to their capacities and must realize that to ask for greater enlightenment is irreligious.

These ideas lead to Newman's third perspective on dogma: the idea that dogma is both crucial for and only understandable within a particular community. The idea that language is understood by its use joins with the idea that certain formulations give one access to the underlying sacred impression. Together they create a view that sees dogmatic language as the means by which a community regulates its life. As "development equals translation into a new language,"[48] regulation is essential if the community's life is not, over time, to fragment and lose its central vision. Dogma, then, is that language which the community, at a particular time, sees as causing correct action and reflecting its guiding vision. Dogmas are to be viewed in light of the practical life of the ongoing community. Serving the religious community's realization of itself, they can be understood only in light of the fellowship and devotion of that community.

Newman sees dogma as an attitude expressing more than a subjective judgment, as a means of contacting a preverbal master vision, and as a way of regulating the actions of a particular community. Such a view differs from the conceptual model of truth generally regnant in the Catholicism of Newman's time. That model saw truth as available in clear ideas and thought teaching meant proposing clearly defined propositions. Using Pears' cogent description of various responses to modern philosophic problems shows how much Newman differed from his Catholic contemporaries. Newman clearly fits the subtle positivist or perhaps even Kantian romantic type, while normal Catholicism fits the pseudoscientific mode. Newman either argues in the "psychological or anthropological form: 'That is how people are,'" or he argues that the "central truth of religion . . . cannot be caught in the network of language, but . . . can be apprehended through it."[49] Historical circumstances forced Newman to relate to a mode of thinking and a criterion for religious truth that was, at best, uncongenial and, at worst, an inadequate vehicle for his own ideas. Though Newman would use and did defend the reigning model, his ideas differ substantially from it.

Dogma as a Necessary Element in Theoretic Religious Expression.   Given Newman's differences from traditional Catholic perspectives on dogma, another perspective is needed. The modern comparative study of religion's discussion of the types, forms, and kinds of religious thought can provide that perspective. Seen in light of this approach, Newman's religious thought aims neither to contemplate questions nor to resolve, in any recognizable sense, certain basic religious tensions. Rather it focuses on the religious usefulness of ideas and wishes to maintain rather than solve, or perhaps even probe, basic tensions. Newman sees religious thought as most religious—most aware of its distinctive subject—when it faces what might be called "irresolvable by revelatory and productive tensions." Two different but related insights are the irreducible givens on which such thought works—e.g., grace and free will; Christ as fully God and fully man, Christ as "both Pastor and agnus, priest and sacrifice."[50] Not only must both sides of the tension be maintained but moreover any resolution that even diminishes either side must be rejected. Indeed, because seeing both sides is revelatory and productive, a resolution need not be sought. Keeping the tension's irresolvability in mind and developing a tolerance for such tensions may be of considerable religious significance in making clear one's relation to the sacred. Certain questions, then, will remain unasked or be only partly analyzed because religious problems are treated only if they affect action and are worked through only in light of their consequences for behavior. Not the problem and its solution but the religious life animates Newman's religious thought. His type of thinking aims to form character and to shape action rather than to solve abstract theological questions.

Newman's view of theology as a form of practical reason, as previously examined in the *Via Media* preface, exemplifies this type of religious thought. Many have seen dogmatic reflection as belonging to Aristotle's theoretic reason. Newman, however, sees it as belonging to Aristotle's practical reason. Dogmatic reflection does not so much express necessary truth as it applies general principles to particular situations in order to guide correct action. In that part of the *Nicomachean Ethics* where the idea of practical reason is most fully developed, Aristotle remarks that the goal of ethical study lies in the actions engendered and people formed by it, rather than in the analysis itself. Indeed, this idea is particularly appropriate for religious thought. If the salvatory transformation of individuals is religion's goal and if basic polar tensions characterize its most significant insights, then forming religious language with the aim of guiding and persuading is not only a defensible activity but one especially congenial to the nature of the subject. If language produces a specific orientation, a certain sort of life—so that to imagine a language is to imagine a way of life—then to create and sustain a language is to create and sustain a way of life. This kind of theological reflection attempts to create a language that will save by forming proper attitudes and setting correct orientations.[51]

Seeing Newman from this perspective raises questions about the truth of such statements. Our final chapter will investigate this more fully, but we can note that Newman's emphasis on the formation of character always works in the service of what he understood to be religious truth. He neither looks to an idea's functional effectiveness in maintaining communal life nor sees a world in which people's limited nature forces them to think or act in ways they know to be accommodations to frailty. The practical mode of his religious thought works in light of what he saw as true.

Given this description, dogma's role can be clarified by reformulating Wach's ideas about the reasons for and forms of religious thought.[52] Wach argues that religious thought originates in religious experience and employs the ideas, symbols, and stories a culture gives. This expression in thought is as normal as is expression in social groups or in the actions of service or devotion. The impetus for expression in thought is varied. It arises, for instance, from the spontaneous need to give form to deeply held beliefs or complex emotions; or from the desire either to communicate with others or to propagate ideas; or from the wish to articulate coherently one's own or a common perspective; or from the attempt to meet the challenges posed by conflicting ideas, new situations, or different kinds of knowledge. All religious people in some fashion, at some time, express their religion in a theoretic way, although few rigorously work at it.

Most important for our purposes, theoretical religious expression has specific forms. A variety of forms can be enumerated; for example, sacred writings, creeds, and confessions of faith. Myth, doctrine, and dogma, however, are the three most important forms. Each of the three is an independent type; however, they may be deemed three levels rising toward increasingly precise propositional formulations. Myth can be described as a story about events that exhibits sacred reality and therefore defines a mode of being. Myth—probably the most evocative, surely the least precise—utilizes symbols, events, and persons in a narrative form that allows for considerable flexibility in exact wording. (Applying a modern understanding of myth to Newman raises a bevy of questions that need not be examined here. His emphasis on "real" events and, particularly, on the "master vision" may be profitably approached, however, by way of contemporary reflections on myths.) The doctrinal level asks questions of the myths and then formulates clear, propositional answers that subsequently may be correlated with one another. Dogmatic formulations arise when persons or institutions decide that certain doctrinal answers more fully express religious truth than do others and therefore must be affirmed, if membership in a particular religious community is desired.

A clear exemplification of these forms is found in those myths, doctrines, and dogmas concerning Mary in Roman Catholicism. A brief description of them clarifies the abstract structure. The basic myth concerns a woman's accepting the charge to bear and be mother to the Redeemer. Subsequently questions are asked of the story: What sort of person must she have been to accept such a request? What does her maternal relation to the Redeemer mean? What kind of sexual relations could she have had? Answers to these doctrinal questions proliferate until certain ones are determined to be true and acceptance of them becomes a criterion for membership in the community. For example, she was conceived without the faults normal to humans, and death brought her a distinctive kind of consummation. A story, when reflected on, leads to questions, answers, and finally explicit definitions of proper and improper views.

In general, then, dogma refers to the choice of those propositions that most accurately express what is believed to be true. Defined in terms of social institutions, dogma refers to those propositions by which a body of people define their central tenets in order to clarify them and, perhaps more important, to exclude some people. Dogmatic propositions are those statements that, if affirmed, bring membership in a specific body, and, if denied, bring exclusion. (Numerous questions arise, of course, about exclusion. For example: On what ground will such a judgment be applied—assent, or action, or attitude? What is the reference, if any, to the excluded person's religious state?) Defined in terms of the person who affirms dogma, however, dogma refers to the person's conviction that certain propositions express the truth. The doctrinal level is constituted by searching, hesitant weighing, and continuous discussing, but at the dogmatic level only certain answers are acceptable. Indeed, dogma is religiously significant precisely because only certain answers are acceptable. Of the three, only the mythic and dogmatic levels express a state that shows a salvatory relation to the sacred and a saving perspective upon the world.

Religious thought is different from other kinds of thought. Because religious reflection is based on religious experience, reports of sacral events, and an overall mythic perspective, its thought processes and results have distinctive origins and therefore distinctive characteristics. Because religious reflection is one of the three basic expressions of religion, a distinctive relationship exists with the ethical, devotional, and social life of the community from which it comes and to which it speaks. Religious thought's distinctive character arises from its sources and its life within a specific ambience. Its special genealogy, goals, and forms necessitate a particular approach to and judgment of it.

This distinctiveness of religious reflection appears most clearly in the spontaneous movement to dogmatic formulation. Doctrinal reflection manifests the normal human activity of asking questions. Dogma, however, shows the religious need for firm answers. The doctrinal level fails to reflect salvation, the essence of religion, because it lacks the solidity of firm resolutions. Because religious man is a questioner, firm statements that reflect answers are necessary to the completion of his religiosity. Anything less than such statements leaves the self without a proper base and the community without adequate guidance. Dogma completes humanity's natural religious impulses because, like myth, it is a medium for and expression of salvation. The final fulfillment of religion must incorporate dogmas and instruments for the proclamation of dogmas. Without them, humanity's natural religiosity is incomplete.

Conclusion Concerning Dogma.   The preceding ideas show that Newman's position on dogma, if uncommon and under attack in his day, is not unusual in human religions. Newman attempts to validate these common forms of religious thought against modern deformations. He argues against those types of religion, such as pietism and a form of Liberalism, that try to rest either in religious experience or on the mythic level. These religions see propositional reflection as able only to reach the doctrinal level, or they question whether any proposition can express the truth better than any other proposition, or they argue that what people think and say is unrelated to their religious state. Newman argues that their religion is truncated and their fulfillment hindered, because they have not proceeded to the completion dogma represents. The possession of dogma is a crucial part of the salvation that religion mediates to people.

The critical problem the opposing position sees in dogma is whether any statement can capture clearly the mysterious reality of religion. For those opposing Newman, only certain statements about morality may be called dogmatic, as they express reality clearly or at least more clearly than their contraries or mutations. For example, the statement that innocent life ought not be taken without compelling reason is truer than its denial. Moreover, one also expects those who deny such a statement to behave in a certain fashion. But the same cannot be said about religious statements or, at the least, cannot be said except about a particular religious statement at a particular time in history. Dogmas may adequately reflect religious reality for one historical period, but they cannot reflect it for all historical periods.

Newman recognizes this problem, but he argues that a basic part of the complete possession of religion is the possession of authoritative statements. To deny dogma is to deny completeness, to deny the fulfillment of all the religious drives, to deny people full access to religious reality. Such a response does not really meet the more subtle question, however: Do dogmas reflect only the reality of a particular time? Newman's answer here is not entirely clear. The *Development*, in particular, does show an acute sense of how particular historical situations call forth specific dogmatic responses. Moreover, a variety of kinds of dogmatic statements are articulated, e.g., defensive ones and recapitulating ones. To some degree Newman realizes how specific dogmas arose in relation to specific situations and thereby reflect the problems, language, and general perspectives of particular periods. But he also affirms their continuing truth, although always emphasizing the need for and fact of an ever-continuing interpretation. Dogmas remain a sacred gift, but one whose context must be recognized and whose reinterpretation must be pursued.

Whatever the incompleteness in Newman's account, certain elements are obvious. Dogmatic definition has a practical goal; it aims at a fuller religious life, not just at speculative solutions. Dogmatic formulations and interpretations are placed inside a community with a past and future. Dogma is the fulfillment of religious people's reflective inquiry, although it is based in religion's expressions in action and society. To sever dogma from this context, treating it like a simple factual statement, is to misunderstand it. The truth-claims and the importance of dogmatic statements are understandable only if one sees that their goal is practical action, their matrix is communal, and their sources are religious experience, myth, and doctrine.

Dogma is the paradigmatic test case of how Newman's authority model relates to normal forms of life. The problem of authority's relationship to normal human functions arises from Newman's abstract argument for an authoritative religion. Starting from the premise that an authoritative revelation exists, Newman argues that such a revelation needs interpretation and therefore demands somebody able to judge correct and incorrect interpretations. This argument leaves Newman with the problem of reconciling religious authority, which is a supernatural gift, with the fallible functionings of normal life. Four of his later writings present a portrait of that ideal, authoritative religion that would complete natural forms. In that portrait, the whole religious community in its spatial width, temporal length, and varied functions is the authoritative agent. Such a community will also contain and honor a plurality of individuals while furnishing protection to the unsophisticated and a forum of discussion for the sophisticated. An infallible teaching authority will exist, but theology will be the ultimate regulator of this ideal authoritative community. This model's incorporation of the ideas of change and pluralism shows that authority need not violate the normal processes of life. However, it also raises the question whether authority, in effect, is not destroyed. The just completed examination of dogma, where the problem is most acute, reveals Newman's response. He views dogma as an attitude expressing more than a subjective judgment, as a means of contacting a preverbal sacred impression, and as a way of regulating the actions of a particular community. Seeing ideas on dogma from the perspective provided by the comparative analysis of religious thought enables us to understand more clearly what dogma's role is, for Newman, in actualizing the human religious potential.

4

Liberal Religion

Six First Principles of Liberal Religion

The discussion and criticism of Liberal religion is perhaps the most prominent thread in the tapestry which is Newman's life work. For example, the Biglietto speech, delivered on becoming a Cardinal and looking "upon the world and upon the Holy Church as in it, and upon her future," takes Liberal religion as its main subject. It did so because for "thirty, forty, fifty years I [Newman] have resisted to the best of my powers the spirit of Liberalism in religion." Newman never gives, however, a clear, unified description of Liberal religion. His writings on the subject cover fifty years and are usually polemical. Moreover, those writings often reflect either the diversity of English religious Liberalism or the still greater diversity of the "Liberal spirit." English religious Liberalism ranged from Low Churchmen through Platonists to non-Christian Theists or Pantheists, while the Liberal spirit, as Newman said, by the second half of the nineteenth century was no longer just a party but rather was the educated lay world.

Nevertheless, a discernible view of Liberal religion emerges from Newman's writings. While he thought that "in detail, and in character, it varies," he also thought that its general nature is "one and the same everywhere." His approach to a characterization of Liberal religion is well put when he says:

> It must not be supposed that I attribute [Liberal religion] . . . to any given individual or individuals; nor is it necessary to my purpose to suppose that any one man as yet consciously holds, or sees the drift, of that portion of the theory to which he has given assent. I am to describe a set of opinions which may be considered as the true explanation of many floating views, and the converging point of a multitude of separate and independent minds . . . I may be describing a school of thought in its fully developed proportions, which at present everyone, to whom membership with it is imputed, will at once begin to disown, and

I may be pointing to teachers whom no one will be able to descry. Still, it is not less true that I may be speaking of tendencies and elements which exist.[1]

In the vocabulary of our study, Newman describes a type of religion. A type points to certain definable attributes that distinguish one phenomenon from others, but it does not imply the existence of a functioning entity that exactly corresponds to the type. Liberal religion is not, however, an abstract type like natural religion. Newman does refer to specific schools, movements, or men as personifications of Liberal religion. Nevertheless, the general idea of typological characterization holds. Liberal religion is neither revealed nor natural religion. It is, for Newman, a third type of religion, the religion that deforms Christianity and stunts fundamental religious impulses.

The type is best understood by uncovering what Newman saw as Liberal religion's first principles, the underlying notions that formed its religious outlook. There are six such principles: (1) human nature is good; (2) private judgment is obligatory; (3) deity is a principle discoverable through examination of evidence; (4) revelation is a manifestation not a mystery; (5) useful goods are primary; and (6) education is salvatory. The first pair reflects its general vision of humanity, the second pair its view of deity and the world's relation to deity. The final pair focuses on the new "salvatory" social matrix that can fulfill humanity.

Newman sees the opposition between Liberalism and Christianity as a conflict of first principles. First principles are those "propositions with which we start in reasoning on any given subject matter." They are "those assumptions rather than objective professions" that cause the basic differences in opinions between men. "Men differ from each other, not so much in the soundness of their reasoning as in the principles which govern its exercise."[2] Differences in principles, then, distinguish positions. Moreover, they control thought as the very information that might change one's thinking is filtered through the principles. This chapter's major business will be the explication of each of Liberal religion's first principles. As background, however, a brief explication of all the principles and some comment on Newman's attitude to Liberalism are needed.

Liberal religion thinks people have a fundamentally unhindered capacity to fulfill themselves; they have the ability to know the good and to realize it through proper action. People are neither irreversibly divided against themselves nor estranged from proper worldly and religious fulfillment. Growing from this view is the idea of people's right, indeed obligation, to judge for themselves on all religious matters. Human beings must exercise autonomous judgments; they must emerge from a slavish dependence on authority and accept only what is congenial. Relying in such judgments on an analysis of publicly available evidence, Liberal religion sees God as a principle in basic continuity with the world, and not as a person transcendent to and different from the world. The divine is that principle underlying the world's unified order. Because any revelation is only a limited manifestation of this principle, rather than the mysterious gift of a transcendent personal deity, the particular forms of the revelation must be penetrated until their universal content is clear. Moreover, ideas arising from this revelation, indeed all ideas, must be tested by their usefulness to the person or the society. Ideas are not to be judged by ultimate standards. Rather they should by judged by the criterion of whether they lead to a just society. A just society will fulfill people completely, in large part because its educational system can train people to actualize their total potential. Because human beings are basically good and useful goods are the criterion by which to judge ideas and actions, proper education can develop good human beings and thus a just society. This complex of ideas undergirds Liberal religion as Newman understood it.

Newman's Attitude to Liberal Religion

Newman's attitude to Liberal religion is complex. Occasionally he appears to see only simple-mindedness or unalloyed evil in Liberal religion, but his more balanced view is respectful if critical. He thinks the vital struggle of modernity is not between Protestants and Catholics, or even perhaps between Christianity and other religions, but between traditional religion and Liberal religion. Unlike most other struggles, that "stern encounter" involves two different "real and living principles, simple, entire, and consistent, . . . rush[ing] upon each other, contending not for names and words, or half-views, but for elementary notions and distinctive moral characters." The struggle is especially momentous because, to Newman's mind, Liberal religion leads inexorably to atheism. As the *Apology*'s famous statement puts it, there is "no medium, in true philosophy, between Atheism and Catholicity, . . . a perfectly consistent mind, under those circumstances in which it finds itself here below, must embrace either the one or the other." "There are but two alternatives, the way to Rome, and the way to Atheism: Anglicanism is the halfway house on the one side, and Liberalism is the halfway house on the other."[3] Put in the vocabulary of this work, the poles Newman sees are the religious and the nonreligious, what develops and what distorts humanity's religious potential. Liberal religion, for Newman, is so far along the continuum toward nonreligion, is so out of touch with religion's roots, that it can only corrupt the religious potential. Liberal religion defines itself as a religion and bears many of a religion's characteristics, but it cannot actualize humanity's religious nature.

This view underlies Newman's passionate rejection of any attempt to use the principles of Liberal religion to reformulate Christianity. Any attempt to reform Christianity by means of Liberal ideas can only create a halfway house on the road to the rejection of all religion. The only two real human possibilities are religion and nonreligion; Newman attempts to destroy all middle positions in order to drive people to one or the other extreme. As he said, "I fully grant that my mode of reasoning . . . tends . . . to drive people into one extreme or the other." For him the real issues are set, the battle truly met, only if the frailty of mediating positions is recognized. One must either "take Christianity, or leave it; do not practice upon it; to do so is as unphilosophical as it is dangerous . . . you [Liberals] dishonestly pick and choose, and take as much or as little of it as you please. You either accept Christianity, or you do not: if you do, do not garble and patch it; if you do not, suffer others to submit to it ungarbled." When most sympathetic, Newman recognizes the integral impulse motivating the Liberals. He realizes Liberals reinterpret Christianity in order to make it more real for themselves and more efficacious in a world that is rapidly losing belief. But, to him, the cruel irony is that their way of saving Christianity is bound in time to destroy it. "The [Liberal] School, as such, will pass through . . . [various stages] to that 'God-denying Apostasy,' to use the ancient phrase, to which in the beginning of its career it professed to be especially opposed."[4]

Newman's opposition to Liberal religion is not, however, the whole story. He recognizes, though rarely publicly expressing his view, that Liberal religion contains important insights. Indeed, his reformulation of Christianity is constituted to a significant degree by his incorporation of Liberal insights—e.g., the historicity of religious life, the importance of personhood in belief. In Newman's own terms, Liberal religion is a set of half-truths about religion: "part of what they say is false, part is true, but misapplied." At times their half-truth is just that of "secular ethics," but more often it is the half-truth of "civilized understanding." In either case the danger is clear, because "we know, even from the common experience of life, that half the truth is often the most gross and mischievous of falsehoods."[5] Simple falsity can never win and keep adherents, but half-truths are attractive because they do contain some truth.

As Liberal religion is a modern reinterpretation of religion, Newman's complex attitude to Liberal religion reflects his complex attitude to modernity. Various descriptions exist of the modern, but most agree that modern people have a distinctive consciousness or at least a distinctive set of problems, principles, and attitudes. Newman often implies that modernity is not distinctive. He says it merely represents what happens, both bad and good, when men become "civilized," become sophisticated about the world's working. Not one but many enlightenments have occurred in the West's history; Liberal religion is just one among many civilized religions that have appeared in Western history. Such a position is more defensible than one that argues modernity has created a unique situation, but certain factors do make modernity distinctive. One factor is put well in Peter Berger's statement that though a similar consciousness has existed at various times, "with the beginning of the modern era in the West this form of consciousness intensifies, becomes concentrated and systematized, [and] marks the thought of an increasing number of perceptive men."[6] Attitudes once held by only a few are now held generally. Moreover, other distinctive factors probably also divide the modern era from other eras—e.g., the sense of history, a critical self-reflection on the act of belief, a recognition of the plurality of viable religions, a grasp of the effect of society on thought and action. Newman did say humanity was soon "to enter upon a new cycle of sacred history" and perhaps the unique situation of a "world simply irreligious."[7] He is aware that modernity has created some new and significant problems.

Newman's relationship to modernity, and thus to Liberal religion, exemplifies how his thought often contains undrawn implications. Newman may not draw certain implications because he simply fails to see where his thoughts lead. He also probably thought, particularly after his conversion, that the situation was inappropriate for the pursuit of some issues.

In most cases, however, undrawn implications exist because Newman stands, or tries to stand, in two worlds at once, a traditional Christian one and a modern one. Most of his major works turn on the attempt to relate traditional religion to some aspect of modernity: in the *Development*, historicity to doctrinal affirmations; in the *Grammar*, skepticism to assent; in the *Idea*, secular education to religious nurture; in the *Apology*, human beings as changing creatures and self-conscious perceivers of their own perceptions to human beings as unitary beings and believers. Throughout his life, he focused on the problem of modernity's effect on religion. Many people in the nineteenth century did that, but Newman lived with the tensions of that time, tensions that are still with us, in an especially profound way. He is a particularly interesting figure because he tries to stand in a traditional and a modern world; he is a particularly challenging figure because he argues that one can and must stand in both worlds; he is a particularly complex figure because his work reflects the tensions of those two worlds. Nowhere is this problem clearer than in his treatment of Liberal religion, where he criticizes its practitioners' use of modern insights but then often attempts to use those insights himself.

Newman, then, sees Liberal religion as a halfway house between the religious and the nonreligious that tends toward the corruption of humanity's basic religious potential. That simple view is complicated, however, by his recognition that Liberal religion contains true insights which he himself can selectively use in his own reflections on Christianity. He remains fundamentally opposed to Liberal religion only insofar as it is a coherent set of ideas and attitudes that other people use to reinterpret Christianity completely. This enterprise is flawed, he thinks, because Christianity and Liberal religion are two different types of religion. Any attempt to synthesize them will change Christianity into an entity that tends toward the nonreligious. Our main aim here is to explicate the abstract type "Liberal religion," but we will also note Newman's rejection or acceptance of certain Liberal insights.

Human Nature as Good

The first underlying principle of Liberal religion is a belief in the inherent goodness of human nature. No fundamental impediments exist to a human realization satisfactory to both the individual and the society. The negative theophany that Newman thought conscience mediated is denied. Conscience's judgments show only specific shortcomings that effort can overcome. Human beings are not seen as divided against themselves, as fallen short of what God and the self desire, and as bound to be both unhappy and judged by God. Such a view of man entails, Newman thinks, a generally bright, optimistic view of the world. Basically satisfied with themselves, the Liberals must view the world in a way that highlights its bright side. Liberal religion then takes "the brighter side of the Gospel,—its tidings of comfort, its precepts of love; all darker, deeper views of man's condition and prospects being comparatively forgotten. . . . Conscience is no longer recognized as an independent arbiter of actions. . . . Everything is bright and cheerful. Religion is pleasant and easy; benevolence is the chief virtue; intolerance, bigotry, excess of zeal, are the first of sins."[8] This view of human nature leads to an overall vision in which possibility, satisfaction, and harmony are preeminent.

Newman's opposition to this view is not only clear, but it also reveals some of his central ideas. At his most polemical, Newman accuses Liberalism of a naively optimistic view of human nature that denies both conscience's and history's testimony about human evil. Lulled into optimism by a lack of self-examination, a belief in progress, and a society temporarily at peace, this view is painted as hopelessly shallow. Indeed, such a view overlooks estrangement and therefore must also deny real relief. These ideas exemplify how Liberal religion lives on half truths; it is attractive because of the truth contained but it is dangerous because of the truth missing.

Newman is right, of course, that either self-examination or historical awareness shows that some views of human goodness are naive. Viable bases for the idea have existed in the modern period, however. The contrast between these viable notions and Newman's own ideas exemplifies a clash in first principles. One such notion is a rebirth of that classical vision exemplified by Aristotle. It recognizes potentially destructive elements within human nature but affirms that people, or at least some people, can control them. With the rebirth of this view, there resurfaces a fundamental issue that has often haunted the Western tradition: to what degree can human beings control all their disordered aspects and by themselves attain a harmonious fulfillment of self? The calm surety of the *Nicomachean Ethics* stands against the passionate perplexity of Augustine's *Confessions*.

The other, more distinctively modern view also recognizes that evil forces move in people, but this view thinks elements outside human nature cause them. Rousseau exemplifies this position with his statement that human dividedness corresponds to the division between natural and civilized humanity. Human evil is only a provisional state. Properly constituted social life will allow for the flowering of humanity's natural goodness. The classical and Enlightenment visions differ, but they share the idea that people can be restored because they are fundamentally good and because all their evil depends on elements that can be changed. Furthermore, they agree that a properly constituted society will allow for, or even cause, people to realize their true selves. The right social arrangements will furnish the salvatory matrix through which people can fulfill themselves. With these affirmations, the problem of human evil changes from a religious or metaphysical question, resolvable only by reference to higher realms, to a social or political question, resolvable only by changes in social areas.[9]

Newman condemned such views largely because they denied conscience's negative theophany. The viability of both visions is evident, however. Historically, Liberalism reflects a post-Enlightenment, "classical" idea of human nature's native ability to overcome estrangement. Newman, however, holds to an older, postclassical, pre-Enlightenment, "Christian" view. His view does differ from the traditional Christian view in one important way, however. Unlike traditional Christians, who knew the opposite view had existed but had been displaced, Newman knew his view had been dominant but now was being replaced by the opposite view. Newman must then examine the contrary view and even admit it carries a partial truth. Newman did think conscience assured him that the "Christian" view was true, but his historical position precludes him from being able to hold to that idea as if no real alternatives exist.

These two views not only represent different historical epochs, but they also illustrate that massive and mysterious shift in Western people's perception of themselves generated by the Enlightenment. That shift is perhaps even more important than the shift in the opposite direction completed in late antiquity. Previously, Western Christians saw themselves as divided and detestable creatures; now at least some saw themselves as either potentially or actually good. The gap between the views is wide enough to make statements from one view sound almost preposterous to listeners from another view. Consider, for example, Aquinas's statement that part of the blessed's happiness in heaven is watching the damned's sufferings in hell, human evil being so clear that to see its punishment is a blessing. Similarly, note Luther's comment that he fears to possess the freedom to realize himself because his depravity is so great that his damnation will then be inevitable. Basic concepts like freedom (for the Liberal the essential condition of self-actualization) or eternal suffering (for the Liberal a barbarism to be rejected) have completely different meanings in the traditional view.

The opposition between Newman and Liberal religion on many issues often rests on their differing sense of human potentiality. Moreover, the Liberals' reconstitution of Christianity around their vision of human goodness must, for Newman, lead to a new religion. Based in a partial view of humanity, Liberalism is bound to generate a new, imperfect religion and corrupt what it attempts to reform. Flawed at its very root, Liberal religion can bear only bitter fruit.

Private Judgment as Obligatory

Private Judgment's Various Senses, Background, and Presuppositions.   The second principle of Liberal religion is the right, indeed the obligation, of people to judge for themselves on important matters. People's basic criterion for judgment should be what they think is rationally demonstrable or what they find congenial with their emotional state. Liberal religion sees the opposite attitude, requiring individual judgment to submit to authoritative truths, as perhaps the most destructive of all human attitudes.

Newman usually labels this idea "private judgment," but he gathers enough divergent ideas under that one rubric to necessitate separating out the various meanings. In later writings, private judgment often specifies that sphere within Catholicism where individual conscience and interpretation may or even must work. Here legitimate private judgment guards against lifeless submission to papal authority. Another meaning, particularly evident in early works, differentiates Protestant and Catholic by means of private judgment. Protestants interpret the Bible by means of private judgment, Catholics by means of the Church and tradition. Still another meaning refers to the general ethos that counsels people to exercise independent judgment in all areas of life. Two other meanings refer especially to Liberal religion, though they are never clearly distinguished by Newman. They refer to what might be called the rationalistic and pietistic wings of Liberal religion. The rationalist sees reason, the pietist the emotions as the criterion for individual judgment. These two meanings are most important to us, but some comment on the general intellectual climate that gave birth to them is helpful.

For many in the Enlightenment, dogma rather than doubt or insufficiency of knowledge was truth's worst enemy. Dogma is, in Cassirer's phrase, "the attempt to anticipate the goal which knowledge must attain and to establish the goal prior to investigation." The dawning sense of human beings' extraordinary ability to know and affect their environment, which Liberals saw in science, is mortally wounded neither by ignorance nor by doubt, which time and careful investigation will overcome, but only by dogmatism. The human mind is subject to delusions and mistakes, but both can be overcome. Only the prejudice of dogma can finally thwart the pursuit of truth. A line from Bayle's *Dictionary* puts it well: "the obstacles to a good examination do not come so much from the fact that the mind is void of knowledge as that it is full of prejudice." The clearest statement of the basic ideal, however, is Kant's famous definition of Enlightenment: "Enlightenment is man's exodus from his self-incurred tutelage. Tutelage is the inability to use one's understanding without the guidance of another person. This tutelage is self-incurred if its causes lie not in any weakness of the understanding, but in indecision and lack of courage to use the mind without the guidance of another. 'Dare to know' (*sapere aude*)! Have the courage to use your own understanding; this is the motto of the Enlightenment."[10] Because the tutelage is self-incurred it can be overcome if human beings will courageously reject both authorities and dogmas and seek the truth. This widespread questioning of the use of external criteria to guide judgment underlies Liberalism's second principle.

The Liberal ramifications of this general idea are already evident in Newman's early attempt to describe eighteen principles of liberalism. Of these, principle five, for instance, is perhaps his most provocative general statement about private judgment: "It is immoral in a man to believe more than he can spontaneously receive as being congenial to his moral and mental nature." People's subjective state is to be the measure for judging the acceptable. Any submission to something not immediately and spontaneously congenial is ruled out. This idea of accepting only what is congenial necessitates (as principle three of the eighteen says) that "no theological doctrine is anything more than an opinion which happens to be held by bodies of men." People with similar private judgments may form a group, but that group's ideas just reflect what some individuals find spontaneously congenial to their moral and mental nature. The implications of this position are massive; as Newman puts two primary ones (in principles six and seven of the eighteen): "No revealed doctrines or precepts may reasonably stand in the way of scientific conclusions"; and "Christianity is necessarily modified by the growth of civilization, and the exigencies of time."[11] If religion's reality depends only upon personal acceptance, it must be modified by the needs of various times, and it must change when faced with objective realities like the findings of science. Private judgment emphasizes, then, that religious affirmations are not responses to objective truths. Any religious community is just a group of people sharing certain subjective responses. Such a community's affirmations will change as cultures change and must always be modified when they meet the "objective" results of science.

The perspective rests on two presuppositions: the ideas that human nature is good and that ultimate truth is inaccessible. If human nature is good, people can trust their judgments, but if it is flawed, trusting what it finds congenial will lead to error. Moreover, asserting that human nature is good also implies that people will find only one thing congenial. Newman, however, argues that different things may be congenial to different parts of a person. One aspect of a person (the desire for immediate gratification) might find congenial something that another part (the conscience) will not. Newman sees people as divided. A person's different aspects are drawn to different satisfactions. Liberal religion sees people as unified. Drawn to a single and congenial goal, people need not accept authority in order to grow toward a goal that at first they find uncongenial.

The other idea underlying private judgment (an idea which will reappear in other principles of Liberal religion) is a skepticism about humanity's ability clearly to know ultimate truth. The "fundamental dogma [of the position] is, that nothing can be known for certain about the unseen world. This . . . [is] taken for granted as a self evident point." "You may have opinions in religion, you may have theories, you may have arguments, you may have probabilities; you may have anything but demonstration."[12] That such a skepticism is crucial to private judgment may seem strange given Newman's frequent equating of Liberalism with rationalism. It makes more sense, however, when Newman's analysis is seen as reflecting the growth of Liberal religion. Particularly in its early stages, Liberal religion did emphasize reason's role either in the general pursuit of evidences for Christianity or in the more particular attempt to know God from a scientific analysis of the world. But this approach generated few self-evident religious truths. As that fact became clearer, the criterion of truth tended to become the internal testimony of the heart, only aspects of which might be reasonable. Reason continued to set the standard for the clearly knowable, but feeling became the real source of belief and action inasmuch as little religiously important was clearly knowable.[13] By this means, and particularly in the minds of ordinary people, the rationalist and pietist wings of Liberalism were fused. The idea of human goodness combines with the ideas of religious knowledge's frailty and religious feeling's validity to generate the view that the self is the only real source of authoritative judgment.

Significant portions of this position attract Newman, as his work on Christian belief shows: e.g., his emphasis on the personal character of belief, or on the integral role of emotion, or on the difficulties in rational knowledge of ultimates. Moreover, Newman agrees with private judgment's emphasis on the need for individual decision in religion. As an early work says, "without private judgment there is no responsibility; . . . a man's own mind, and nothing else, is the cause of believing or not believing, and of his acting or not acting upon his belief." As this is clear, "the question in dispute [is only] . . . what are the means which are to direct our choice, and what is the manner of using them."[14] This subtle point is the real hinge on which the argument swings; here as elsewhere Newman sees the Liberal view as a half-truth parading as the full truth.

Newman's Criticism of Private Judgment.   Newman opposes the Liberal idea of private judgment because he thinks it excludes revelation and fallaciously describes the decision process in humans. The very notion of revelation demands some suspension of private judgment. Moreover, people normally accept authority and limit private judgment in the beliefs they accept and decisions they make. Newman argues that "no revelation [is] conceivable which does not involve a sacrifice of private judgment."[15] Revelation involves the reception of something humans are unable to give themselves. Therefore, revelation and private judgment cannot coexist; one must be denied or at least modified. Our discussion of Newman's authoritative model showed how subtle this question is, but clearly some elements of revelation are authoritative enough to demand a suspension of individual judgment. A never-ending war between authority and private judgment may exist, but that war occurs because both factors exist. To eliminate the given called revelation, with its demands on private judgment, is to eliminate religion.

Newman also argues that private judgment's sphere is very limited. Most human knowledge and action moves by means of implicit authoritative guidance. People may either desire to exercise independent judgments or think they do so, but in reality they neither want to nor can. The human knowing process is necessarily, if often unconsciously, guided by authority. First principles exemplify this external guidance. People reason from first principles; they do not freely reason about them. Normal reasoning, however, also shows the same process.

> However full and however precise our producible grounds may be, however systematic our method, however clear and tangible our evidence, yet when our argument is traced down to its simple elements, there must ever be something assumed ultimately which is incapable of proof, and without which our conclusions will be . . . illogical. . . . For instance, we trust our senses, and that in spite of their often deceiving us. . . . We consider that there is so strong an antecedent probability that they are faithful, that we dispense with proof. . . . Again: we rely implicitly on our memory, and that, too, in spite of its being obviously unstable and treacherous. . . . . [This is] the state in which we find ourselves by nature with reference to the acquisition of knowledge generally,—a state in which we must assume something to prove anything, and can gain nothing without a venture.[16]

Throughout his analysis of knowledge and judgment, Newman highlights those areas where acceptance of authority is normal and limitation of private judgment is natural. Indeed, showing his distrust of purely intellectual ideals, Newman argues that most people either spontaneously reject or modify private judgment. He even argues that the only possible reasons to accept private judgment are either an acceptance of total pluralism or an unfounded belief that the truth is so clear that independent judgments will lead everyone to the same conclusions.[17] In actual life people accept numerous ideas on trust because of authority. For Newman, then, private judgment conflicts, by definition, with any possible idea of revelation—and thus religion—and rests on a flawed notion of the human decision process.

*Deity as a Principle Discoverable
through Examination of Evidence*

The Physical Theologians.   The third and fourth principles concern the
character of and means for knowing God or the ultimate religious
object. (This connection between how one knows and what one knows
is basic to Newman.) Liberal religion sees the sacred as a principle
known through various manifestations in the natural and historical
process. The third principle concerns the acquisition of knowledge
through the natural process, the fourth principle the acquisition of
knowledge through the historical process. The third principle asserts
that the sacred object can be discovered and its character defined by
close attention to the evidence available in the natural world. The position of the specific school of thinkers that Newman usually refers to is
clearly inadequate. Hume demonstrated their argument's philosophic
incoherence and the development of science undermined their factual
base. With this school, then, we must distinguish between the actual
proponents of the principle and the more general notions the principle
points toward.

Newman focuses on that school which argued to God from the
design of the natural world. Their greatest success lay in the eighteenth
century, but the ideas continued to thrive, in both popular and sophisticated forms, in Newman's lifetime. These thinkers asserted that
reflection on the natural order could both prove God's existence and
articulate his character. Newman entitled their approach Physical Theology to differentiate it from Natural Theology, which "properly
comprehends man and society." He thought Physical Theology was
"really . . . no science at all, for it is ordinarily nothing more than a
series of pious or polemical remarks upon the physical world viewed
religiously." Its attempt failed to meet those philosophic tests set by
Hume, that "acute, though most low-minded of speculators," in his
critiques of arguments from design. Newman thought reflections of the
divine might be found in nature, but they were evident only because of
previous belief. As he said, "for 40 years I have been unable to see the
logical force of the argument [from design] myself. I believe in design
because I believe in God; not in a God because I see design." Rather
than a serious attempt at proof, Physical Theology is "a certain view
taken of Nature, private and personal, which one man has, and
another has not."[18] Moreover, not understanding science's changeable
character, it is "powerless against scientific anticipations, for it is merely
one of them [a scientific theory]." Changes in the scientific perspective,
such as the shift from a static to a developmental view brought by
Darwin, will invalidate its findings. Dependent on scientific findings,

such a theory must reflect any shift science undergoes; as Newman bitingly puts it, "if 'the Spirit of God' is gas in 1850, it may be electro-magnetism in 1860."[19] Physical Theology lacks both philosophical in-tegrity and a sense of the instability of scientific findings.

The most basic flaw of Physical Theology, however, is using scientific research on the natural world as the basis from which to judge the validity of all approaches and conclusions. This flaw reveals that the issues here go beyond the ideas of a school that is now of only historical interest. The more general question is how to approach and character-ize the ultimate religious object as that object is seen outside of revela-tion. Newman recognized that Physical Theology could be seen as part of a tradition longer and often more cogent than its own. He comments that it is part of a two-thousand-year-old tradition or, more polemically, that in every age it is the creed of shallow people who think themselves enlightened and philosophic. Seen in this larger context, the issues are more significant and the battle more vital.

The Substantive Issues: The Use of Evidence and the Specification of Religion's Ultimate Object.   The appropriate approach to evidence about religion and the characterization of the ultimate sacred object are the important general issues that Physical Theology generates. Both these issues raise questions crucial to the difference between the fulfillment and the de-formation of human religiosity. The relation of evidence to religious reflection is critical to Newman's overall disagreements with Liberal religion, as the reliance on evidence provides an alternative to New-man's reliance on authority.

The Liberals' reliance on evidence comes close to being a principle of their religion. The issue takes different forms in different places, however. For example, the personal appropriation of evidence crucial to the principles of private judgment and of revelation as manifestation differs from the attitude toward evidence when deity is pursued by means of an examination of the natural world. Moreover, the question of evidence's role consumes a major portion of both the *Oxford Sermons* and the *Grammar of Assent.* Here, however, we shall focus only on Lib-eral religion's desire to use evidence drawn from the natural world, evidence which all people supposedly will find compelling, as a basis for understanding religion's sacred object.

The Liberal ideal is that "prejudices and mental peculiarities are excluded from the discussion; we descend to grounds common to all; certain scientific rules and fixed standards for weighing testimony, and examining facts, are received. Nothing can be urged, or made to tell, but what all feel, all comprehend, all can put into words." Indeed, "nothing properly can be assumed but what men in general will grant as true; that is, nothing but what is on a level with all minds, good and bad, rude and refined." Newman thinks this portrait is flawed because important evidence is neither clear nor independent of the observers' state. This portrait overlooks the subtlety of religious evidence and the influence of the perceiver's spiritual character on what evidence he finds compelling.

> Commonly the evidence for and against religion . . . is not of . . . [an] overpowering nature. . . . [It need not be because] most men must and do decide by the principles of thought and conduct which are habitual to them; that is, the antecedent judgment, with which a man approaches the subject of religion, not only acts as a bearing this way or that,—as causing him to go out to meet the evidence in a greater or lesser degree, and nothing more,—but, further, it practically colours the evidence, even in a case in which he has recourse to evidence, and interprets it for him.

The Liberal view of evidence collapses faith into a limited kind of reason. Faith is no different from reason if "it turns out merely to be a believing upon evidence, or a sort of conclusion upon a process of reasoning, a resolve formed upon a calculation."[20]

Newman argues that belief is more than an unwarranted acceptance. But he also emphasizes the differences between belief and an acceptance compelled by evidence. He works, then, between the two poles of faith as independent of evidence and faith as a result of evidence. Each pole is for him a half-truth. Although never denying faith's relation to evidence, he emphasizes that faith interprets evidence. "Faith, considered as an exercise of Reason, has this characteristic,— that it proceeds far more on antecedent grounds than on evidence; it trusts much to presumptions, and in doing this lies its special merit." Indeed, "we decide one way or another, according to the position of the alleged fact, relatively to our existing state of religious knowledge and feeling." Viewing evidence by means of, say, presumption and a properly tuned heart, faith interprets evidence. Simple evidence is less important than the viewer who interprets it; indeed evidence is significant only if the perceiver is in a proper state. Belief arises from a multitude of things that work in a subtle, delicate interaction—e.g., desire, moral character, love, antecedent probability, appropriate first principles, the mysterious movement of outside spiritual forces. When questioned by others or querying themselves, people can delineate evidence for their belief. Such evidence, however, is not belief's total cause, and therefore it cannot be expected to compel others. Although playing a role in faith's decision process, evidence attains real prominence only in faith's rational explanation of itself. In Newman's phrase, evidences "are not the essential groundwork of Faith, but its reward."[21] Rather than the groundwork which generates faith, they are the reward which makes its coherence explicit.

Newman's concern here is not just to win an argument about the character of various mental processes. More crucial for him is that the misreading of evidence's role in religious belief engenders an attitude that corrupts people's natural religiosity.

> Is not this the error, the common and fatal error, of the world, to think itself a judge of Religious Truth without preparation of heart? . . . [In] the schools of the world the ways toward Truth are considered high roads open to all men, however disposed, at all times. Truth is to be approached without homage. Every one is considered on a level with his neighbor; or rather the powers of the intellect, acuteness, sagacity, subtlety, and depth, are thought to be the guides into Truth.[22]

The attitude illustrated by Liberal religion undermines real religious growth and understanding. In overlooking the subtle process of selecting and interpreting evidence, Liberal religion overlooks people's normal religious movements and corrupts humanity's natural religiosity.

The other general issue generated by Physical Theology concerns the specification of religion's ultimate object. This question relates closely to the question of evidence because, for Newman, certain kinds of approach generate certain kinds of objects. Approaching deity through conscience gives a judging deity; approaching deity through nature gives only a divine principle. A scientific attitude leads to a truncated vision of God because it is concerned only with those phenomena which people see, hear, and handle. A scientific approach cannot rise to a full vision of the sacred. It begins "with matter . . . [so] with matter it will end." As in studying man, religion focuses not only on the human body but also on the "living principle, acting upon it and through it by means of volition," so in physical science, religion must look "behind the veil of the visible universe, [where] there is an invisible, intelligent Being, acting on and through it, as and when He will."[23] Just as physiology is unable to deal with the human spirit, so physics is unable to deal with deity.

Science pushed beyond its proper sphere of inquiry leads to the disastrous consequence of seeing God as a part of the world and therefore robbing the word "God" of any real meaning.

> Nothing is easier than to use the word [God], and mean nothing by it. The heathens used to say, "God wills", when they meant "Fate"; "God provides", when they meant "Chance"; "God acts", when they meant "Instinct" or "Sense"; and "God is every where", when they meant "The Soul of Nature". The Almighty is something infinitely different from a principle, or a centre of action, or a quality, or a generalization of phenomena.

The use of this approach, Newman argues, results in only three qualities being attributed to the Supreme Being. The three are Power, Wisdom, and Goodness and "of these, most of Power, and least of Goodness"; "it speaks only of laws . . . identifying Him [God] with His works." It relates human beings to a Divine Principle, not a Divine Agent. That shift not only corrupts Christianity, it also stunts humanity's basic religious potential. Where in their picture of deity, Newman asks,

> are those special Attributes which are the immediate correlatives of religious sentiment? Sanctity, omniscience, justice, mercy, faithfulness. . . . [What does it] teach us, except very indirectly, faintly, enigmatically, of these transcendently important, these essential portions of the idea of Religion . . . of duty and conscience? or a particular providence? and, coming, at length, to Christianity, what does it teach us even of the four last things, death, judgment, heaven, and hell, the mere elements of Christianity? It cannot tell us anything of Christianity at all. . . . Indeed, a Being of Power, Wisdom, and Goodness, and nothing else, is not very different from the God of the Pantheist.[24]

Newman's view here reflects his general idea that Liberal religion is a superficially attractive approach that destroys religion by attempting to reinterpret it. Moreover, his desire to undermine middle positions in order to make options clear shows in his preference for an outright profession of atheism rather than a profession of naturalistic pantheism. "I really doubt whether I should not prefer that he should be an Atheist at once than such a naturalistic, pantheistic religionist. His profession of Theology deceives others, perhaps deceives himself." Such a profession stops someone from recognizing, for instance, that the only "practical safeguard against Atheism in the case of scientific inquirers is the inward need and desire, the inward experience of that Power, existing in the mind before and independently of their examination of His material world." The progeny of this Liberal reinterpretation of religion is Atheism; the reinterpretation can but corrupt what it misguidedly tries to save. Like all halfway houses, it is bound not only to fail but also to deceive, to create perspectives that, although called religious, draw the lifeblood from religion. Real religion can arise only from the experience of conscience and received gifts. Its base is never the mere evidence that anyone, religious or not, can perceive. True religion can never arise from those "who have never been careful to obey their conscience, who cultivate the intellect without disciplining the heart, and who allow themselves to speculate freely about what religion *ought to be*. . . . [To] lay much stress on works on *Natural Theology,* [is wrong because Religion] . . . is something *relative to us;* a system of commands and promises from God *towards* us." The Liberal approach leads people to forget their own hearts. That, in turn, generates a rejection of revelation because their selves are unprepared and therefore unresponsive. Indeed, because conscience, the one origin of religion, has been stunted, revelation, the other origin of religion, can never be accepted. "Conscience has been silenced. The only information they have received concerning God has been from Natural Theology, and that speaks only of benevolence and harmony; so they will not credit the plain words of Scripture. . . . This indeed is the creed of shallow men, in *every* age, who reason a little, and feel not at all, and who think themselves enlightened and philosophical."[25] Newman argues, then, that this attitude toward evidence and the view of deity it generates not only are wrong, but also stunt the growth of humanity's religious potential.

The third principle of Liberal religion argues that a dispassionate investigation of the natural world leads one to religion's ultimate object—that deity is a principle discoverable through examination of evidence. The results of the Physical Theologians are rejected because of their philosophic inadequacies. On the larger question of the correct approach to and characterization of the ultimate sacred object, however, Newman's opposition moves beyond just this school to the general option it represents. He argues that the method advocated and the picture of deity presented will undermine true human religiosity. Whatever the particular historical form, this principle will always overlook religion's real springs and consequently generate a superficial religion and a truncated view of deity.

Revelation as a Manifestation not a Mystery

The Liberal Idea of Revelation as a Manifestation.   In an early essay, Newman characterizes an important Liberal notion as the belief that revelation is a manifestation not a mystery. This belief is the fourth in the list of six Liberal first principles. It concerns revelation's character and reception and, focusing on the temporal expressions of the divine, is the historical analogue of the preceding principle.

Newman's analysis in that essay serves to introduce the general principle. Of special importance are the Liberal ideas that any particular revelation indicates an ever-present situation; that revelation's encasement in ambiguous historical events makes its meaning dependent on the observer's ability to perceive; and that particular revelations need to be criticized and systematized because revelation's object is, at least in theory, completely understandable.[26]

For Liberal religion, revelation manifests an understandable and ever-present situation; it neither unveils mysterious, transcendent realities nor records unique, world-changing events. The half-truth in the idea is that "when Providence would make a Revelation, He does not begin anew, but uses the existing system. . . . Thus the great characteristic of Revelation is addition, substitution." Orthodoxy, however, also teaches that

> there are facts revealed to us, not of this world, not of time, but of eternity, and that absolutely and independently; not merely embodied and indirectly conveyed in a certain historical course . . . but primary objects of our faith, and essential in themselves. . . . In a word, it has taught the existence of *Mysteries* in religion, for such emphatically must truths ever be which are external to this world, and existing in eternity;—whereas this . . . system teaches nothing but a *Manifestation, i.e.* a series of historical works conveying a representation of the moral character of God; and it dishonours our holy faith by the unmeaning reproach of its being metaphysical, abstract, and the like.

This position, for example, resolves the Incarnation into a "moral Manifestation of God in the person of Christ." Similarly, it views the Atonement "as a mark and pledge of God's love," whereas, for Orthodoxy, "Christ's death is . . . a sacrifice acting in some unknown way for the expiation of human sin."[27] Notions of Christ's divinity or of a transaction that effects expiation are seen as peripheral, metaphysical ideas. Revelation's basic content is simply to show that the universe is formed so that people may legitimately believe a Christlike life manifests what ought to be, what is finally supported and validated. Revelation makes manifest an ever-present situation.

A direct corollary of this approach is the view that revelation consists basically in historical events. This situation heightens the role of the observer of revelation. " 'Manifestation' far more naturally fits on to a history witnessed by human beings, than to dispositions made in the unseen world." Revelation is not an objective given. It is an ambiguous set of events whose meaning depends upon an individual's perception. As Newman puts it:

> Revelation, as a Manifestation, is a doctrine variously received by various minds, but nothing more to each than that which each mind comprehends it to be. Considered as a Mystery, it is a doctrine enunciated by inspiration, in human language, as the only possible medium of it, and suitably, according to the capacity of language; a doctrine *lying hid* in language, to be received in that language from the first by every mind, whatever be its separate power of understanding it; entered into more or less by this or that mind, as it may be.

Orthodoxy believes Revelation shows facts faith can receive but not understand. Liberalism believes that the rationale of or object behind the facts is also intelligible. Manifestation means there exists "a system comprehended as such by the human mind," or at least one that can be comprehended more and more perfectly if one is diligent. Orthodoxy, however, sees not a "revealed *system,* but [rather] . . . a number of detached and incomplete truths belonging to a vast system unrevealed."[28]

The idea that the divine can be understood does not contradict the principle of private judgment. That principle does say that revelation can only be what each person says it is, while this principle does say people can penetrate through a particular manifestation to an understanding of the universal truth. The contradiction is only apparent, however. So far as Newman is concerned, some standard always covertly exists for measuring individual judgments. More important, the two approaches can easily harmonize in practice. Viewing revelation as a manifestation does not, in practice, lead people to draw a clear picture of the sacred. Rather it leads them to analyze critically the content of their own and other people's revelations. People do not feel bound to the specific contours of one revelation, as that is merely one manifestation of an omnipresent divine reality. Instead they "criticize and systematize the Divine Revelation,"[29] in order to achieve a more perfect understanding of the divine. As Newman develops the position in this essay, Liberal religion defines revelation in terms of those historical points at which a universally present divine is manifest in humanity's historical experience. It then counsels people to go beyond any particular revelation and seek the underlying essence of all revelations.

The Liberal position on revelation stresses the limits of humanity's knowledge. Because revelation manifests the divine in history, the contingencies of the historical situation limit human understanding. But the Liberal position also stresses the possibilities of understanding. Because a static, immanent universal is manifest in revelations, human beings can penetrate through various historical manifestations to gain further understanding. (Newman's own position might be said to reverse this point. He would argue that although much is given in revelation it remains impenetrable.)

On the one hand, then, Liberal religion argues that any human understanding of a divine manifestation is severely limited by the existence of the manifestation and the recipient in a particular linguistic, cultural, and conceptual environment. Revelation manifests rather than gives the divine, so that significant aspects of the divine must remain forever hidden. Traditional attempts to characterize the divine fully not only fail but also lead either to the creation of false idols or to meaningless discussion and dissension. Accepting historical finitude means recognizing that the divine cannot be completely comprehended.

But, on the other hand, Liberal religion also argues that one may be able to reach that essence which transcends the spatial, temporal limitations of the manifestation. If people stop focusing on revelation's particulars, if they look through them to the universal, comprehension is possible. Christ's importance, for example, should not be sought in the unique quality of his personhood or action. Rather it should be sought in his teachings as they manifest an abstract universal. To use contemporary language, a particular revelation's universal meaning becomes evident only when one cuts away those aspects of the revelation that are solely products of its historical setting. For example, one should recognize that men of the first century A.D. personalized God or believed in miracles. Recognizing this enables one to penetrate through the limited forms of expression to reach the revelation's universal meaning. Such penetration shows the Atonement is not a mysterious transaction involving Christ, God, and humanity, but is an exhibition of the ever-present divine love. Similarly, the Resurrection is not about bringing a dead man back to life but is a statement about how the universal spirit manifested by Christ continues to live and be effective.

To employ an evocative formulation of Newman's—which he rarely uses and unfortunately never developed—Liberal religion sees Christianity as a religion of principles not doctrines, of general ideas not specific mysterious givens.[30] Revelation brings the gift of general ideas or attitudes, not the gift of specific rites, doctrines, or reports of how cosmic transactions make possible the expiation of sin or the deification of humanity. The divine is most adequately grasped, not by an attachment to a single revelation, but by a view that looks through specific revelations and includes all the existing, varying, and limiting manifestations of the sacred. This procedure alone leads to that one principle manifested by and standing behind all particular revelatory expressions. Liberals think, "There is a system of religion more simply true than Christianity as it has ever been received."[31] To seek this system is the true aim of religious people; to find it involves moving beyond the particularities of any specific manifestation. If Christianity is to find this system, it must recognize the limits of its manifestation and move beyond them.

Newman's Idea of Revelation as a Mystery.   For Newman, such a view of revelation is insufficient or, put more neutrally, different from the view that underlies both natural religion and Christianity. Newman's own view of revelation having been discussed, the general points of oppositions are clear. For example, the transcendent, impenetrable personhood of the revealer; the mysterious character of revelation; the con-

crete givenness of revelation. The exact meaning of these differences is
hard to specify, however, because Newman never clearly works out a
theory of revelation.

This indefiniteness is exemplified by Newman's treatment of "mystery," the idea he contrasts with "manifestation." Newman's analysis
often goes little farther than the assertion that the only crucial problem
is discovering whether something is a mystery which must be believed.
As he says, "I can believe it . . . *if* I know for certain that I *ought* to
believe it." He even sanguinely adds that it is a "great comfort . . . to
know that he ought not lose time on a point, or to fidget himself, but to
say . . . 'It is unanswerable . . . it is one of those things which we must
take upon faith.' "[32]

When he does analyze mystery, the examination, though evocative,
is usually brief and often strewn with unanswered questions. Generally,
he treats mystery as an attribute of a certain kind of abstract statement:
"A mystery is a proposition conveying incompatible notions, or is a
statement of the inconceivable." Statements of the inconceivable concern past or future events that seem impossible or even unimaginable.
One example is God's incarnation of himself. "What! Son of God taking human flesh, impossible! . . . we refuse to admit a course of doctrine so utterly unlike any thing which the face of this world tells us of."
Another example is the promise that "our bodies shall rise again and
live for ever . . . [this is one of the] truths addressed solely to our faith,
not to our reason, because we know so little about the 'power of
God' . . . that we have nothing to reason *upon.*" Knowing the body only
as presently existent, understanding so little of God's power, we have
no materials to reason with. The conveying of incompatible notions
finds a clear theological example in the proposition that God has no
beginning. "It distorts our mental sight and makes our head giddy to
have to say (what nevertheless we cannot help saying), that He had no
beginning. Reason brings it home clearly to us, yet reason again starts
at it; reason starts back from its own discovery, yet is obliged to endure
it." One may recognize, for a variety of reasons, that God must be
without beginning, and yet still be unable to fathom the idea's meaning
because the ideas of "a being" and "no beginning" are incompatible.
Mysteries, particularly those that convey incompatible notions, arise
from the differences between real objects and our notions about them.
The problem, then, lies not in the object but in our subjective perception of it. "Our notions of things are never simply commensurate with
the things themselves; they are aspects of them, more or less exact."
Because "notions are but aspects of things; the free deductions from
one of these aspects necessarily contradict the free deduction from
another. After proceeding in our investigations a certain way, suddenly

a blank or a maze presents itself before the mental vision." The real object is a unified complex of various elements that our notions, as an inadequate reflection of the real object, can form only in a contradictory way. Consequently, "an alleged fact is not therefore impossible because it is inconceivable; for the incompatible notions, in which consists its inconceivableness, need not each of them really belong to it in that fullness which would involve their being incompatible with each other. . . . Hence, when we try how to reconcile in the moral world the fullness of mercy with exactitude in sanctity and justice . . . we feel we are not masters of our subject."[33]

Newman's analysis contains a problem we have seen elsewhere. "Something" is given in revelation, but understanding just what it is, how it is grasped, and how it is clearly expressible is very puzzling. Newman's analysis of mystery reflects the general problem in Newman's account of revelation: he tries to uphold apparently opposed positions. On the one hand, he emphasizes the sacred object's inscrutable character. On the other hand, he argues for an irreducible something that sets clear limits as to what can be said or done.

Newman opposes the Liberal idea of revelation because it denies the givenness of revelation. Denying this eliminates one of the two poles he wants to uphold and therefore destroys the balance he thinks must be maintained. The cogency of his own alternative to the Liberal position is unclear, however. He might employ an empiricist model and see surety about revelation, like that about sense, as arising from a self-authenticating impression. He could then add to that model the notion of a continuing divine assistance.[34] If so, there is some meaning to his notion that a mysterious, objective core is grasped but not understood. The gap in his account of the character and acceptance of revelation thus becomes understandable. Unfortunately, that gap also means we can never really comprehend his alternative. Such a position does exemplify, however, that type of thinking discussed when analyzing Newman's view of dogma. Newman's religious thought maintains rather than solves, or even probes, what we called "irresolvable but revelatory and productive tensions." The Liberal theory is condemned because it resolves the tension and thereby overlooks one-half of a full view of revelation. It overlooks the religious fact that people feel grasped by a revelation that, however incompletely understood, remains a transcendent gift containing a substantive core available nowhere else. This sense of what has been received and where it has come from binds religious people to the particular outlines of their given revelation. Moreover, it leads them to realize that full penetration is impossible. In trying to penetrate the mystery of revelation, Liberal religion corrupts religious people's basic response to revelation.

Useful Goods as Primary

The Liberal Idea.   The fifth principle is that useful goods are more important than integral goods. Human beings ought to pursue only those ideas and actions that are of direct use to the individual and to the community. This idea took an English form in Utilitarianism, but it arose from a general shift in viewpoint that was partly fueled by a long-standing disquiet about religion's effect on society. Echoing the emphasis on humanity's limited knowledge of integral goods, this principle develops the positive criterion that everything ought to be judged by its usefulness. Although large questions about life's integral goods will remain unanswered, human happiness will be unimpaired. People need not concern themselves with areas other than those where usefulness applies. Indeed, by basing education on the principle of use, people can create a just society that meets all human needs.[35]

This position argues that integral values, if existent, are unknowable. People must turn to the knowable if ever-changing arena of human activity to formulate values. These values will be dependent upon the changing needs of the individual and his community. Therefore, a calculus of what is useful to the greatest number of people becomes the instrument for making decisions. Although the idea has partial analogues in the past, it represents a significant shift in the Western perspective. Indeed, Newman's opposition may be particularly fervent because this principle attacks both the West's classical and Christian heritages.

Put abstractly, in this shift the "made" replaces the "given" as the basic category. Only the "making," not the finding, of truth is possible. Compassionate action, for example, is seen neither as natural nor as the proper response to a sacred command, but rather as necessary if the general good of the society or of the individual is to be realized. Human action ought to reflect variable human needs, not given absolutes. People do not exist in a world where they discover absolute standards. Rather, they exist in a world where standards arise from the shifting needs of the social group. People make their good by attending to complex group needs, rather than find their good by attending to some higher stable realm.

Hannah Arendt argues that this view witnesses to a massive change in Western ideas. It inverts the traditional hierarchy of thought over action, contemplation over labor, and philosophy over politics. Theory changes from "a system of reasonably connected truths which as such has been not made but given to reason and the senses [into] . . . a working hypothesis, changing in accordance with the results it produces and depending for its validity not on what it 'reveals' but on whether it 'works.' " This in turn means that values are social commodities that have no significance of their own, but, like other commodities, exist only in the ever-changing relativity of social linkage and commerce. . . . The "good" loses its character as an idea, the standard by which the good and the bad can be measured and recognized; it has become a value which can be exchanged with other values, such as those of expediency or of power . . . [so that] ideas finally become mere values whose validity is determined not by one or many men but by society as a whole in its ever-changing functional needs.[36]

The Liberal position on the primacy of useful goods rests on certain premises. One is the goodness of human nature; people can know a common good and be depended on to modify their own desires to seek it. Another is that people control their destiny firmly enough to create the social reality they desire. A final one is that a just, peaceable society fulfills people totally. Flaws in any of these premises would destroy the position's workability. For example, it fails if significant numbers of people cleverly seek only their own good; or if people are unable to control societal events; or if a properly constituted society still leaves people unfulfilled. But if these premises are true, a coherent position emerges. Usefulness is the primary criterion and the creation of a good person or society is the primary goal; together they determine the worth of all acts and events.

Newman's Distinction between Useful and Integral Goods.   Newman's argument with this position has many facets. For instance, he questions each of the position's underlying premises. For us, however, the critical point is his defense of the distinction between useful and integral goods, especially as it applies to religion. This distinction differentiates what is good in itself from what is good only as leading to some other goods. As Aristotle, whom Newman quotes, wrote in discussing possessions, "of possessions, those rather are useful, which bear fruit; those *liberal, which tend to enjoyment.* By fruitful, I mean, which yield revenue; by enjoyable, where *nothing accrues of consequence beyond the using.*" (I call "integral" goods what Newman, following Aristotle, calls "liberal" goods.) Newman himself, in his defense of the distinction's application to education, defines the liberal as follows: "that alone is liberal knowledge, which stands on its own pretensions, which is independent of sequel, expects no complement, refuses to be *informed* (as it is called) by any end, or absorbed into any art, in order duly to present itself to our contemplation. . . . [This kind of] Knowledge . . . is then especially liberal, or sufficient for itself, apart from every external and ulterior object."[37]

Simply put, Newman's argument is that two categories exist—

"good" means one thing, "useful" another. This simple distinction is complicated, however, because the good always has results. " 'Good' indeed means one thing, and 'useful' means another; but . . . though the useful is not always good, the good is always useful. Good is not only good, but reproductive of good; this is one of its attributes; . . . it overflows, and spreads the likeness of itself all around it." Physical health provides the clearest example. "Health is good in itself, though nothing came of it, and is especially worth seeking and cherishing; yet, after all, the blessings which attend its presence are so great, while they are so close to it and so redound back upon it and encircle it, that we never think of it except as useful as well as good, and praise and prize it for what it does, as well as for what it is, though at the same time we cannot point out any definite and distinct work of production which it can be said to effect."[38] We seek health for itself, not for the abilities that arise from it. The state of being healthy is in itself a desired and enjoyed good. Nevertheless, health is useful; it brings further pleasures or goods both to oneself and to others.

The idea that the good generates the useful seems to invalidate the distinction between the good and the useful. Clearly, this abstract distinction, like most, only imperfectly captures the mixed currents of actual life. Nevertheless, it aids our understanding by marking off the various aspects of those currents. The distinction's clarification of educational questions illustrates this. For example, liberal education's justification, unlike its useful counterpart, rests both on its distinguishable sort of knowing and its tie to utility. Moreover, the distinction clarifies the different aspects of any single educational phenomenon. The student of anatomy, for instance, understands that his study is justified both for its usefulness (it helps him become a doctor) and in itself (it is intellectually gratifying, and it trains the mind). Most important for us, the distinction shows that certain activities are valuable in themselves; they need not be rejected as worthless if they lead to no useful goal. This distinction frees activities like education or religion from the tyranny of utility, from the need to reject everything that is not directly useful. Some activities are valuable whatever the social determination of their usefulness.

Newman also employs the distinction between the useful and the good in his argument for both a variety of goods and a hierarchy among them. He accepts the notion of useful goods—even that utility is the basis of evaluation in certain areas—but he rejects the notion that useful goods are the only or the highest goods. His position on this is most clearly exemplified by his writings on medicine. Medicine's

> province is the physical nature of man, and its object is the
> preservation of that physical nature in its proper state, and its

restoration when it has lost it. . . . [But] bodily health is not the only end of man, and the medical science is not the highest science of which he is the subject. . . . He has a mind and a soul; and the mind and soul have a legitimate sovereignty over the body, and the sciences relating to them have in consequence the precedence of those sciences which relate to the body. And as the soldier must yield to the statesman, when they come into collision with each other, so must the medical man to the priest; not that the medical man may not be enunciating what is absolutely certain, in a medical point of view, as the commander may be perfectly right in what he enunciates strategically, but that his action is suspended in the given case by the interest and duty of a superior science, and he retires not confuted but superceded.[39]

A doctor, for example, may tell a missionary in the tropics that death or great physical harm will come if the missionary remains; but the doctor cannot, solely as a doctor, make the judgment that loss of bodily health necessitates that the missionary leave.

The Liberal failure to recognize the distinctions between and hierarchy among human goals has particularly disastrous consequences in religion. Religious ideas come to be judged by their usefulness; religion is what it does. Liberal religion tested religion's usefulness by asking whether religion formed moral character or led to a just society. This testing often judged religion by its ability to form moral character. Starting from the premise that revelation works on an individual's affections, it moves, via the principle of use, to the notion that religion is validated or invalidated by its effect on character. As Newman's comment on a Liberal work succinctly puts it, "the reasonableness of a religion, and therefore its claim on our acceptance, consists in there being a direct and natural tendency in belief in its doctrines to form that moral character which it recommends." "The Atonement is [important, for instance, not] . . . in its relation to the attributes of God and to the unseen world, but in its experienced effects on our mind, in the change it effects when it is believed." Similarly, when applying the principle of use in a wider social context, religious ideas and practices were judged by their effect on societal life. Judgments about religion are made in terms of whether personal or societal well-being is produced. Newman clearly, if rhetorically, states his opposition to this idea in the *Apology*'s statement:

> The Catholic Church holds it better for the sun and moon to drop from heaven, for the earth to fail, and for all the many millions on it to die of starvation in extremest agony, as far as temporal affliction goes, than that one soul, I will not say, should be lost, but should commit one single venial sin, should tell one

> wilful untruth, or should steal one poor farthing without ex-
> cuse. . . . She has it in charge to rescue human nature from its
> misery, but not simply by restoring it on its own level, but by
> lifting it up to a higher level than its own . . . [all of which
> means] that a lazy, ragged, filthy, story-telling beggar-woman, if
> chaste, sober, cheerful, and religious, has a prospect of heaven,
> such as was absolutely closed to an accomplished statesman, or
> lawyer, or noble, be he ever so just, upright, generous, honour-
> able, and conscientious, unless he had also some portion of the
> divine Christian grace.[40]

Newman will, in other writings, modify this uncompromising assertion
that religion is not to be judged by any criteria of worldly usefulness.
As with other Liberal principles, he accepts parts of the idea of usefulness: as a criterion for certain social issues; as a significant if lower-level
good; as an important issue of integral goods. But use should neither
define all religious action nor, more important, stand as the single
criterion defining religion's value.

Education as Salvatory

The Liberal Idea that Education Can Fully Actualize People.   The last principle claims that education is "salvatory"—that the particular sort of
intellectual and moral training signified by the word education can
actualize humanity's full potential. The nurture of people in schools
can effect everything necessary for a realization of full humanity. This
principle gives concrete form to many of the preceding abstract ideas.
In so doing, it furnishes a practical answer to the question of how
people are to become what they ought to be. The educational community becomes the new church; educational endeavor the new road to
salvation; educational theory the new theology. Education will actualize
the potential goodness of humanity, will free and guide the exercise of
private judgment, will make possible the study of the various natural
and historical manifestations of religion's object, and will explicitly employ the idea of use to form better people and societies. Education
sums up in practical form what was, for Newman, a complete but
inadequate view of the nature of and means for salvation.

Liberal religion's practical solution resembles the classical idea that
the proper state can perfect humanity. The analogy is imperfect, as the
classical community had clear religious aspects and sought the complete
fulfillment of only some citizens. Nevertheless, the analogy shows the
vision's grandeur and antecedents. Moreover, it illuminates how Newman's efforts resemble those of the Church Fathers. Like them, he

defends Christianity against a complete but different view of the nature of and means for salvation.

Newman thinks the Liberal believes that

> Education is the cultivation of the intellect and heart, and Useful Knowledge is the great instrument of education. It is the parent of virtue, the nurse of religion; it exalts man to his highest perfection, and is the sufficient scope of his most earnest exertions.
>
> Physical and moral science rouses, transports, exalts, enlarges, tranquilizes, and satisfies the mind.... [It] makes us know our duty, and thereby enables us to do it; by taking the mind off itself, it destroys anxiety; and by providing objects of admiration, it soothes and subdues us.
>
> And, in addition, it is a kind of neutral ground, on which men of every shade of politics and religion may meet together, disabuse each other of their prejudices, form intimacies, and secure co-operation.

Liberal religion, "instead of the Church's authority and teaching[s] . . . substitute[s] first of all a universal and thoroughly secular education, calculated to bring home to every individual that to be orderly, industrious, and sober is his personal interest." As Newman succinctly puts the Liberal position: "Virtue is the child of knowledge, and vice of ignorance."[41] Thus greater knowledge leads people to an understanding that generates correct behavior and personal happiness. According to the Liberal, education can replace religion and lead humanity to final happiness.

Newman on the Limited Actualization Education Brings. Newman criticizes this idea in two places. In *The Tamworth Reading Room,* he focuses on the attempt to educate common people by means of informal reading rooms. In the *Idea of a University,* he focuses on the attempt to educate an elite in universities. Newman attacks any attempt to influence common people by means of the establishment of reading rooms. He argues, among other things, that real education is too difficult and time-consuming for worthwhile results to arise from such a meager measure.[42] Newman's cogent insistence on the need for extended education undercuts any idea that all people can be saved by such education. A universal education scheme does, of course, solve that particular problem. The question still remains, however, as to how much native intellectual ability is needed for education to succeed. Clearly, certain people of very low intelligence are redeemable in a Christian context but are bound to be almost unaffected by education.

With the question of an intensive education undergone by an elite, Newman faces a more real issue. Here the question is whether the

Liberal idea is correct under the best of circumstances. Newman never denies education's importance, but he thinks it cannot generate human fulfillment because it can only train the mind. Education does train the mind to view any single item from all possible perspectives and then to see how that item fits into the widest conceivable framework. Education seeks to form an imperial intellect that

> is based, not so much on simplification as on discrimination. Its true representative defines, rather than analyzes. . . . Taking into his charge all sciences, methods, collections of facts, principles, doctrines, truths, which are the reflections of the universe upon the human intellect, he admits them all, he disregards none, and, as disregarding none, he allows none to exceed or encroach. His watchword is, Live and let live. He takes things as they are; he submits to them all, as far as they go; he recognizes the insuperable lines of demarcation which run between subject and subject; he observes how separate truths lie relatively to each other, where they concur, where they part company, and where, being carried too far, they cease to be truths at all.[43]

The perfection of mind that education attempts to generate consists, then, in the ability to view things accurately, to recognize and order both the variety of relevant facts and the various possible perspectives on any particular fact. This process leads to that overall view that allows one to see things both in themselves and in their relationships. Accuracy about particulars, overall knowledge, and enlightened vision together make up that perfection of mind education can generate.

This perfection of mind is an integral good and it will even produce useful goods, but these goods are not salvatory. They can neither answer humanity's ultimate questions nor generate the power necessary for social well-being or self-actualization. In general, "a university training is the great ordinary means to a great but ordinary end; it aims at raising the intellectual tone of society, at cultivating the public mind, at purifying the national taste, at supplying the true principles to popular enthusiasm and fixed aims to popular aspiration, at giving enlargement and sobriety to the ideas of the age, at facilitating the exercise of political power, and refining the intercourse of private life."[44]

Newman's opposition to this principle of Liberal religion is most clearly focused in his analysis of education's effect on humanity's fundamental problems. When most polemical, he argues education is unable to touch any of people's basic conflicts. As he says, "who was ever consoled in real trouble by the small beer of literature or science?" Moreover, it can never change character, it is "the mere lulling of the passions to rest by turning the course of thought." If one can "quarry the granite rock with razors, or moor the vessel with a thread of silk;

then may . . . such keen and delicate instruments as human knowledge and human reason . . . contend against those giants, the passion and the pride of man." His more balanced presentations, however, admit education is effective but argue that it is incomplete. Indeed, it cannot maintain even its own gains without the addition of religion. The training of secular education does have a legitimate place; it is the necessary

> first step . . . in the conversion of man and the renovation of his nature, is his rescue from that fearful subjection to sense which is his ordinary state. . . . Religion seems too high and unearthly to be able to exert a continued influence upon us; its effort to rouse the soul, and the soul's effort to cooperate, are too violent to last. . . . Religion indeed enlightens, terrifies, subdues; it gives faith, it inflicts remorse, it inspires resolutions, it draws tears, it inflames devotion, but only for the occasion . . . [;] what we need then is some expedient or instrument, which at least will obstruct and stave off the approach of our spiritual enemy, and which is sufficiently congenial and level with our nature to maintain as firm a hold upon us as the inducements of sensual gratification. It will be our wisdom to employ nature against itself. . . . This then is the *primâ facie* advantage of the pursuit of Knowledge; it is the drawing the mind off from things which will harm it to subjects which are worthy of a rational being.

Even this gain will be subverted, however, if the obligations and real objects mediated by religion are missing, because "that very refinement of Intellectualism, which began by repelling sensuality, ends by excusing it."[45] As part of a developmental process crowned by religion, education can generate an important if preliminary kind of human improvement. By education alone, however, only a modified kind of control, soon destroyed, is possible. The destruction is often painted as inevitable, but the portraits of virtuous pagans, gentlemen, and others show exceptions. Newman's point probably is that only a few elite can maintain the highest level. Most important, education alone can never duplicate what religion does; it can never harmonize the self or mediate final meaning.

We can structure education's possible effects by focusing on what are, for Newman, the stages in human development. In the most abject stage, people move from uncontrollable passions, seek only their own good, and generate chaotic disorder in themselves and society. A higher stage shows that minimal self-control brought about by enlightened self-interest and the desire for material goods. Education can produce this form of self-control. Moreover, all do benefit from a person's recognition that general goods like social order arise from such self-control. (If people are clever enough to remain undetected, however, they can pursue their own self-interest. This stage provides no compelling reason for seeking the common good.) At a still higher stage, education employs nature against herself and leads to a type of morality, self-control, and fulfillment. This achievement, however, is not only incomplete but also frail; it is bound to sink to a lower level unless the stage is completed by religion. The highest stage accepts the actualization of the lower stages but crowns them with religion's new power and vision and thereby both maintains and perfects all the lesser achievements.

Put in a more theological or philosophic scheme, intention can be seen as the means of evaluating actions. Purity of intention is the most general criterion for establishing praise and blame. Educational nurture, at its lowest level, violates this criterion. It just affirms that "detection, not sin . . . is the crime; . . . and decency is virtue"[46]—decency meaning the outward appearance of good. Intending one thing (self-protection) and acting differently (aiding another) is blameworthy. The more important criterion, however, is not merely the intention's purity but rather the intention's goal. Each act's value depends on its goal. At the lowest level, people form themselves according to aesthetic standards; at a higher level, they seek a social good, at a still higher level, they pursue an abstract principle of good; at the highest level, they are directed to God. Newman argues that education can generate only the lowest level. Moreover, he thinks that all other levels will in time (except with a few people) fall back to the level that violates the general criterion of pure intention. More important, the highest level, the key to religiosity, can never be caused by education. Despite a question as to how self-conscious the intentional relation to deity must be, particularly given Newman's emphasis on the role of implicit processes, the general scheme is clear. The notion of pure intention divides good actions from bad, and the levels within pure intention, levels determined by the goals sought, establish the value of the actions. For Newman, then, education cannot be that matrix which fulfills humanity. It may mediate a pedestrian if important fulfillment, but to believe it can do any more is a delusion.

The Character and Viability
of Liberal Religion's Overall Perspective

These six principles form Liberal religion's perspective. The following brief sketch of that perspective stresses the integrity and religiosity of the Liberal vision, the integrity because Newman's depiction sometimes obscures it, the religiosity because the last chapter will critically analyze it. A prior question, however, is whether any single Liberal perspective exists. Are there not just a set of discrete and often contradictory principles, held to by various people at different times, to which Newman, writing on various occasions, responds? There clearly are strains, if not outright contradictions, among the various principles. The different views of evidence have already been noted and other instances can be cited. For example, insofar as the idea of the useful rests on a skepticism about the availability of ultimate answers, it appears to conflict with those principles that speak of a divine principle that is manifest in nature and history. Moreover, strains exist inside Liberal religion, for instance, the tension between its rational and pietistic wings. Nevertheless, a reasonably coherent view emerges, if one remembers the type of portrait sought, realizes the incoherences which plague any view, and recognizes that certain principles will be to the forefront in certain situations.

Liberal religion rests on two bases. One is that people have within themselves the fundamental resources to overcome any difficulties they face. No basic, irresolvable divisions exist in people's moral nature; people are not fundamentally split by their desires and their obligations, or their passions and their reason. Moreover, no questions that are critical to people's spiritual well-being are without adequate answers. The other base is that Liberal tradition lacks final religious answers. Although it has contact with a sacral realm through nature and particular revelation, that contact renders deity quite imperfectly, must be used tentatively, and needs to be filled out from other sources.

These two Liberal ideas substantially modify Newman's notion that estrangement and relief are religion's sources. The sense of estrangement is modified so much that it almost ceases to exist; it means little more than that reachable goals are now temporarily beyond one. The sense of relief does remain but only in much diminished form. What is received is understood to have neither finality nor transcendent saving power. Neither ultimate answers nor ultimate means of salvation are received. Instead, significant manifestations, but only manifestations, are given or, more precisely, seen.

This perspective leads to the idea that people must accept only those aspects of the sacral manifestations that they find personally congenial. Moreover, the character of both the sacral manifestations and the community that mediates them does not allow for passive reception. A personal appropriation is necessary, and it is trustworthy because a person's judgment is trustworthy. All people, then, are called to a full, self-conscious appropriation of all the religious attitudes and ideas they hold. Both the natural and the historical worlds provide readily available information by which to make the necessary judgments. The natural world even provides, at least for the more intelligent, persuasive enough evidence to lay all possible doubts to rest.

The sacred object thus discovered in the natural and historical arenas is best described as having the attributes of power, wisdom, and goodness. These attributes must be understood to have only muted personal analogues. For example, love refers only to the existence of a world where people feel at home and find their greatest happiness through the love of others. Religion's final object does not contain other perfections that people call personal—such as will, mercy, or judgment. To personalize deity by saying that deity makes particular judgments on people or wills specific things for people is to engage in unwarranted anthropomorphic speculation at best and crass superstition at worst.

These preceding ideas affect the evaluation of specific practices by means of the notion that all actions should be judged by whether they are useful to the individual or to the society. Abstract discussions about, say, ritual actions that have consumed so much time are to be replaced by practical discussions on how to alleviate concrete human problems. Religion is to focus on worldly needs, not otherworldly standards or pursuits. The concrete means for solving problems will be education. Education will help people understand themselves and their world and generate both proper action and personal fulfillment. The essential functions of the traditional religious community will be taken over and purified by this new salvatory community. Its teachers, for instance, will serve as the new priests, the new mediators of meaning, but they will be unencumbered by the useless ritual functions or lack of learning that plagued their traditional predecessors. Without recourse to mystery, they will mediate to people a body of ideas that brings personal actualization. The educational community itself will be an ongoing group into which people are initiated, through which they attain salvation, from which they receive support, and to which they return to give aid. Only the nonproductive aspects of traditional religious communities are excluded in this new salvatory community.

Such, in outline, is the Liberal religious vision, as Newman understood it. This position is coherent and, given its premises, it meets all basic human needs. Moreover, the position becomes much stronger if certain principles are modified so that they meet Newman's criticisms but do not lose their basic meaning. An unqualified idea of private judgment is inadequate. Nevertheless, modifications can be made that do meet Newman's most telling criticisms and yet do not surrender the basic idea that people must decide religious issues on the basis of what appears congenial to them. Even Newman himself, when struggling with the idea of authority, recognized the power of that idea. Similarly,

Newman's criticisms of Physical Theology are cogent. Nevertheless, the more general questions of evidence's role or of the appropriateness of attributing personal qualities to deity allow for more than one cogent answer. The viability of the other principles is clear. The native goodness of humanity can be argued for without overlooking the obvious evils that humans do; revelation can be seen both as a gift and as something limited by its existence in a particular history; usefulness can function as the basic criterion for religiosity; and a new educational community can be imagined that would mediate the modified fulfillment Liberals see as all that is possible.

The Liberal religion that Newman opposes is not, then, a straw figure, even though Newman the controversialist sometimes treats it that way. Rather, as Newman himself sometimes recognized, Liberal religion is a serious attempt to reconstitute religion so that it can respond to modern attitudes, ideas, and problems. Certain problems the twentieth century has found most pressing are only hinted at by Liberal religion—for example, the diversity of man's various religions and the social scientific perspective on man as the maker of his cultural world. They may indeed raise questions Liberal religion cannot answer. These questions, however, set new problems for Newman also. Moreover, both Newman and Liberal religion have resources to begin to meet these questions. Liberal religion, then, does have an integrity; it does represent a serious attempt by modern people to reconstitute their religion in order to make it more acceptable. The Liberal attempt to be both modern and religious brings up real questions and represents a new type of religion.

5

An Evaluation of Two Aspects of Newman's Analysis

This concluding chapter evaluates the adequacy of Newman's position on two questions that reflect the wider import of this study: the relation of Christianity to other religions and the view that Liberal religion deforms humanity's religious potential. "Evaluation" is a treacherous word. All too often, it means little more than "I agree or disagree." Internal evaluations, those that stay within the subject's own world of discourse, can legitimately point up many problems: for example, failures to reach desired goals; or internal inconsistencies where statements at one place do not agree with, follow from, or stand in harmony with statements at other places. External evaluations, however, either query the subject's premises or pose questions different from those the subject posed. An external evaluation may just either pit different views against each other or judge people by problems they never envisioned.

Newman's unsystematic presentation makes even internal failures difficult to pinpoint. Moreover, to demand strict coherence from Newman is to bring him before a bar whose inadequacies he often analyzes. He points out, for example, that coherence may be strained by personal growth, that insights may outrun logic, and that particular audiences may demand different forms of expression. Finally, Newman's overall perspective makes external criticism impossible in many areas because it stresses, for example, the existence of self-validating internal perceptions and the need for spiritual preparation.

Nevertheless, evaluations are important. They both reveal the outlines of Newman's position and clarify his work's possible relevance. The preceding chapters analyzed Newman's work in its own context. Although these chapters presented an abstract reconstruction and criticized him at points, they emphasized the viability of the answers he gave to the problems he set. If sometimes using contemporary language, if sometimes highlighting those aspects of his work that could best meet modern criticisms, the previous presentation emphasized the viability of Newman's vision, given the world he lived in. Now, however, Newman will be evaluated as to his relevance.

"Relevance" is a word that has various connotations today. In this context it means only that Newman's ideas can be seen to illuminate, or to be illuminated by, certain contemporary problems that he did not directly address. The search for relevance involves drawing out implications Newman only hints at, taxing him with information he was unfamiliar with, and asking questions different from those that he asked. Such activity may present an erroneous picture and therefore may do a disservice to the man supposedly honored by being called relevant. Careful attention to Newman's ideas meets many of these problems, but certain other factors also embolden us. Newman saw his work as beginning probes needing development rather than as a finished edifice. The tentative approach of the "private" Newman makes this particularly clear. The man of the letters and notebooks often uses a very different tone from that of the self-assured public man. Furthermore, Newman himself was acutely aware of how historical changes create situations that demand the reformulation, not the mere repetition, of the ideas of past figures if those ideas are to be fully understood. Moreover, Newman's attempt to stand in both the modern and the traditional Christian worlds leaves many implications undrawn and many questions only partly asked. Finally, all who have in any way been caught by Newman's vision need to recognize that his ideas often appear strange to contemporary eyes. That situation is exemplified by Reardon's statement that "in the end Newman's positive teaching leaves us incredulous."[1] Recent works often see him as an odd museum piece. Although quite admirable, the piece is from a strange era; it ought to be respectfully viewed but not actively engaged. Those who recognize that, like any person, Newman is bound by his time, but think that, like certain people, he may also speak to different times, should exhibit their ideas to others.

The Relation of Christianity to Other Religions

The Problem Presented by the Diversity of Human Religions. The diversity of human religions is the major stumbling block in any attempt to analyze the relationship of Christianity to other religions as Newman did. This diversity is dramatically exemplified in Chenshiah's comment: "The supreme longing of the Hindu, to escape from *samsara*, Christ does not satisfy, [just as] the Lord's gift of rebirth does not appeal to the Hindu. Thus the correspondence of longing and satisfaction fails."[2] Although Newman's typological description of natural religion is commendable in many ways, it fails to reflect the radically different judgments and structures evident in human religions, as noting some examples shows.

His basic dichotomy of estrangement and relief is sound. Reading estrangement, however, in terms of guilt before a judging, personal God is inadequate for, say, Vedantic Hinduism or sophisticated Taoism. Similarly, although community is an essential expression of religion, the difference between natural and differentiated religious communities leads to important distinctions in organization. For example, natural community has neither an official priesthood nor the possibility of a conversion that is other than a rite of passage. Moreover, some personalized mediator (Newman's meritorious intercessor) is a common feature of religion, but that mediator may be a mythic figure, or the holder of a hereditary sacral position, or, as in some forms of Buddhism, a figure true adepts pass beyond. Finally, certain fundamental notions—such as the importance or even existence of the individual—may differ so radically in different religions that apparently general ideas have, in fact, totally distinct meanings. For example, reconciliation may destroy rather than preserve individuality, while estrangement may refer not to part against part, but to any single part as it remains distinct from an undifferentiated whole. Similarly, the possibility of religious community may arise not when individuals become themselves, but only when individuals cease to be individuals. General categories, although helpful and necessary, can mislead by appearing to unify what is, in actual fact, disparate. For example, differences in the object from which people are estranged—e.g., a personal God, Brahman, or the Tao—give each estrangement a distinct character. The single category only appears to bring unity.

Such diversity means that accounts of the relationship of religions, at anything but the most abstract level, will be exceedingly difficult. Such accounts are probably limited to relating particular aspects of definite religions. Indeed, any more comprehensive explanation may be ruled out simply on the practical grounds that no one can have the necessary informational background. A book like G. van der Leeuw's *Religion in Essence and Manifestation* is inconceivable today, for instance. No person has the available, necessary, detailed information on various traditions. The comparativist need not have a specialist's knowledge of each subject, but even the knowledge that is necessary for cogent comparative generalizations cannot be encompassed by a single mind. This situation does not, of course, rule out the possibility of examining the relationship between Christianity and other religions. It does, however, make the task more difficult and the resultant relationship more complex than Newman realized.

Four Contemporary Models of the Relationship of Religions.   We can best approach the question of the relationship between Christianity and other religions by examining the four most common contemporary models of the relationship among religions. Examining each of these models enables us to see the strengths and weaknesses of Newman's ideas. Moreover, such an examination enables us to understand more clearly not only what Newman actually says but also the directions in which his thought moves. The four models are: (1) one religion is true and all others are false; (2) a single essence underlies all religions; (3) one religion is the fulfillment of all others; and (4) a plurality of true religions exists and a person just affirms one. (These four models are highly theoretical. No specific thinker clearly corresponds to each option.)[3] Although we will examine each model, our focus is on the fulfillment model, which Newman clearly reflects, and the plurality model, which much of his thinking leads toward. Apart from their relationship to Newman, these models are also the most viable. Although the first two models contain important insights, they are fatally flawed. Indeed, the first two models are best seen as setting poles of a problem the last two models attempt to resolve.

The first model maintains that truth exists in one religion and falsehood in others, however the truth and falsity are titled: e.g., heathenism/true religion; natural religion/revealed religion; superstition/ spirituality. (This model, incidentally, is still prevalent today. Despite statements to the contrary, the diction, approach, and general view of many Christian theologians often reflect it.) The problems in the model are numerous. Perhaps most basic is its evident lack of sympathetic understanding. It does not recognize that, at the least, certain elements of worth exist in other religions and that, at the most, certain attitudes accepted by adherents of the true religion find their clearest expressions in other religions. A related problem arises from the recognition of how much of the condemned tradition is present in the affirmed tradition. That recognition leads to separating out the true and false parts of the affirmed tradition, an almost impossible task. Another more abstract question concerns how one can declare the sacred is evident only in one place, particularly if, as most Christians contend, a merciful and powerful deity exists.

The second model asserts that all religions seek unity with an identical object or attitude. This position takes a variety of forms, but it usually argues that all religions move toward the same goal, distinctions arising only from unimportant historical elements. The goal pursued is normally spelled out either as mystical union or as an attitude of love— either mysticism or ethical action being taken as the defining mark of religion. The major difficulty with this model is that mysticism covers many different kinds of experiences and that love covers a great diversity of attitudes.[4]

Both models contain insurmountable difficulties. They also, however, contain significant insights. These insights form the poles the next two models attempt to synthesize. The one pole emphasizes the similarities in religious response to the world or, put more theologically, the existence of one sacred object or sphere. The other pole emphasizes the distinctions among religions and the consequent need to make judgments as to which ones reflect reality. The one pole's vague statements of unity stand in tension with the other pole's specific delineations and call for decision.

The fulfillment and plurality models seem to exhibit the difficulties of any position attempting to mediate between poles. The fulfillment model's apparent difficulties evaporate, however, if it is seen as a form of theology. The plurality model's apparent difficulties evaporate, however, if certain insubstantial changes are made. Newman reflects the fulfillment model and might be seen as moving toward the plurality model. He can reflect both models because the two models only appear to answer the same question. Actually they answer separate questions and therefore may exist side by side. The fulfillment model responds to the theological question of how to articulate one's own religion in relationship to other religions. The plurality model responds to the question of how to embrace only one religion and yet take account of those distinctions among religions that allow for no clear model of their relationship. This distinction between the models must be recognized if they are to coexist and, more important, if the character and viability of each are to be understood.

The Fulfillment Model as a Form of Theology.   The fulfillment model is best understood by examining how it responds to two major problems. These responses illustrate how the fulfillment model offers a theological perspective on one's own and other's religions, rather than a perspective on the objective relationships among the world's various religions. The first problem arises from the distinctions among religions. The fulfillment model functions smoothly only if the religions considered have no fundamental distinctions—for example, where one religion has many mediating deities and another religion only one. Significant questions arise when such basic continuities are not operative, e.g., when in one of the religions deity is not a central idea or the individual is not a basic category. To say that Christianity's concept of God or of personal integrity fulfills religion *x*, when religion *x* denies the reality of both God and personhood, is to employ the idea of fulfillment when the idea of truth and falsehood is more apt. Speaking of Christianity as fulfilling Liberal religion is hard to imagine, for example.

The second problem is that many of the model's usual arguments lose their force when they are set in a larger informational context. For example, if a criterion of fulfillment is the organization of all lesser realities around a transcendent deity, Islam may fit the criterion better than Christianity; if the incarnation of spirit in matter is the criterion, certain primitive religions go further in this direction than Christianity; if the assimilation of divergent ideas is the criterion, Buddhism may be more exemplary than Christianity. Even if certain criteria for fulfillment are agreed on, non-Christian religions may best exemplify fulfillment.

This difficulty is solved by using what can be called the art of balancing statements. Rather than fixing on any idea's apparent meaning, one uses that idea only as it fits into a group of contrasting ideas that are delicately balanced against one another. The criteria for usage, the measurement for artistry in balancing, are set by the community's practice. The community thinks one use is truthful, another use nonsense or heresy. The following example shows how this art of balancing statements can operate. In response to the information that x religion's deity is a more transcendent focal point than Christianity's—that being the current operative criterion for fulfillment—one turns to the criterion that deity must be related to worldly processes and judges x religion by that. In response to the information that y religion's deity is more closely related to worldly processes than Christianity's—as that is now the criterion of fulfillment—one returns to the notion of transcendence and judges y religion by that. Islam, for instance, could mount an excellent argument for being the revelation "with credentials," given, among other things, its revelation's character and its relation in time to both Judaism and Christianity. The Christian, then, would just employ other criteria, such as the need for development or the importance of deity's relation to the world. The believer works from a set of interrelated ideas using some at some points, others at other points. This kind of procedure is clearly defensible. The criteria for measuring fulfillment, however, are not as clear as they are in our usual thought, where, for instance, one may cogently argue that a mongoloid does not fulfill the notion "human," nor Edgar Guest's verse the notion "poetry."[5]

The fulfillment model responds to the problem of radical religious diversity with judgments about the true and false. It responds to the problem of other religions' possession of distinctive strengths by balancing statements. Both responses lead one to ask how exactly the argument for fulfillment is, then, to be understood. To use Newman's own phrase about Physical Theology, the argument seems to be a set of pious comments on the structure of the religious world as that world is seen by religious men. In both Physical Theology and the fulfillment model, only the believer can understand and use the statements correctly. The two are analogous, but that relationship is neither necessarily bad nor something Newman must find distasteful. The differences between the religious and the natural worlds make such an approach defensible in one area but problematic in another area. The fulfillment model, then, tells us little about the objective relationship of the world's various religions, but it tells us a great deal about individuals' views of their own religion. The fulfillment model does not illuminate the objective interrelation of religions, but it does offer a particular perspective on a particular religion. For example, the fulfillment model provides Newman with the means for viewing Christ as the "idol" who breaks all idols including the idolatrous part of himself, and it guides Newman's particular development of the need for and character of dogma.

Such a perspective on the fulfillment model indicates that it is a part of theology rather than of the comparative study of religion. Schematically, the comparative study of religion concerns descriptive statements about religions and their relation, the philosophy of religion concerns those normative statements such descriptions might imply, and the theology of religions concerns the examination of a personal and traditional faith in light of the other two. The fulfillment model analyzes religions from a particular normative standpoint that is not publicly demonstrable but that is viable and explainable. As with any theology, it shows considerably more about a religion's, or a religious person's self-understanding than about the objective character of the world. Being a part of theology, its contributions to theology must be the focus for evaluation.

The theological importance of the fulfillment model arises from the changes in diction and therefore view that its new insights bring. The fact that the Roman Catholic acceptance of the idea of salvation outside the Church caused almost no new general formulations exemplifies how a simple recognition alone may cause no real change. A theology of religions sets a new frame for statements about, for example, the nature of the Church, the uniqueness of Christ's actions, and the role of sacramental efficacy. It represents the establishment of a new horizon within which theologians work, a new attitude by which they work, and a new set of problems and facts on which they work. Such a perspective does more than merely modify some traditional formulation.[6]

Perhaps most important, the perspective of a theology of religions forces theologians to clarify the basic judgments that underlie their religion, the critical first principles that define their religion. For example, the reality of individuation, the existence of an uncontingent realm, the excellence of a differentiated community, the need for a personal concretization of religion, the fact of judgment upon the self, are all fundamental ideas that must be recognized, clarified, and then affirmed or denied. Contact with any opponent stimulates such reflection, as Newman's contact with Liberal religion shows, but the issues are heightened when one faces powerful religious opponents. For example, the argument about the evil inherent in human nature can be made whether the opponent is Liberal religion or Confucianism's Mencian wing. But if Confucianism is the opponent, the tension increases because Mencius's argumentation is considerably more cogent than Liberalism's, as it is based on a clear recognition of human evil, self-actualization's difficulty, and the sacral character of goodness. Moreover, Mencius's view is the exfoliation of a general cultural outlook and a long tradition that shows both effective action and profound reflection. If the comparative arena is opened up, the different options have a cogency that arises from the work of individual geniuses and a long intellectual tradition. Perhaps more important, these options also represent religious views to which millions of adherents have been committed and from which numerous spiritually compelling ideas, figures, and institutions have arisen.

Furthermore, the new perspective of a theology of religions aids theologians in their continuing task of distinguishing the central elements in a religion from the products of particular times and attitudes. A comparative analysis of culture's effect on religion sets this question with a sharpness that is otherwise impossible. Moreover, such a perspective confronts theologians with new and potentially powerful symbols for beliefs and new and potentially significant modes for action and organization. Finally, such a perspective raises and highlights the question of the distinctiveness of the theologians' religion. For example: What are the unique possibilities it offers? What are the situations of those outside it? What exactly does "outside" mean, especially for those who never were and perhaps never can be inside?

A theology of religions working from the fulfillment model cannot solve objectively the question of the relationship of religions. It can, however, make a significant contribution to that re-understanding, re-working, and re-formulating of ideas, attitudes, and structures that is theology. The challenge is greater, in most ways, than the challenge involved in theology's relation to philosophy or social science, because theology must face powerful and conflicting spiritual visions as well as the necessary limitations a cultural setting imposes on people. To put the statement more theologically, this perspective shows how revelation is never a simply controllable given. Instead, revelation is a novelty that constantly moves people out of themselves and into a struggle that is informed by the idea that though some finality is possessed, not all that is possessed is final. The question of whether revelation has been adequately apprehended and expressed is brought to the forefront. In the answer to that question lies the challenge, the danger, and the possible productiveness of a theology of religions. Newman, of course, did not fully accept all these challenges and work them through. The perspective on Christianity that emerges from viewing him in light of these challenges shows, however, the potentialities in such an approach.

The Pluralism Model.   The pluralism model accepts the diversity of religious affirmation as an indisputable given. It concludes that no more can be said than that a plurality of true but different religions exists. The pluralism model may lead in two directions. One affirms no religion, arguing that no single one is acceptable because all religions are relativized when they are seen as one among a plurality of religions. A second joins pluralism with the affirmation of a single religion and is our concern here. The following analysis will deal with its basic character, some needed reformulations, and its possible application to Newman.

The position's two most important, if fragile, presuppositions are best expressed by Ernst Troeltsch. One presupposition is that Christianity's "primary claim to validity is . . . the fact that only through it have we become what we are, and that only in it can we preserve the religious forces that we need. . . . We cannot live without a religion, yet the only religion that we can endure is Christianity, for Christianity has grown up with us and has become a part of our very being." The second presupposition is that "a truth, which, in the first instance, is a *truth for us* does not cease, because of this, to be very Truth and Life. What we learn daily through our love for fellow-men, viz. that they are independent beings with standards of their own, we ought also to be able to learn through our love for mankind as a whole—that here too there exist autonomous civilizations with standards of their own. . . . In our earthly experience the Divine Life is not One, but Many. But to apprehend the One in Many constitutes the special character of love."[7] The idea that a person's cultural situation makes only one religion endurable and the idea that apparent pluralism need not conflict with higher unity are essential to the position.

The position's character is best seen through its disagreements with the other models we have discussed: religions are neither simply distinguishable as true and false, nor just expressions of one essence, nor organizable into a hierarchy. Religions are just different. The argument may be made that the pluralist position must become one of these other positions. If the existence of a sacred object is affirmed, logic can be said to lead in one of three directions. The sacred object is expressed only here, or everywhere in similar fashion, or here in its most developed form. The pluralist response to such an argument is that no such statements can be made because such questions are unanswerable. The pluralist position combines a surety about people's ability to make personal statements with a skepticism about their ability to make general statements. Its skepticism arises from its notions of the weakness of reason and of the limits to understanding imposed by people's cultural circumstances. Its surety arises from an inner asurance that salvatory power exists in one's own particular religious ambience. A person knows only that salvation is present in his own situation and that others have said salvation is also present elsewhere. One can be sure about one's own situations. On others' situation, one has only the assurance that arises from reports. Such reports, however, are presumably true, given, for example, the sanctity present in other traditions and the probable existence of sacral reality in different places.

The overall approach is cogent, but it must be reformulated to allow for certain "nonpluralistic" judgments. The position overstates a defensible position about the limits of knowledge. It runs afoul of certain difficulties that plague any skeptical view: For example, if there is a plurality of *x*, must not the *x* be common to all? Must not the statement that all statements are relative itself be relative? More important here, the results of comparative studies in religion cannot be so easily dismissed. The pluralist model must admit that religious phenomena show certain similarities, must recognize that some people can enter sympathetically into other religions, and must acknowledge that at least some small-scale comparisons are possible. All these pointers toward "nonpluralistic" judgments may be carefully limited; they may be called too abstract or too few in number to have real meaning. They must be recognized, however.

Moreover, the pluralist model overlooks how its own affirmations make necessary certain judgments about different perspectives. For example, a Taoist mystic or an African tribesman may refuse to save a drowning person—the mystic because of a view about how people should relate to the natural process, the tribesman because the person is not a member of the sacred tribal community. Those judgments would be condemned and that condemnation implies some universal criteria. The pluralist may argue that few such judgments will be made or that they are of a practical moral character. However, even if few, they still exist, as even if moral (and they arguably involve a religious perspective), they still are judgments. The pluralist who saves the drowning person might reply that the situation is extraordinary and the act done only on subjective moral grounds. To the rejoinder that such judgments are more than subjective and moral, the pluralist's response is weak. The only argument is that knowing how one would act oneself need imply neither legislation for others nor a sense of the religiously based value of the individual. To the rejoinder that the situation's extraordinariness makes no significant difference, the pluralist responds that the fewness of instances is significant. That response, however, admits the existence of some exceptions to the espoused position. The judgments implied by the pluralist's affirmations necessitate certain modifications in the position. These reformulations are not so major, however, that they change the position's character; it remains a distinct option.

Newman and the Pluralism Model.   Newman does not explicitly hold to the pluralism model, but elements in his thought do point toward it. Newman's disquiet with pluralism is evident, for example, in his statement that private judgment is wrong simply because it "leads different minds in . . . different directions," and such a situation is intolerable to religious people. "If, indeed, there be no religious truth, or at least no sufficient means of arriving at it, then the difficulty [of divergent results] vanishes: for where there is nothing to find, there can be no rules for seeking, and contradiction in the result is but a *reductio ad absurdum* of the attempt. But such a conclusion is intolerable to those who search, else they would not search; and therefore on them the obligation lies to explain, if they can, how it comes to pass, that Private Judgment is a duty, and an advantage; and a success, considering it leads the way not only to their own faith, whatever that may be, but to opinions which are diametrically opposite to it."[8] Private judgment, for Newman, is inadequate just because it leads to a plurality of beliefs.

Nevertheless, other elements in Newman's thought point toward pluralism. Newman's sense of the limitations of the human knowledge, particularly in the religious realm, leads to considerable hesitancy about large, speculative generalizations. Moreover, his notion of religious affirmation, with its emphasis on interiority and the personal appropriation of evidence, makes difficult either a public defense of belief's rightness or an understanding of dissimilar beliefs. Finally, his view of faith as a practical principle, when combined with his emphasis on a guiding providence, asserts that people have only that light needed for immediate decisions. Taken together, these ideas paint a religious life wherein people must simply accept the possibilities present in their immediate situations. People know only that religious actualization is possible for them in their particular circumstances. People recognize that a more general understanding is perhaps impossible, certainly extremely difficult, and surely unnecessary to their own religious actualization.

These motifs lead to some startling "pluralistic" statements in Newman. One example, from a fascinating examination of faith and superstition, concludes by defining superstition as a "faith which falls below that standard of religion which God has given, whatever it is." Another example is the statement that "what is common to all Christians, as distinguished from good men under other Dispensations, is that, however the latter were justified in God's inscrutable resources, Christians are justified by the communication of an inward, most sacred, and most mysterious gift." A final example is the notion that because "we cannot, if we would, move ourselves literally back into the times of the Fathers," we must recognize, for example, "that the taste for poetry of a religious kind has in modern times in a certain sense taken the place of the deep contemplative spirit of the early Church. . . . Poetry then is our mysticism. . . . Identity of appearance is not the law on which the parts of the creation exist."[9] In all these statements, Newman's pluralistic tendencies find quite striking expression.

Newman's idea of first principles also points toward pluralism. For Newman, first principles are those basic notions or attitudes that control perception and action. They are, in large part at least, unchangeable as they filter the very information that might change them. Newman often uses this idea to explain why some people cannot be persuaded to accept traditional Christianity. He argues that no evidence or argument can convince someone who lacks the appropriate first principles. At this level, he simply posits true and false principles. At another level, however, his view is analogous to that notion of discrete, culturally conditioned perceptual patterns that underlies the pluralist position. Like pluralism, it sees a few first principles, such as a respect for other people, as drawn from knowledge of human nature, but sees most first principles as determined by the inescapable view a culture gives. Newman never develops this aspect of his idea of first principles, in large part because of his ignorance about both divergent cultures and the social scientific analysis that highlights this point. His thinking moves in that direction, however. When Newman says first principles specify the irreducible difference between people's basic ideas and are a crucial limitation on our knowledge, his view resembles modified pluralism.

Several strands in Newman's thinking, however, seem to invalidate this resemblance: his assertion that some views are better than others; his belief that people are responsible for their first principles; and his conviction that conscience gives clear, true information about both moral absolutes and deity's character. Newman often does simply assert that some views are better than others, but other factors in his thought undermine such a simple dichotomy. The idea of natural religion and the triadic scheme that results from it means that few polar oppositions exist. Furthermore, although there are issues where Newman believes right and wrong are clear, in many cases he thinks the question is more or less open. Moreover, the relation between implicit and explicit reasoning is important, especially given the problems that arise from any attempt to measure implicit understandings. In addition, the distinction between the "public and private" Newman must be remembered, as the private Newman is much less likely simply to reject opposing views. Finally, the differences between Newman's stated position and his thought's apparent implications must always be kept in mind. Newman not only makes judgments on the truth and falsehood of positions, he also emphasizes the need to make such judgments. His stance on this issue, however, is far more complex than it may appear to be.

Another strand that seems to invalidate the pluralistic position is Newman's emphasis on individuals' responsibility for their first principles. This emphasis reflects an idea (and a dilemma) that reaches back at least to the Aristotelian idea of habits. Newman's explicit position is reasonably clear. Ward once asked him "if he did not believe that man was *responsible* for his first principles and that wrong first principles, were, to a great extent, the outcome of wrong habit, morally blameworthy *in the long run,* though perhaps *hic et nunc* invincible? . . . [He answered:] 'I quite agree with you . . . and that is what you must urge on your young men.' "[10] Such an attitude arises for a clear reason. If first principles control perception and action, people are responsible for what they do only if they are responsible for their first principles. Because we want people to be responsible for their actions, we must hold them responsible for their first principles. Newman's other arguments for assuming this responsibility rest on a variety of related notions: for example, the existence of free choice and the idea that all people had clear-cut choices as to what habits or first principles to adopt. Such a position has always been hard to demonstrate, but social scientific findings on environment's effects on the formation of character make establishing its validity even more difficult now. While some sort of responsibility can and perhaps must be argued for, the problem is far more complex than Newman's analysis shows. Indeed, the question reaches into some of the most critical aspects of current discussions among religion, philosophy, and the social sciences.

Given all this, those aspects of Newman's thought that militate against his acceptance of a pluralist position need modulation. The character of certain first principles may necessitate that one argue both for their correctness and for people's responsibility to possess them. For example, people should be praised for regarding other people as important and condemned for regarding them as without value. Numerous other notions, however, are more clearly dependent on the cultural situation. For example, the answer to the question of whether people's first responsibility is to the aged in their family or to the aged generally is dependent on divergent cultural factors. Responsibility for first principles may be argued for in certain instances, but such instances are fewer than Newman thought.

The information presented by conscience also seems to invalidate a pluralistic perspective. Conscience may generate absolutes. It may, for example, declare that the value of people means one must see to their welfare (however differently welfare is understood), and even protect them from injury or death when possible. Nevertheless, the particular cultural perspective influences conscience. Even if conscience produces the same basic experience, the explication of that experience depends on the ideas regnant in the culture. For example, Mencius's "conscience" tells him that people are to be especially regarded, gives that perception a religious sanction, and informs him of the character of religion's sacred object. But the cultural context differs and Mencius does not stress that object's judging personhood. If Newman's ideas on conscience are put in a comparative frame, they will encounter powerful alternative explanations that uphold much, perhaps even all, of what he thinks is crucial but in a form that causes significant modifications in his formulation.[11]

Certain components in Newman's thought do militate against extending his ideas toward the pluralistic model, but these components may need modification. Newman clearly did not move toward pluralism. The impetus for such a shift was missing as he did not face a really pluralistic world. Radically different religious perspectives were neither a part of the culture nor a recognized fact of human life. Even Liberalism reflected many of Western religion's sureties or presumptions.[12] Newman might never have shifted toward pluralism because the shift would have involved his reformulating certain key ideas. Nevertheless, the shift would harmonize with aspects of Newman's thinking. Moreover, this model is more viable than Newman's own proclaimed position. Even its difficulties are more complex and real than those that Newman suffers from. Newman, then, may be said to reflect the fulfillment model and possibly tend toward the pluralism model. Seeing him in terms of these two models involves making some important changes in his thought—large ones in relation to the pluralistic model, less important and probably more congenial ones in relation to the fulfillment model. One view of the direction and character of Newman's work indicates, however, that he would not have found such an evolution distasteful.

Liberal Religion as a Deformation of Humanity's Religious Potential

Newman boldly attacks Liberal religion and the set of modern attitudes it represents. His claim that it deforms human religiosity is momentous enough to demand detailed examination. To undertake such an examination, however, we must sort out and develop a variety of issues that Newman often mixes up or fails to develop. His basic argument rests on the idea that humans have a religious potential that is defined by the pursuit and reception of ultimates. A religion such as Liberalism, which neither pursues nor presents ultimates, must then be a quasi religion that deforms the human religious potential.

We can best begin by distinguishing a descriptive and a normative approach in Newman's analysis, recognizing that he often fails to distinguish them clearly. The descriptive approach tries to show the definable characteristics of various human activities and to distinguish their differences. For example, it shows that although political and familial activities interact in a variety of ways, they have distinctive attributes. The normative approach evaluates the descriptive approach's results. The descriptive approach argues only that Liberal religion differs from either natural religion or Christianity because it fails to meet criteria established by those religions. Distinctions but not value judgments are made; a map is drawn but specific areas are not commended to the traveler. The normative approach, however, makes judgments and commends areas. It judges that Liberal religion deforms the human religious potential and therefore leads people to an incomplete fulfillment. This judgment rests on the idea that human nature has a specifiable religious potential that can be defined in terms of the pursuit and reception of "ultimates." The crucial notion here is "ultimacy," but some comment is also necessary on Newman's argument for the existence of a specifiable human nature.

Newman's argument focuses on both internal and external evidence. The internal approach argues that certain perceptions of the self tell a man not only what he is but also what all people are. Such perceptions ought to lead people to use them to define not only themselves but also all other people. For example, the internal perception that one ought not take innocent life without compelling reason defines not only one's own character but also that of all humans. Those who act differently may be called less than human, stopped by force, or perhaps even killed. This approach works from a developmental model. It asserts that a set of potentialities will grow to a certain form but only if they are unimpeded and properly nurtured. (This model differs somewhat from most traditional Western models of human nature but in ways that aid rather than destroy those models. Indeed, the traditional model's emphasis on such things as telic causality, free will, and habits points toward a developmental model.) Questions about how one knows one's nature or disagreements about human nature's characteristics are reasonably easy to answer with this model. Indeed, the model allows Newman to take account of, but not be challenged by, much difficult evidence.[13]

The external approach focuses on the evidence that religious activity of certain definable types is widespread. This approach yields only fragile results because the developmental view means contrary evidence may be discarded as merely the reflection of unactualized potential. Although Newman never faced the problem, he could, for example, answer modern ethnographic findings about unreligious "primitives" with this notion of undeveloped potential.

Clearly the internal perception of certain defining potentialities is the crucial element in Newman's argument. External evidence is not unimportant; the extent of human religious activity is an important corroboration of the internal testimony. For Newman, however, such evidence cannot be conclusive. Newman's emphasis on internal perception makes his position unassailable, if also unfalsifiable. Such an emphasis also means that few who do not already agree can be convinced. That fact did not overly trouble Newman as he thought only certain people could understand certain matters. As the old example puts it, the tone deaf person's lack of appreciation for music creates no problems for the music lover. Such an example is somewhat misleading, as the results of nonappreciation are more telling in religion than in aesthetics. Moreover, if moral or religious blindness is not explained by social or physical reasons, problems arise about human responsibility and perhaps even divine direction. Nevertheless, Newman's emphasis on internal perception replaces possible discussion with what he would call a clash of first principles.

Human Religiosity Defined by the Pursuit and Reception of Ultimates. The human religious potential Newman points to is defined by its pursuit and reception of ultimates. Ultimacy, or its analogues, is used by many contemporary theorists to differentiate religions from "pseudo" or "quasi" religions—those phenomena that bear many of religion's marks but lack its full character. These differentiations become important with the rise of numerous "new religions" such as humanistic psychology and Marxism, but they can also illuminate Newman's analysis of a similar problem. Certain problems bedevil the usual formulation. They arise from its intellectual framework, however, and can be solved by transposing the idea from a neo-Kantian to an Aristotelian framework.

Ultimacy need not be defined to be used. Discovering an adequate definition will be either impossible or of little use, but understanding its appropriate usage is both possible and sufficient. As Aristotle argued concerning the word "good," the ability to define is not critical to certain discussions. Aristotle focuses only on places where exactitude is unnecessary because the aim is action, but his point also covers cases where the aim is a description of action. Furthermore, ultimacy need not primarily refer to emotional experience. The main reference may be instead to a general perspective upon the world. The usual emphasis on experience in discussions of ultimacy arises, in large part, from the use of Romantic ideas to answer problems created by neo-Kantianism and the rise of science. Moreover, an observer's description rather than a participant's self-description must underlie any analysis of ultimacy. Accepting as ultimate whatever anyone calls ultimate is unproductive. Finally, the distinction between ultimacy as a philosophic idea and ultimacy as a criterion to distinguish different religious activities needs to be emphasized. The philosophic notion looks to some basic reality—Being, Tao, Brahman—but the descriptive notion looks to a standard by which to differentiate activities. As used in this analysis, then, ultimacy will not be defined, nor have emotional experience as its main reference, nor be focused on self-description, nor be used in a philosophic sense.[14]

Instead, this defining criterion for religion will be viewed as a function of two elements: the pursuit of a sacred object and the acceptance of a sacred foundation. The pursuit of a sacred object arises from a negative theophany, an experience that leaves one disquieted with the human condition. This disquiet rests on a relationship, however inchoate, to some ideal that judges what is normally seen. This relationship can be specified in many ways: for example, theorists of religion, like Wach or van der Leeuw, call it the drive for salvation or the tension between the given and the possible; Scholastic theologians call it the natural desire for the vision of God. The human drive to ultimacy appears in people's inability to accept life as it is, in their demand for a something beyond what they have, in their unwillingness calmly to accept various insufficiencies. The drive surfaces in the asking of certain abstract questions: What is the point of it all? Why is there something rather than nothing? But it also surfaces in the asking of certain more personal questions: Why do the innocent suffer? Why do one's finest hopes die by one's own or other's hands? Perhaps the clearest example of this drive is the protest against death. People's idea that something is radically amiss if humans die arises not simply from their sense of what they lose; it arises also from a belief that human life has a value and human relations have apparently enduring qualities. As a pursuit of the sacred, ultimacy refers to that set of desires, emotions, and questions that cuts against any simple acceptance of life. This pursuit shows humans live in the light of some ultimate.

A sacred foundation, ultimacy's other aspect, is a given which places a person within a world of meaning. The foundation's ultimacy is revealed by its authoritative character. The foundation is not questioned, rather questions are answered in terms of the foundation. Whether expressed by sacred texts, laws, myths, communities, or dogmas, this foundation places people in a cosmos and guards them from chaos, or it frees people from a fallen world and carries them to a higher one.[15] The ultimacy of this foundation exemplifies religion's character as a reflection upon the passive voice, as a reflection upon what is done to or for rather than by one. Vouchsafed to rather than produced by people, this foundation irrevocably places people into a world where meaning and power are both evident and available. The sacred pursuit and the sacred foundation interact: the pursuit arises from an inchoate sense of the foundation, and the foundation appears only if the pursuit exists. Together, they specify how ultimacy characterizes religion.

A quasi religion, on the other hand, is defined by its lack of a full sacred pursuit and foundation. Religious needs and questions either go unrecognized, or they are falsely dissolved by the belief that they cannot be answered. The foundation, in turn, either lacks the needed answers and power, or it is unable firmly to place someone as it can be manipulated by people. In a quasi religion the sacred pursuit and sacred foundation, the impetus and the fulfillment, fall short of attaining ultimacy.

Liberal Religion as a Quasi Religion. Newman thinks Liberal religion is a quasi religion that corrupts the human religious potential. His description rests on the idea that all people have a nature that has a religious potential whose defining characteristics are the pursuit and reception of an ultimate foundation. The need and reception aspects have both an intellectual and an action component. The intellectual component covers people's desire for and reception of ultimate answers, however imperfect is the translation of those answers into propositional form. The action component concerns people's desire for and reception of ultimate means for reconciling the self with itself, other people, the world, and sacrality, however imperfect that reconciliation may be as it appears in everyday life. People have two separable needs: the need to understand and the need to act in accordance with that understanding. Newman often points out how knowing and doing interact, but the distinction between them is useful in understanding Newman's criticism of Liberal religion.

Liberal religion neither asks ultimate questions nor sees ultimate difficulties in action. No basic conflicts in the self plague human beings, and no important but apparently unanswerable questions perturb human beings. Lacking the full scope of the religious search, Liberal religion will also necessarily lack the full scope of the religious reception. Its knowledge and means of actualization will meet only those difficulties it sees, leaving untouched the ultimate problems that animate the true religious search. Liberal religion's inadequacy is exemplified by its treatment of death. Death apparently violates the human quest for ultimacy and religion must respond to that. Liberal religion fails because it does not face the apparent tragedy death represents. (The adequacy of those religions that recognize the problem but differ in their answer fits into the problem of Christianity's relationship to other religions. A position such as that of the *Chuang Tzu,* for instance, would be judged wrong on the criterion that individuals are valuable.)[16]

Examining Newman's criticism of Liberal religion in this fashion may appear to complicate the issue needlessly. Does not Newman's criticism simply rest on his belief that a final revelation has set a standard that shows Liberal religion is inadequate? Clearly this approach does exist in Newman, but to focus on that solution is to overlook my earlier arguments against reading Newman in terms of a simple true/false dichotomy. Moreover, the idea of natural religion introduces subtleties that invalidate a simple revelation/no-revelation model.

More important here, a crucial element in Newman's description of natural religiosity is his depiction of the complex interrelation between need and reception. This interaction is clear when we view Newman's analysis of conscience's relationship to God in terms of the ideas of need and reception. Such an analysis also highlights Newman's opposition to Liberal religion's seeking God through objective reflection on the natural or historical world. Newman starts from the Platonic/Augustinian formulation that human beings can never discover the truth unless they already know it. People must have something within themselves that corresponds to the truth, that makes the truth self-validating when it is discovered. Indeed, people are impelled to seek truth's full manifestation by its inchoate manifestation within themselves. Human beings are driven to the truth, by the truth. The problem this formulation tries to answer is intensified by the reflective self-consciousness that marks modernity. Sophisticated moderns characteristically step back from the known to the subject who knows. This act of "knowing we know" establishes any truth as but one among other truths. Moreover, such self-consciousness means that sophisticated moderns can never simply believe in a given truth because they know they sought and found the truth. That recognition changes their relationship to what they discover, unless the seeking itself is impelled by the truth. Unless truth, when found, is recognized as what not only was sought but what impelled the seeking, knowing will be undercut. For all people, but particularly for modern people, need and reception are intertwined. The possible reception creates the need just as the need points to the reception.[17] This relationship modifies any simple view of Newman's ideas on sacred pursuit and reception.

This view that need creates reception can, of course, be criticized by the argument that needs, by one device or another, will discover or create their solutions. For example, my need of love generates my love. Such an analysis can, in theory, explain anything, but alternative explanations do exist. People, for instance, do need love, but they often rightly balk at having all their loves explained as simple creations of their needs. They may point to their own recognition of how their loves differ. Some clearly arise just from need but others show different motives. More important, the very idea of need must be closely examined. Needs may be seen as ignoble impulses that manufacture false solutions, but they may also be seen as potentialities that enable a person to reach an actualization. Neurotics who cannot feel a need for love, at least consciously, will not find love, but their humanity is thereby damaged. Their twisting of a natural need causes a deformation of their humanity.

Applying these ideas to religion generates the claim that certain religious needs define humanity's full potentiality. If these needs are unrecognized their satisfactions cannot be found, and a human potential is therefore deformed. The critic may counter that a real need will never go unrecognized. The respondent replies, however, that human nature has potentials that are actualized only if they are unimpeded and properly nurtured. He points to the example of those neurotics who think they feel no need of love. The critic can counter that such a view may explain the neurotic but only an unjustifiable arrogance is responsible for the assertion that those people who feel no religious needs are analogous to the neurotic. The response notes that such a criticism proves nothing. Most important, the criticism fails to consider that the modern cultural milieu fails to nurture, or even positively impedes, the recognition of religious needs because it emphasizes material well-being, the solution of social problems, and a skeptical approach to traditional beliefs. Newman himself thought the battle with Liberal religion was important precisely because it, like neurosis, deforms a basic human potentiality. That claim is momentous and perhaps arrogant, but the conflict is significant enough that such sharp personal judgments are demanded.

The idea that religious needs exist and can be deformed explains why Newman thinks Liberal religion can be seen as a corruption of humanity's basic religiosity. Moreover, the relation of need and reception further explains the deformed character of Liberal religion. Liberal religion's stunted need can only lead to its impoverished reception, with its meager analogues to religion's defining characteristics. For example, the educational community, unlike the Church, has little authority, slight transhuman reference, and no answers to central problems like the relationship of the dead to the social community. Moreover, the Liberal idea of revelation can neither place people in a world of evident meaning nor establish them in relationship to some final goals. Perhaps most telling, ritual forms are either nonexistent or only intermittent, artificial activities. Liberal religion has no notion of sacred actions loosing mysterious power or putting people into the mysterious ambience of a sacred remembrance. Liberal religion is a religion of principles or general notions. It thereby lacks the concrete's mysterious power to stir emotions, set views, and establish an overall direction.[18] Indeed, Newman's stress on the concrete's role in traditional religion underlines the ultimacy of the religious need and reception. The concrete is important because it touches people at a level that the notional cannot reach. When Newman says no man will martyr himself for a conclusion, he points up his conviction that intellectual principles can mediate answers to some questions, but that they cannot generate the total commitment needed to face ultimate problems like death. Rite is essential, for instance, largely because its real images and actions create an ambience from which flow ultimate answers and ultimate means.

Three Responses to the Idea of an Ultimate Foundation.   Should one accept this analysis—and given Newman's understanding of Liberal religion it makes sense—one substantial question still remains: Is it possible for a modern to accept the notion of an ultimate sacred foundation? Moderns recognize the variety of sacred foundations that people have lived by. They also understand how historical circumstances influence such foundations and how people must exercise private judgment. These ideas seem to invalidate any acceptance of a sacred foundation.

The modern West has generated three responses to this problem. The first is similar to what Newman calls Liberal religion. The need is so moderated that a reduced foundation is acceptable. Modernity may make impossible any affirmation of a traditional sacred foundation, but a new view of the human quest makes a lesser foundation quite acceptable. Significant difficulties exist for such a solution, however. Some arise from its failure to face certain pressing questions. For example, the radical diversity—perhaps contradictoriness—of various religions may undercut any notion of a single principle manifesting itself in divergent historical situations. Moreover, a social scientific perspective on people as the makers of their cultural worlds may undercut any employment of utility as a viable mode for decision, as well as rob the religious foundation of any transhuman reference. A more basic problem, however, is that descriptively this solution creates only a quasi religion while normatively it involves a corruption of humanity's religious potential.

The defender of Liberalism might argue that Newman has defined what religion is, has even articulated the integral need to which it responds, but has failed to face fully that such a religion is not an option for moderns. Because modernity makes impossible the acceptance of traditional kinds of religiosity, new forms must be created. A respondent may argue that Newman has absorbed enough modern insights to modulate the conflict. The defender of Liberal religion, however, will no doubt point up that Newman's very absorption of modern insights is double-edged. The haunting ambivalence in Newman arises from his mixing of modern and traditional ideas, as is evident in his analysis of the relation of authority and private judgments or in his view of revelation as a transcendent something that is still enmeshed in the processes of history and culture.

The respondent may reply that Liberal religion is obviously too frail a vessel to carry the weight of a new religious community. The defender, however, can point up the viability of Liberal religion's vision and, more important, the existence of Liberal religious possibilities that are not exhausted by Newman's idea of Liberal religion. (Newman never really faced the more weighty Liberal alternative; he knew Schleiermacher, for instance, only through a second-hand report on his Trinitarian ideas.) The debate continues, but Newman is correct in emphasizing the newness of Liberal religion. Even if Liberal religion has possibilities that Newman did not know about, even if more new kinds of religion may exist in the Christian tradition than Newman would readily admit, Liberal religion is a new kind of religion. Austin Farrer puts this point well in his discussion of Whiteheadian Christianity. He admits to being unable to show the absolute untenability of what he calls half-theologies, or to remove "their attractiveness for minds whose religious attitude they fit or form." But he still declares it "often becomes evident to the orthodox student of such systems that their authors are simply articulating a strange religion. . . . [Their God], for example, must be human enough to have a natural need of his creatures. It is apparently a matter of no concern that he should be divine enough to save their souls alive. Here is a rival doctrine about that divine charity which is the heart of our religion."[19]

A second view, generated by the modern West, affirms the need for the ultimate but simply denies the possible reception of any sacred foundation. (The existence of a potential does not necessitate the existence of a fulfillment; need affects reception only if one assumes something exists to be received.) This alternative can be loosely labeled nonreligious existentialism. It sees human beings as trapped with a potential they cannot fulfill, as strangers thrown into a world that is unable to meet their deepest needs, as creatures victimized by a cruel joke. This view is bleak but clear: the quest exists but the answer does not. People must work out their lives in the light of that situation. The viability of this solution is evident—indeed, Newman shows a strange respect for it.

A third alternative is Newman's attempt to affirm both the sacral quest and the sacral foundation. His answers cannot be our answer for reasons already indicated—e.g., incoherencies in argument, new intellectual problems, the erosion of certain accepted sureties. Nevertheless, Newman posits an important alternative—he both makes clear the goal and gives invaluable aid to the traveler. His analysis of questions such as human religiosity, the sacral foundation's character, the marks of religion, and the religious quest's relationship to its resolution provide both significant models and substantive materials.

Newman in his personal way faced the problems modernity sets for religion. If one accepts his argument—which I find convincing—that Liberal religion's solution so deforms man's given religiosity that it fails as a substitute for traditional religion, then only three options remain. First, the quest may be affirmed but the foundation denied; both Liberal religion's halfway house and Newman's own solution can be rejected. Second, Liberal religion may be reconstituted in light of Newman's criticisms and those more persuasive Liberal schemes he never knew. Its character will clearly differ from traditional religions, indeed it will probably be a quasi religion, but it may be the only possible religion that modernity allows. Third, Newman's own attempt may be carried forward. With his help, the attempt may be made to see how, in modernity, a religion may have that sacral foundation that fulfills the religious quest.

Notes

The abbreviations used for Newman's works are explained in the Bibliography. Pages in the references to these abbreviated titles refer to the uniform edition, Longmans, Green, and Co. For works by others I give the author's name only, or name and date when more than one work by the same author is cited. Complete references are in the bibliography.

If a work is not in the bibliography, I give a full citation.

Chapter 1

1. For an analysis that does not share my misgivings, see Döpfner. For an explication of my views on the general idea's possibilities and problems, see my articles of 1970 and 1971.

2. *U.S.*, p. 17. (See *U.S.*, pp. 17–18 for Newman's own use of the idea, but note this work is early.) Natural religion is examined in many works. Two studies that both differ in approach and cover most of the problems are: van der Leeuw, pp. 591–601 especially; and Evans-Pritchard. See de Vries for an overall view.

3. *Idea*, pp. 252–253. Materials relevant to Newman's study of Western classical religions are contained in A6.22 at the Birmingham Oratory, but no sure means exist to judge the extent of Newman's knowledge of the diversity of man's religions. The published works contain few references to religious traditions other than Christianity. His catalogued library is an ambivalent source of evidence, as what it contains may either have been unread or not all that was read. It has, however, only one book on Eastern religion: Carolyne de Sayn Wittgenstein née Iwanowska, *Bouddhisme et Christianisme* (Rome, 1868). A gift from the authoress, it was unread; the pages are uncut. Newman did have Max Müller's *Introduction to the Science of Religion, Four Lectures Delivered at the Royal Institute with Two Essays on False Analogies and the Philosophy of Mythology* (London, 1873). Though in a letter of 24 August 1873 he says, "I have read your book with great interest," most of the pages are uncut, particularly after the first half, and there are no notations.

4. *P.S.*, VIII, p. 185. For another example of this harshness, see the treatment of Islam in *Diff.*, I, pp. 339ff. Also see *G.A.*, p. 440, for a statement about Judaism and Christianity's unique communication with deity.

5. Van der Leeuw, p. 23; cf. p. 679. One analysis uses, in the main, an older generation of comparativists, especially the line that runs from Otto to van der

Leeuw and Wach. These men, being closer to Newman's intellectual world, often provide a more helpful perspective on him than do some more recent comparativists.

6. *G.A.*, p. 419. Newman's discussions of religion show only some awareness of this phenomenological distinction but in the *Grammar* he shows a considerable sensitivity about the point. Moreover, perspectives that tried to show Christianity's family resemblance to other religions were called by Newman an external view of Christianity. Although they worried him, he recognized the viability of their approach. (See *Ess.*, I, pp. 207–209 particularly, but also pp. 187–188.) Finally, *The Idea of a University* uses the external/internal distinction and may be read as validating both. (See *Idea*, pp. 23ff.; 60–71; 75ff.; 350.)

7. For a classic if dated exposition of this approach, see van der Leeuw, pp. 591–597; 671–678. Pages 592–593 make an important distinction between two kinds of typology. A critical evaluation of the whole approach is contained in Penner.

8. See Sillem, 1969, pp. 127–139 for balanced, general comments on this. Sillem specifically points to Boekraad's and Walgrave's works as examples; Walgrave suggested the retitling of the *Grammar*.

9. *G.A.*, p. 498. See *Ess.*, II, pp. 208–209, 242, where a similar point is argued in a somewhat different fashion. The point also underlies the *Development*'s argument that Christianity can be approached and analyzed as a given fact.

10. See Sillem, 1969, pp. 134–136. The *Grammar*'s criticism of Gibbon exemplifies the need for both stages; see *G.A.*, pp. 459ff.

11. Ricoeur, p. 202. An important criticism of Ricoeur's emphasis on belief, a criticism also relevant to Newman, is found in Jay J. Kim, "Belief or Anamnesis: Is Rapprochement between History of Religions and Theology Possible?," *Journal of Religion*, 52 (1972), 150–169.

12. See *Idea*, pp. 181–183; *H.S.*, I, pp. 161ff. Although Newman's evocation of these types is incomplete, it resembles Wach's (1967) analysis of how different social classes correlate with different religious movements.

13. *Dev.*, pp. 325–326. Newman's most interesting discussion of typology in religion occurs in *Dev.*, pp. 174–178, though there the major point is that types may endure through apparent change.

14. *G.A.*, pp. 117, 390; *Ward*, II, pp. 330–331 (from a letter of 25 June 1869). For other references to conscience's importance and content, see *P.S.*, I, p. 216; *P.S.*, II, p. 18; *U.S.*, pp. 18–19; *O.S.*, pp. 64–65; *Diff.*, II, pp. 248–249. To understand Newman's account one must hurdle the barriers represented by his refusal to pursue certain abstract questions (see *G.A.*, p. 115), and his adjustment of his ideas to the particular audience addressed. (See the differences between the treatments in *G.A.* and *Diff.*, II.)

Secondary works on conscience are numerous, but two that work from different approaches and set most of the issues are: Walgrave, pp. 71–93, 201–241, 342–357; and Sillem, 1964, pp. 377–401. Also worth noting are: Boekraad and Tristram; and Cameron, pp. 210–217 especially.

Walgrave's work (see pp. 148, 288, 342) contains the best sustained argument for conscience's crucial role in Newman's work. In relating Newman to contemporary Existentialist ideas (see p. 289), however, he often fails to account fully for aspects of Newman's ideas, especially the relation to a judging, personal God and to a given nature. Moreover, Walgrave makes conscience so general an idea that it almost loses all specific content. (See pp. 35–36.)

15. I note Newman's relation to the Augustinian tradition in order to highlight a view of his work on conscience that is different from, say, that of Cameron (see pp. 210–217), who relates him to the empirical tradition. For example, the Augustinian idea that certain human judgments reflect eternal exemplars in the mind of God is undeveloped by Newman, but it underlies his notion of conscience (see *U.S.*, pp. 99–119).

The relation to Augustine raises the question of Newman's position on universals. Walgrave, whose account is the best balanced, thinks Newman was unaware that he had described two different kinds of abstraction—one concerning sensible quality, the other spiritual values. See Walgrave, pp. 81–89; but also note Zeno, pp. 52, 64–72; and Boekraad, pp. 190ff., 301–302.

16. See *O.S.*, p. 66; *U.S.*, p. 131; *P.S.*, V, pp. 123–125; *Diff.*, II, p. 240. Walgrave and particularly Boekraad have pointed out the affinity of these ideas with the ideas of those Existentialists who pose an opposition between true selfhood and the voice of the crowd. See Walgrave, pp. 230ff., and Boekraad, pp. 247ff.

17. *G.A.*, p. 105. Newman, *The Philosophical Notebooks*, II, pp. 47–48. The special signs in the quotation are employed by the editors of *The Notebooks* to reproduce the manuscript faithfully. See p. 3 for a full explanation of the signs. The sign ≤ ≥ indicates an addition between the lines; the sign < > indicates a simple alternative, usually written over the word which it might replace.

18. *G.A.*, pp. 113–114. Newman's distinction raises questions as he also argues a person can lose one of the two aspects. (See *G.A.*, pp. 105–106.) The loss of the judicial sense is easy to understand, but feeling an obligation without also distinguishing good and evil poses difficulties. Granting that some discrimination between actions must exist, Newman's point seems to be that for many acts such discriminations remain in the background. For many unsophisticated people, and for all of us in our less sophisticated moments, conscience just commands. (See *G.A.*, p. 106.) Seen in this light, Newman's distinction makes sense.

19. Another point to consider is Newman's assertion that conscience's judgment is retributive rather than remedial. Newman thought retributive judgments expressed the human ability to know moral truth, to act on that knowledge, and to hold all people fully responsible for their actions. He recognized that most moderns feel uneasy with the idea, but he thought conscience taught it. (See *G.A.*, pp. 391, 419.) Realizing the concept's momentousness, he did not accept it easily, and he did modify his early views on this issue. (See Bouyer, pp. 62, 65; and *P.S.*, IV, pp. 87–88.) Nevertheless, he believed it was essential to the Christian ethos, was clearly taught in the Bible, was harmonious with the evil evident in the world, and, most important for our purposes, was validated by conscience. (See *U.S.*, pp. 99–119.)

20. *G.A.*, p. 65. These experiences underlie and validate abstract moral ideas. Exactly how the instinctive recognition relates to an actual moral code is not clear, but Newman appears to see the following process: the instinctive apprehension of value in an individual instance, the generalization of that to a notional system, and the application of that generalization back to particular notions and real events. (See *G.A.*, pp. 64–65 particularly, but also *U.S.*, pp. 183ff.) For analyses of Newman's ideas here, particularly in relation to instinct as a part of conscience, see Walgrave, pp. 347–354, 149, 330, as well as Boekraad, pp. 145–146, and Zeno, pp. 95–96, 135, 231–232, 240–241.

21. *P.S.*, I, pp. 216–217. My analysis stresses the experience's self-validating character and the obligatory judgment's basis in a Good. A different approach could stress that conscience testifies to the constitution of our nature, and that

we have no choice but to trust and obey our nature. (See *G.A.*, pp. 347, 351–352.) This approach raises the question of whether human nature is a contingent fact or an ontological reality. The two differing approaches are exemplified by Boekraad (pp. 256ff.) and Walgrave (pp. 71–93 and 334 ff.). Unfortunately, neither addresses the questions our third problem introduces. Walgrave's analysis is the most satisfactory. He argues that Newman's judgment need not reach reality, it must merely be one that provides a base for practical judgment. Humans must use their nature, as it is all they have, but whether or not it is "real" in some metaphysical sense is a different and perhaps unanswerable question.

This question also touches on the exact character of moral certitude for Newman. For a general description, see *G.A.*, pp. 318, 495–501; and Boekraad, pp. 287ff. For its strongest form, see *G.A.*, p. 65; *Apo.*, p. 15; and Walgrave, pp. 330ff.

22. *G.A.*, pp. 354–356. One of the few places where Newman specifically addresses this problem is when he asks the question "how can an oracle be divine, which is not infallible in its answers?" He responds that "conscience errs, not in principles, but in details. There is always something true in its dictates. There is in no races of men a feeling of its being sin not to kill children and old men [sic]. If [—men] <Jews> thought that putting the Apostles to death was doing God service, what conscience really told them was that blasphemy should (according to the Mosaic Law) be punished with death, not that the Apostles were blasphemers. Truth and falsehood are ever intermingled here below." (Newman, *The Philosophical Notebooks*, II, p. 58. For an explanation of the special signs in the quotation, see note 17, Chapter 1. The sign [—] refers to a deleted word; if the word is legible, it is given.) The passage from a notebook is not a finished argument, and it cannot be weighed too heavily. But it does affirm that a command of conscience, though correct in principle, may be wrongly applied.

23. *Idea*, pp. 514–515. The idea of conscience's "weakness" is a major motif in Newman. See *O.S.*, pp. 64–65; *S.D.*, pp. 357–358; *Diff.*, II, pp. 253–254; *G.A.*, pp. 422–424; *P.S.*, II, pp. 17–21; and *U.S.*, pp. 120–135.

24. *G.A.*, pp. 115–116. Newman never attempts to explain fully why conscience is constituted in such a fashion. Rather than attempting to probe the "why," he described only the "what," the knowledge that one has a nature, is free, and yet is caught in a destructive matrix.

25. *G.A.*, p. 349; also see pp. 228, 231. In *U.S.*, pp. 80–81, this abstract statement is filled out and directly related to conscience in a passage comparing normal growth to that of a "Teacher of Truth."

26. *G.A.*, p. 390. (See p. 116, where the sense of obligation, "if duly cherished, may expand, deepen, and be completed.") See also *Diff.*, II, pp. 259, 336–362; *Dev.*, pp. 86–87; *G.A.*, pp. 389–390; *D.A.*, pp. 258–259; *Ess.*, I, p. 391; and *The Philosophical Notebooks*, II, p. 62. Turning his attention to the problems of what a person is and how, given that situation, conscience can be developed rather than destroyed, he stresses the need to habituate oneself to proper attitudes and actions. (See *Dev.*, p. 325, and *G.A.*, pp. 118, 120–121.)

27. See *G.A.*, pp. 42–74, for an analysis of notional assents such as opinion and credence. For a position close enough to allow for comparison with Newman, yet distinct enough to raise the central questions about conscience's origins, see Niebuhr, pp. 74–75 especially. One of the best, and surely most winning, general presentations of the problem is Berger, 1967. For the application to religion see Berger, 1969. A cogent exposition and criticism of Berger is

found in Van Harvey, "Some Problematic Aspects of Peter Berger's Theory of Religion," *Journal of the American Academy of Religion,* XLI, 1 (1973), 75–93.

28. Wach, 1951, p. 34. The theory is also developed briefly in Chapter Two of Wach, 1967, but the fullest discussion occurs in Wach, 1961. Also see Kitagawa, 1967, pp. 31–53.

29. *V.M.,* I, pp. xl–xli. This preface was written for the reissue of an early attempt to validate the Anglican Church as a middle way between Roman Catholicism and Protestantism.

30. *G.A.,* pp. 392, 389; *U.S.,* p. 19. For Newman, those ideas that arise from self-examination are indisputable truths. They furnish the criteria for judging the worth of religions or religious practices. Liberal religion, for example, falls short of true religion by denying the judging personhood of Deity, while a religion that sacrifices humans denies the moral sense's judgment about people's value.

31. *Apo.,* p. 217; *G.A.,* p. 397; *Apo.,* p. 217. Newman uses these two perceptions to "validate" the Fall. (*See Apo.,* p. 218.)

32. *G.A.,* p. 398.

33. *G.A.,* p. 400. A further discussion of this issue occurs in the last chapter's third section where the relationship of "need" and "reception" is analyzed.

34. Van der Leeuw, pp. 339–340, 681–682. (Also see pp. 83–90, 101–102, 107–108, 147–149, 173–177, 463–471, 509–514, 517, 528.)

35. Eliade, 1959, pp. 11–14. Mircea Eliade, "Structures and Changes in the History of Religion," in G. H. Kraeling and R. M. Adams, eds., *City Invincible* (Chicago, 1969), p. 366. For an excellent analysis of Eliade's work see Jonathan Z. Smith, "The Wobbling Pivot," *Journal of Religion,* 52 (1972), 134–149; pp. 142–149 contain critical comments. Eliade and Newman do differ radically as to the role given to a judging, personal Deity, perhaps because the theological frame influencing Eliade's work is Eastern Orthodoxy, while Newman's work has a significant Protestant component.

36. *G.A.,* p. 403.

37. *G.A.,* pp. 402–403; *U.S.,* p. 285.

38. *G.A.,* p. 403.

39. Van der Leeuw, pp. 23–36, 83–90, 101–105, 147–158, 182–187.

40. See particularly Chapter 11 of Otto. Otto, like Newman, opposed rationalistic explanation and insisted on the primacy and irreducibility of religious people's feeling response to the Holy's presence in the world. Both also emphasize the need to rid oneself of presuppositions as to what must be and the need to unify oneself with perceived appearance.

41. Friedrich Heiler, *Prayer, A Study in the History and Psychology of Religion,* trans. S. M. McComb (New York, 1922). See *P.S.,* VIII, p. 145, for ordinary actions as sacramental actions. Newman's desire to show prayer's universality clearly exhibits his method of approach. Although noting differences in particulars and recognizing the need to judge practice's suitability, he argues the type "prayer" is clear (see *G.A.,* p. 404).

42. *V.M.,* I, p. lxix.

43. Wach, 1961, p. 97. For an enumeration of common rites, see *P.S.,* VIII, p. 5.

44. *G.A.,* p. 404. (Also see *Moz.,* I, pp. 205–206.) The character of revelation as viewed by Newman and by Liberal religion is analyzed in Chapter 4.

45. Van der Leeuw, p. 566. This section contains an important discussion of phenomenology's relation to revelation.

46. *U.S.*, pp. 27, 25; *Ess.*, I, pp. 41–42.

47. *Mix.*, pp. 309, 264.

48. For a brief description of the variety of theories about sacrifice, see de Vries, pp. 198ff. Note that modern work, like A. E. Jensen's, uncovers information that raises questions about the generality of Newman's ideas.

49. See van der Leeuw, pp. 350–359. Newman's presentation here differs from other more theological accounts. (See *U.S.*, p. 116; *G.A.*, p. 405.) He attempts to match vicarious reparation and conscience's sense of personal responsibility in *G.A.*, pp. 393, 395, 405, and points up sacrifice's various meanings in *S.N.*, p. 189. If all these accounts are correlated with the type prayer, an evocative view emerges.

50. *G.A.*, p. 408.

51. Helmuth von Glasonapp, *Der Jainismus, Eine indische Erlösungsreligion* (Berlin, 1925), p. 359. Quoted in Wach, 1961, p. 117. (Also see Karl Jaspers, *Socrates, Buddha, Confucius, Jesus*, trans. R. Mannheim [New York, 1962].)

52. Van der Leeuw, p. 667. This aspect of van der Leeuw's work illustrates the interaction between the apologetic and the objective approaches to religion. Van der Leeuw argues the observer's views must inform any work at critical points, and his book is pervaded by a powerful theological vision. See Przywara, 1922, pp. 63–65, for an analysis of how Newman relates to the Patristic use of Mediator as a synthetic notion.

Chapter 2

1. The connotations of the Greek "economy" *(oikonomia)* differ from those of its English counterpart, although both do refer to the production, distribution, and consumption of "wealth." See Prestige, pp. 57–67, for an analysis of the word's various meanings in Patristic literature.

2. *U.S.*, pp. 340–341; 344; 342; 340. See *Ari.*, p. 75, for a clear description of revelation as an economy. For a good analysis of this idea in Newman see Nédoncelle, pp. 202–263.

3. *Apo.*, p. 299. Newman in the *Arians* says that the *disciplina arcani* and economy are scarcely distinguishable, but he later saw that economy was a larger category of which the *disciplina arcani* is a particular expression. (See *Ari.*, p. 65, and *Apo.*, pp. 241–242. *V.M.*, I, pp. lviii–lix has an eloquent defense of the general notion.) Newman delineates various kinds of secret teaching: concealing a truth completely, if that is possible without deceit; stating a truth only partially; and representing an idea in a form understandable to the learners, if they are unable to comprehend it exactly. Newman felt the first kind was not an example of true economy.

4. *Apo.*, p. 300. See *Ari.*, p. 85, for the case of an apostate; there the outline is lacking.

5. *Apo.*, p. 36. Newman expands this notion into what he calls the sacramental or mystical principle, the view that "the exterior world, physical and historical, was but the manifestation to our senses of realities greater than itself" (*Apo.*, p. 36). For comments on this sacramental principle, especially in relation to mystery, see Keogh.

6. *Ari.*, pp. 79–82. This idea's most extended discussion occurs in the analysis of the Alexandrine Fathers in *Ari*. The book is a historical study rather than a personal statement, but Newman's affinities are quite clear.

7. *Dev.*, p. 181; *U.S.*, p. 33; *Ari.*, pp. 84–85. (See *G.A.*, pp. 385 and 408; *Ess.*, II, p. 231; *Diff.*, I, p. 83.) The question of the salvatory possibilities in other religions is taken up in our final chapter.

8. Wach (1968, p. 77) hints at but does not develop this distinction. The reference is not, of course, to "pure" phenomenology.

9. *S.N.*, pp. 322–323; *O.S.*, p. 25.

10. *U.S.*, pp. 22, 23, 28, 30.

11. *G.A.*, p. 487.

12. *U.S.*, p. 27.

13. One might think a discussion of the relation between natural religion and Christianity would find its center in the *Grammar*'s almost hundred-page treatment of the subject. Newman once remarked, however, that its arguments were for the use of elderly people confronted by local nonbelievers. The remark seems justified by parts, at least, of the argumentation. Significant points are made but other threads are not only flimsy but woven in combinations that leave no clearly defined fabric. Moreover, the distinction between the phenomenological and chronological approaches is muddled, and most arguments are of the chronological sort.

14. This specification of alternatives is more speculative than historical. Chadwick, 1957, sets at least three of these alternatives in a historical framework.

15. *Dev.*, p. 356. For a somewhat different perspective see Newman on Milman's view in *Ess.*, II, pp. 186–248, particularly pp. 230–231, 233.

16. See *Ari.*, pp. 110–115 and particularly pp. 101–104.

17. *Ess.*, II, p. 233.

18. *Dev.*, p. 443.

19. A cogent criticism of reading the *Development* in "psychological" terms is found in Lash.

20. Wach, 1951, p. 51. For statements of the other two views mentioned—Hocking's single generating principle and Tillich's *telos* of existence—see Thomas, pp. 136, 181.

21. *Dev.*, pp. 356; 365 (see *V.M.*, I, pp. lxix ff.). For an example of how this idea might be worked through, using the materials available to a modern comparativist, see Eliade, 1958, pp. 110; 112; 115–116; 119–121. Eliade's approach is not explicitly theological, but his theological thrust is apparent.

22. Neither Scholastic terminology nor Voegelin's terminology has obvious analogies in Newman. The perspectives are similar, however, especially if Scholastic terminology is interpreted by means of a work like de Lubac.

The briefest presentation of this aspect of Voegelin's work is in "The Gospel and Culture," in D. G. Miller and D. Y. Hadidan, eds., *Jesus and Man's Hope* (Pittsburgh, 1971), pp. 59–102. Voegelin sees the process's culmination in the Scholastic distinction between the contingent and the necessary.

23. *U.S.*, pp. 21, 23. On why efficacy is not a criterion for the comparativist, see Wach, 1951, p. 50.

24. *U.S.*, p. 24.

25. *G.A.*, pp. 92–94. (The passage is taken by Newman from his earlier Tamworth papers.) For Newman's general emphasis on the real, see *Grammar*, pp. 12, 29, 36–37, 82, 89, 92ff., and 236ff. He notes the problem in separating them (pp. 38ff. and 75ff.) and defends the notional's correction of the real (p. 146), but he also says a dogmatic creed's importance is its gift of objects to vital religion (pp. 12, 121).

Also note Culler's argument that the *University* scheme makes theology just

another science; see p. 265. It is worth emphasizing that Newman rarely per-
formed as a "scientific" Roman Catholic theologian. The closest approximation
is, perhaps, *Jfc.*, parts of the *Norfolk Letter,* and certain unpublished papers.
With that sort of theologizing, not surprisingly, he was uncomfortable.

26. *G.A.*, pp. 119–121; 34; see *Ari.*, pp. 67–68, and note, pp. 75ff.

27. *U.S.*, p. 26.

28. *V.M.*, I, p. lxxiii. This sense was reinforced by his idea that people have a
propensity to obey, that they will find false objects if they lack true objects. (See
Ess., I, p. 391; cf. *G.A.*, p. 466.)

29. *Dev.*, p. 57; *Ess.*, II, pp. 194–195; *Dev.*, p. 368.

30. *G.A.*, p. 488. For different views on power in religion, see van der Leeuw,
pp. 86–90 particularly; Otto, the opening chapters especially; Wach, 1961, pp.
27–37; Frederick Streng, "Studying Religion: Possibilities and Limitations of
Different Definitions," *Journal of the American Academy of Religion,* XL, 2 (1972),
219–237. Eliade, with his emphasis on kratophanies, might also be added to a
list that could be considerably extended.

31. *Jfc.*, pp. 195–196; *Dev.*, p. 368; *Jfc.*, pp. 317–318. A similar point is made
in somewhat more moderate fashion in *Dev.*, pp. 371–372. Also see Newman's
discussion of superstition (*U.S.*, pp. 117–118; 243ff.).

32. *Jfc.*, p. 144; *P.S.*, V, p. 180; *Jfc.*, p. 219; *G.A.*, p. 488 (cf. pp. 463ff.); *P.S.*,
II, p. 146; *P.S.*, V, pp. 139–140; *P.S.*, II, p. 222; *P.S.*, IV, p. 169; *P.S.*, V, p.
179. (For an analysis and further references see Dessain, 1962, pp. 207–228;
269–288.)

Newman does not hold to a simple sanctification position; his more Protestant emphasis appears in *Jfc.*, pp. 22, 25, 70, 112–113, 179, 230ff. He argues
the Protestant notionally defines what happens, while the Catholic concretely
explains it; conflicts arise only because the notional/real distinction is not
recognized.

33. *S.D.*, pp. 349–350; *P.S.*, V, p. 241; *P.S.*, VIII, p. 30. Newman emphasizes
the gift is "secret" or "hidden." (See, for instance, *P.S.*, V, pp. 295–296; *P.S.*,
VI, pp. 88–89, 209–211, 214; *S.D.*, p. 313.) Some attempts to specify the
change through various images do exist, but they fail to meet the problem (see
Mix., p. 169).

34. *Mix.*, p. 189; *P.S.*, VII, p. 147; *Jfc.*, p. 216 (cf. *P.S.*, V, p. 55); and *P.S.*,
III, pp. 292ff. (Of course, a dialectic between "is" and "can be" saved must
work, given the problems connected with knowing one is saved.) Newman also
argues we know a person through conscience (*U.S.*, p. 29), but it is difficult to
correlate that with the new power that forms one, as that power's personal
qualities are never evident. The correlation can be made only on grounds like
those underlying the argument explained above.

Chapter 3

1. The problem of Newman modulating his ideas in response to circumstances is exemplified by the question of whether aspects of the *Norfolk Letter*
are conservative statements or are muted libertarian statements. Capps touches
on some of the psycho-historical questions.

2. *Ward,* I, p. 588; II, p. 127. The situation is well portrayed in Coulson,
1970, pp. 95–164.

3. *V.M.*, I, pp. lix; lvi.

4. *Diff.*, II, pp. 321–322; *Apo.*, pp. 218–220, with omissions.

5. *Dev.*, pp. 86; 79–80; see *G.A.*, p. 440. An objective authority is necessary because no subjective one is "sufficiently commanding to be the basis of public union and action." (*Dev.*, p. 90.) This description of the "natural" is diminished, but his point remains.

6. Ascertaining Newman's views on Scripture is difficult, especially as he wrote little. His general approach is rather flexible, even though he sometimes is literalistic. For Newman on the dangers of "demythologizing," see *Ari.*, pp. 78–79. But put those statements against his notion of allegorizing interpretations of Scripture (*Ari.*, pp. 56–64) and his overly simple idea of possessing Christ's own words (*G.A.*, p. 449). His most important work in the area is *On the Inspiration of Scripture*. The 1967 edition of this work has a valuable introduction, and its co-editor Holmes has also written an interesting article on these questions; see Holmes, 1971.

7. *Dev.*, pp. 56–57; pp. 56ff. develop these arguments at some length. The problem is particularly acute because the reference is to living ideas. Such ideas possess the mind, become active principles, and lead to new contemplations, applications, and propagations of the idea. (See *Dev.*, pp. 33–38.)

8. *Dev.*, p. 89.

9. *Dev.*, p. 84.

10. From *Church Dogmatics* (London, n.d.), I, 1, 116; quoted in Hans Küng, *Structures of the Church*, trans. S. Attanasio (New York, 1964), pp. 365–366.

11. Newman, *On Consulting the Faithful in Matters of Doctrine*, ed. John Coulson (London, 1961), pp. 63, 67, 73. This "instinct" is communal in the sense that different members support, guide, and correct each other.

See Coulson, 1970, p. 125, and *A.W.*, p. 272, for the effect of the work's reception on Newman. For an extended analysis of the background and character of this work, see Patterson. The Coulson edition of *On Consulting* also has a good introduction.

12. Newman, *On Consulting*, pp. 74–75; 103–104. *H.S.*, I, pp. 209–210, succinctly puts a similar point.

13. A quotation from the review contained in Dessain, 1966, p. 121.

14. *Apo.*, pp. 220–221; 236–237. Coulson, 1970, pp. 138ff., develops and substantiates the idea that Newman's defense is also a criticism.

15. *Apo.*, p. 228.

16. See *Apo.*, p. 240, for a statement of this. Newman does not develop the point, but it is nonetheless important.

17. *Diff.*, II, p. 20.

18. *Apo.*, pp. 237; 238–239; 239; also see pp. 224–230.

19. Quoted in Coulson, 1970, p. 100, from the correspondence with F. W. Faber, February to December 1849; *Apo.*, pp. 225–226.

20. *Apo.*, p. 239.

21. *Diff.*, II, p. 179. Answering Gladstone also furnished an opportunity for responding to Catholic extremists, as Gladstone took their interpretation of Church authority as normative. As Newman said: "We can speak against Gladstone while it would not be decent to speak against [Archbishop] Manning." (Letter to Lord Blachford, quoted in Vincent Blehl, ed., *The Essential Newman* [New York, 1963], pp. 241–242.) Since the *Norfolk Letter* lacks certain distinctions now current in ordinary discussions of such issues, no attempt will be made to relate Newman's ideas to recent technical debates.

22. *Diff.*, II, p. 297.

23. Laski, p. 202. Laski's book overstresses Newman's Liberalism (see p. 207), but it contains an excellent and provocative analysis.

24. *Diff.*, II, pp. 243–244. For possible cases of assistance see *Diff.*, II, pp. 216; 243.

25. *Diff.*, II, p. 259. Conscience is called "the aboriginal Vicar of Christ [so that] . . . even though the eternal priesthood throughout the Church could cease to be, in it the sacerdotal principal would remain and would have a sway" (pp. 248–249). Newman's discussion of conscience here is of little interest. His desire to use some traditional formulations against certain contempories (see p. 247) leads to a wooden repetition of traditional ideas. (For a study that lacks analysis but does collect information on this topic, see Calkin.)

26. See *Diff.*, II, pp. 242, 278.

27. *Diff.*, II, pp. 320, 299, 304. Newman's perturbation over some aspects of the Council was intense. A letter declared, "we have come to a climax of tyranny. . . . For years past my only consolation personally has been in our Lord's presence in the Tabernacle." (Quoted in Coulson, 1970, p. 151, from a letter of 18 November 1870; also see Dessain, 1966, pp. 137–138.) The timing of the Council and the machinations behind it disturbed Newman deeply. Indeed, he was heartened that so little was actually defined. He wrote, "I have no hesitation in saying that, to all appearance, Pius IX wished to say a great deal more (that is that the Council should say a great deal more) than it did, but a greater power hindered it." (*Ward*, II, p. 378.)

28. See *Diff.*, II, pp. 296ff. The section on dogma discusses Newman's relation to this kind of theologizing.

29. On the criteria, see *Diff.*, II, pp. 324–325; 329–330; 302–303. Some implications of this are expressed in a letter in *Ward*, II, p. 379; to Miss Holmes, 15 May 1871. Also note his quoting of Molina—*Diff.*, II, pp. 307–308—on a similar point.

30. *Diff.*, II, pp. 328–329. Newman draws a technical distinction between inspiration and assistance *(assistentia)* to help clarify this. The Apostles were inspired, they had an inward, general gift of infallibility. The Church, however, is only assisted.

31. *Diff.*, II, pp. 339; 333–334.

32. *Diff.*, II, p. 339. "Minimism" had acquired a variety of meanings in the discussions of Newman's day. A letter to Pusey states that he is against some interpretations, but the letter is prior to Vatican I. Also note Newman's distinction, in another letter to Pusey, between doctrines, the voice of a religious body, and principles, the substance of the religion. He says principles are less likely to be defined because they are essential, but he develops the idea inadequately. (See *Ward*, II, pp. 217–223 for the letters.)

33. *Diff.*, II, p. 321.

34. *V.M.*, I, p. xlii.

35. *V.M.*, I, pp. xlvii–xlviii

36. *V.M.*, I, pp. xlviii–xlix. This is a major motif developed at many points. See pp. lxii–lxvii especially, but also pp. li; lvi; lviii; lxxxiii; xcii–xciii.

37. *V.M.*, I, pp. liv–lv; Newman, *The Philosophical Notebooks*, II, *The Text*, p. 167. The note is from 24 January 1867. For an explanation of the special signs in the quotation, see note 17, Chapter One. The sign << >> indicates quotation marks. The first brackets are my addition to the text.

38. *V.M.*, I, p. lxix. For a similar point in relation to devotions, see *V.M.*, I, p. lxxv.

39. *Apo.*, p. 54, italics added; also see *Apo.*, pp. 17–19. See *Ari.*, pp. 142–150 for issues such as the movement from Scriptural to dogmatic language and dogma's relation to heresy. (Also see Harrold, ed., 1948, II, p. 197.)

40. *Ari.*, pp. 76, 36; *H.S.*, II, pp. 452, 223. Newman's treatment of the various religious orders, as well as his choice of the Oratorians, shows his personal perspective. James has evocatively drawn out this side of Newman's general approach, if occasionally in a one-sided fashion. See pp. 214–225; 233–261.

41. See *U.S.*, sermon VII, "Love the Safeguard of Faith against Superstition," pp. 222–250, p. 226 especially. Newman's interpretations of dogma also sometimes show this; see *G.A.*, pp. 132–133; 138–140.

42. Quoted in Coulson, 1970, p. 61, footnote two, from a note to a copy of the *Essay on Development* used for the revision of 1877; *U.S.*, pp. 25; 27; 35.

43. My analysis differs from that of Walgrave, who says, "Very often . . . what is assimilated forms no part of the dogmatic and permanent content of the Church's teaching," citing as examples the use of Aristotle's philosophy in theology and the use of pagan rites in liturgy. See Walgrave, p. 270. The argument may be made about ritual but not about dogma. (See *Ari.*, pp. 142, 150, for an example of how Newman's acumen in respect to the difficulties in Scriptural language is not displayed in his examination of creedal language.)

44. *Dev.*, p. 439; *Apo.*, p. 54; *Essays and Sketches*, II, p. 204. Newman sometimes says attitude implies fact, which is untenable. (See *Apo.*, p. 54.)

45. Many issues are raised here. Coulson, 1970, touches on the subject briefly but well (see pp. 3–37; 154). The perspective of the late Wittgenstein is helpful here, although Newman might have been unhappy with the results. See Richard Bell, "Wittgenstein and Descriptive Theology," *Religious Studies,* 5/6(1969/70), 1–18, and Hudson.

Incidentally, at times Newman seems to hold a position like that of sophisticated modern Fundamentalism, where Biblical language is the only linguistic source for the Christian. (See his speaking of the "new language when Christ has brought us" [*P.S.*, V, p. 44].) The more significant elements in his thought do not, however, accord with this emphasis.

46. *U.S.*, pp. 329; 334; 335; 331; 336; 345–346. The main source for this perspective is the last of the *U.S.* sermons, "The Theory of Development in Religious Doctrine." The relation of Newman's analysis to empiricism is developed by Cameron in his book, pp. 207–217, 222–243 and in Coulson and Allchin, pp. 81–87.

47. *U.S.*, pp. 348–349.

48. A note to a copy of *Dev.*, used for the revision of 1877. Quoted in Coulson, 1970, p. 61, note 2.

49. Pears, pp. 28–29. Pears also notes that positivism is a fourth response. On the particular situation of Newman's time, also see Küng.

50. Newman gives a summary of how various images correct each other in a letter on Mansell to Meynell, 20 December 1859; quoted in Coulson, 1970, p. 60.

51. The "practical type" of religious thought, as well as the abstract question of a typology of religious thought, are developed in my 1975 article, "Toward." Chinese thought, especially Mencius's thought, probably best exemplifies the type, but Newman clearly fits the type—indeed, he is one of the Christian tradition's clearest examples of it.

52. The kind of study pointed to here is still in its infancy, but a few important works do exist. Wach's, 1961, pp. 59–96, underlies my approach, but

Wach is more suggestive than clear, systematic, or even coherent. I have recast Wach's ideas and applied them to Chinese materials in my 1975 article, "Mencius." Streng also has done a fascinating study, and Richards (pp. 173ff. especially) sets some issues extraordinarily well. An interesting if less successful work is Smart.

Chapter 4

1. *Ward,* II, p. 460; *Apo.,* pp. 233–234; *Ward,* II, p. 461; *Idea,* pp. 386–387. The last quotation is taken from a discussion of what Newman calls "the form of infidelity of the day," but the point can be generalized. On the different kinds of Liberalism, see Walter E. Houghton, "The Issue between Kingsley and Newman," in John Henry Cardinal Newman, *Apologia Pro Vita Sua,* ed. David J. De Laura (New York, 1968), pp. 390–392. As our goal is to depict Newman's views on a particular type of religion, certain historical questions are not critical.

2. *G.A.,* p. 60; *Dev.,* p. 179; *G.A.,* p. 143. See *U.S.,* pp. 200–201; *S.N.,* p. 201. The major theoretic problem in Newman's idea of first principles is examined in Chapter 5. Boekraad's long discussion has problems, but it brings together most relevant passages on this subject and discusses the differences between Newman's presentations. See pp. 156–159; 214–241; 276–281; 289; 301–302. Walgrave, pp. 114ff.; 143–146, is also worth consulting. Newman's fullest single presentation is in the *Grammar;* see pp. 61ff.; 221ff.; 237ff.; 269ff.; 305–311; 361–362; 363–378. Newman attempts only a few brief enumerations of the first principles of Christianity (e.g., *Dev.,* pp. 324–325; 184–185) and of Liberalism (e.g., *Apo.,* pp. 260–262). Given the importance of such an enterprise, the absence of a more concerted effort is puzzling.

3. *Apo.,* pp. 98; 179–180; 185. Newman thought the European history of Liberalism showed it aimed to destroy all traditional religion. See the letter to C. L. Blachford, 25 October 1874, quoted in Kenny, p. 144.

4. *The Letters and Diaries of John Henry Newman,* ed. Charles Stephen Dessain (London, 1962), XI, p. 86; Harrold ed., 1948, III, p. 373; *Ess.,* I, p. 95. Sabellianism is the special stage noted. On this point also see *Idea,* pp. 381–382 and *Ess.,* I, pp. 241–242.

5. *P.S.,* I, pp. 319, 310. In this general context, Newman's idea of the differences between the "barbaric and civilized" is worth noting, especially as he sometimes says Liberal religion is congenial to a civilized time. (See *Idea,* p. 218, and *P.S.,* I, pp. 311–312, 319.) But he also argues that the true idea of civilization is synonymous with Christianity (*H.S.,* I, pp. 161–170). Even when Newman equates religion with at least aspects of barbarism, he also recognizes that certain aspects of a "barbaric" temperament cannot operate in a civilized age. See the letter to P. C. Allies, 10 November 1863, quoted in Kenny, pp. 161–162.

On Liberal religion as the half-truth of secular ethics, note that the Biglietto speech says, "it must be borne in mind, that there is much in the liberalistic theory which is good and true; for example, not to say more, the precepts of justice, truthfulness, sobriety, self-command, benevolence." The problem comes only when "this array of principles is intended to supercede, to block out, religion." (*Ward,* II, p. 462.)

6. Berger, 1963, p. 43. Berger's reference is only to the "sociological consciousness," but the point can be expanded.

7. *Ward,* II, p. 416; *The Catholic Sermons of Cardinal Newman, Published for the First Time,* ed. Birmingham Oratory (London, 1957), p. 123. A striking analysis of how the twentieth century differs from its Enlightenment past occurs in Toulmin, pp. 1–130 especially.

8. *P.S.,* I, p. 311–312; see also *G.A.,* p. 416; *U.S.,* pp. 102–104. As Newman said elsewhere, "since 1688 men saw the good in themselves and not the evil." Quoted in Kenny, pp. 129–130, from a letter of 13 March 1831.

9. See Cassirer, pp. 137–160, for a good analysis of this. Cassirer's study is dated in places, but it contains a valuable exposition of the positive meaning of many Enlightenment ideas which more theologically inclined analyses often fail to highlight. See, for example, Barth, pp. 33–79 especially.

10. Quoted in Cassirer, pp. 161–163. This belief emphasizes tolerance, defining it as an open-minded inquiry into a variety of ideas that was bound to uncover the truth. By Newman's time, however, it was turning into the belief that the objective investigation of at least human questions finds not a single truth but many truths, each of which must be tolerated.

11. *Apo.,* pp. 260–262. The eighteen principles of Liberalism appear in the *Apology* as Note A. Newman notes that these principles are more a historical portrait of the Liberal party at Oxford in 1830–1840 than a general philosophic description. He also said that one ought not rely on them alone for his views. (See the letter to C. L. Hutton, 3 June 1865, quoted in Kenny, p. 144.) Nevertheless, his descriptions, particularly of private judgment, are often evocative, although he highlights Liberalism's rationalistic aspect.

Some of the other principles are particularly interesting; see, for example, the use of conscience in the tenth. These principles appear to exemplify only the rationalistic wing of liberalism; see one, two, and four especially. If read more generally, however, they just assert that both people's rational and emotional energies are the final judge of religious truth. For example, in principle one the standard that tests the importance of a religious tenet is whether it converts, whether it causes a change in the total person. (For a strong statement of Liberalism's tie to rationalism, see the letter to C. L. Armstrong, 23 March 1887, quoted in Kenny, p. 132. For a statement emphasizing its more general subjective character, see *Ess.,* I, pp. 33–35.)

12. *Idea,* pp. 393, 387; see *Dev.,* p. 357.

13. For examples of this emphasis on "feeling," see *Idea,* pp. 28, 32, and a note from 23 July 1868 quoted in Vargish, p. 84.

14. *V.M.,* I, pp. 130–131. This work is early. Newman did not, however, change these lines on reissuance, although he does query his solution to the problem (see p. xviii). To my mind, this formulation sets the question that even the later Newman struggled with.

15. *D.A.,* p. 397. See *Mix.,* p. 206; *Ess.,* II, pp. 353.

16. *U.S.,* pp. 213–215. See *V.M.,* I, pp. 132, 138; *S.D.,* p. 50.

17. See *Ess.,* II, pp. 336, 340–341.

18. *Idea,* pp. 61, 40, 9; also see p. 449. The philosophic issue is complex, but, in brief, Newman thought that "God . . . being known only through the visible world, our knowledge of Him is absolutely commensurate with our knowledge of it,—is nothing distinct from it,—is but a mode of viewing it." (*Idea,* p. 40.)

Newman's attitude to attempts to prove God's existence is hard to pinpoint. The *Grammar*'s "derivation" of God from conscience is called an illustration rather than a proof, but he also calls the analysis of conscience his favorite or chosen proof for the existence of God. (See John Henry Newman, *The Philo-*

sophical Notebooks, II, *The Text,* ed. E. J. Sillem, rev. A. J. Boekraad [New York, 1970], p. 67.) He might have accepted those proofs that attempt to clarify the implicitly present; see Versfeld.

19. *Idea,* p. 39; *Letters and Diaries,* XIV, p. 127. Newman's guiding idea concerning the relation between religion and science is that truth cannot contradict truth. (See *Idea,* pp. 466–467.) He thought quarrels between disciplines arise only when one discipline either encroaches on an area it ought not or utilizes inadequate methods to study certain questions. This approach left Newman open to new scientific findings. Darwin, for example, failed to perturb him, though he may not have understood all the implications of Darwin's theory. The particular parts of his resolution are, however, badly flawed, especially where it concerns method: emphasizing theology's deductive character and science's inductive character is, at best, a partial description. See *Idea,* pp. 441–442; 456–479; and Culler, pp. 6–9; 244–247; 265. Thomas Kuhn, *The Structure of Scientific Revolutions* (Chicago, 1968) presents an interpretation of scientific method that is quite different from Newman's, though note the criticisms of Kuhn in Toulmin, pp. 98–123.

20. *Idea,* pp. 229–230; 271; 227; 179. See *U.S.,* pp. 181, 264; Harrold, ed., 1948, II, pp. 204–206. Newman's point is defensible, but it overlooks certain kinds of strict reasoning. See Wicker for a discussion arguing that although Newman's understanding of logic is inadequate, his basic position is sound.

21. *U.S.,* pp. 222; 228; 294.

22. *U.S.,* pp. 198. See *U.S.,* pp. 266–267, for the dangers in any speculative approach. Newman criticizes Liberalism's liberty of thought and mode of inquiry at many places. See for instance, *Apo.,* pp. 255–256; *U.S.,* pp. 197, 200; *Letters and Diaries,* XIV, p. 45, and C.C. A 463 (Birmingham Oratory), p. 89, quoted in Kenny, p. 145.

23. *Idea,* pp. 432–433; 61–62; see *Idea,* p. 434. The idea of "science" here makes no distinction between physical and life sciences, but the point has general applicability.

24. *Idea,* pp. 37–38; 453–454. Newman's rhetorical powers are often exercised on this topic—see the full treatments here; *U.S.,* p. 115; *Idea,* p. 225; and the magnificently polemical passage in Harrold, ed., 1948, II, pp. 209–213.

25. *Idea,* p. 445; *U.S.,* pp. 194–195; *P.S.,* I, pp. 316–317, 319.

26. This work originally appeared in 1836 as Tract 73. Its major concern is a study of two books, but it is much concerned with rationalism, which is "to ask for *reasons* out of place; to ask improperly how we are to *account* for certain things, to be unwilling to believe them unless they can be accounted for." (See *Tracts for the Times,* III, 2 [London, 1839].) Our analysis selects only certain points of the essay and extrapolates from them. On how the two meanings of "manifest" specify the two positions, see *Ess.,* I, p. 69.

27. *Ess.,* I, pp. 194–195; 69–70; 80–82; 82–83. Unlike the preceding principle, this principle seems to contain a notion of a personal deity, but that probably represents only a general comment on how the world's character validates certain ethical imperatives.

28. *Ess.,* I, pp. 74; 40–44.

29. *Ess.,* I, pp. 72.

30. *L.G.,* pp. 121–22. This idea is returned to in Chapter 5.

31. *Apo.,* p. 260. Newman saw Milman's *History of Christianity* as an example of this. (See *Ess.,* II, pp. 208; 216ff.) Cassirer explicates this point well; see p. 189; note especially the two quotes from Diderot, pp. 166, 170.)

32. *Letters and Diaries*, XIX, pp. 530–531. See the response to a criticism of this letter on pp. 548–550. For another clear example of this attitude, see *Ess.*, I, p. 47.

33. *G.A.*, p. 45; *P.S.*, VI, p. 81; *P.S.*, I, p. 276; *Mix.*, p. 266; *G.A.*, pp. 49, 52, 51, 52. Also see *P.S.*, III, p. 156; *Ess.*, I, pp. 166–168; *P.S.*, I, p. 209; *U.S.*, p. 345; *G.A.*, p. 47. The *Grammar* discusses at length the notion of believing what is not fully understood, as is exemplified at *G.A.*, pp. 122–141. For a critical analysis of aspects of this question, see Pailin, pp. 92–197 especially. Note that my account has at times generalized from the mystery of "earthly," real objects.

34. For a further analysis of the empirical model, see J. M. Cameron, "Newman and the Empirical Tradition," in Coulson and Allchin, pp. 76–96; pp. 81–87 especially. Cameron's 1962 essays on Newman are also worthy of note (see especially pp. 204–217; 222–243). This problem can also be approached in the more general terms of Romanticism: see John Beer, "Newman and the Romantic Sensibility," in H. S. Davies and G. Watson, eds., *The English Mind* (Cambridge, 1964), pp. 193–218. The notion of continuing divine assistance could be validated by an approach like the *Development*'s idea that a revelation once given is protected.

35. Newman's attitude to Utilitarianism is hard to specify, as the phenomenon is complex and his comments on it are few. As a purely legislative criterion, for instance, he might agree with some of its ideas. (See *Ess.*, I, p. 29.) He does make some specific critical comments on Utilitarianism: for example, that the hedonistic calculus must take account of the happiness brought by faith in eternal life and that vicarious punishment, as a social "fact," is not recognized. The dearth of specific analysis probably arises from Newman's belief that the differences are so great that not specific criticisms but rather the construction of a counterposition is needed. (See the letter to C. L. Blachford, 22 February 1877, noted in Kenny, p. 137; also see Vargish, pp. 108; 111; 113–115; *Idea*, pp. 381ff.; and *G.A.*, p. 416.)

36. Arendt, pp. 39, 32, 33, 40 with omissions; also see pp. 87–89. Arendt's reflections can be seen as an extension of the foreboding analysis of Newman. For a cogent, commonsense defense of Utilitarianism that, while not fully answering Arendt's question, uses Utilitarianism as a standard but allows for other bases for action, see J. O. Urmson, "Saints and Heroes," in A. I. Melden, ed., *Essays in Moral Philosophy* (Seattle, 1972), pp. 198–216.

37. *Idea*, pp. 109; 108; 111. Note the idea that Liberal knowledge is a permanent addition to the self (*Idea*, pp. 114, 152).

38. *Idea*, pp. 164–165. Newman argues here for a parallelism between the development of the intellect and the body.

39. *Idea*, pp. 508–509. See Culler, pp. 211–226 for a good discussion of this point. Our interpretations differ at certain points; Culler, for instance, formulates the key question in terms of human beings' chief good (p. 223). Aristotle's notions of pleasure—particularly as developed by Urmson—articulate the emotional parallels of useful and liberal activity. See J. O. Urmson, "Aristotle on Pleasure," in J. M. E. Moravcsik, ed., *Aristotle, A Collection of Critical Essays* (Garden City, N.Y., 1967), pp. 323–333.

40. *Ess.*, I, pp. 55, 47; *Apo.*, pp. 221–223. Also see *Ess.*, I, p. 48 and Newman's sixth Liberal principle, *Apo.*, p. 260.

Culler argues that Liberalism sees religion as a purely Liberal (i.e., internally significant) action, where orthodoxy sees it as useful (pp. 216–217). For example, prayer for the Liberal affects only the individual soul, where for orthodoxy prayer is answered and therefore is useful. While my overall interpretation is not as much opposed to Culler's as it might appear, we do differ on his portrayal of orthodoxy as useful. Traditional Christian theology almost always shies away, for instance, from the idea that prayer directly affects God because this implies God's nature is changeable.

41. Harrold, ed., 1948, II, p. 174; *Ward,* II, p. 461; *Apo.,* p. 262. In a somber statement that deals with the problem Liberals try to solve, Newman writes: "The ascendency of Faith may be impracticable, but the reign of Knowledge is incomprehensible. The problem for statesmen of this age is how to educate the masses, and literature and science cannot give the solution." (Harrold, ed., 1948, II, p. 203.)

Note that even the *Idea* does not answer this question, as it concerns only education for the elite. For a fuller explication of the views of both sides, see Culler, and Vargish, pp. 123–154.

42. See Harrold, ed., 1948, II, p. 194. *The Tamworth Reading Room* is a polemical attack. Unlike the *Idea,* it formulates no constructive alternatives.

43. *Idea,* p. 461. See Culler, p. 195, and Vargish, p. 147. The ideal is difficult to imagine but its lesser manifestations do allow the ideal to be recognized in action. In this sense, the educated person's abilities parallel those of the fine tennis player or musician. An abstract specification of their qualities is difficult, but the result is fairly clear. This provides a partial answer to the charge that Newman's view is so idealistic it is without practical meaning.

44. *Idea,* pp. 177–178. The passage continues with a picture that recalls the famous portrait of the gentlemen. (*Idea,* pp. 208–211; on aspects of that kind of portrait, see Triffin.)

45. Harrold, ed., 1948, II, p. 181; *Idea,* pp. 121; 184–186; 202. Also see *Idea,* pp. 115–118.

46. *Idea,* pp. 201–202; see *P.S.,* I, p. 32. I develop these ideas at length in my 1975 article, "Newman."

Chapter 5

1. Reardon, p. 128. Even Vargish's sympathetic account (p. viii) begins by noting the immense gap in sensibility between Newman and us. On Newman's notion of the unfinished character of his work, see Coulson, 1970, p. 162. His work's highly personal character, his writing as a response to specific situations, and his often polemical stance accentuate this unfinished character. (See Coulson, 1970, pp. 105, 145–146; *A.W.,* pp. 272–276; and *V.M.,* I, pp. xx–xxi.)

2. Quoted in Wach, 1968, p. 149. For a striking explication of the distinctions between Buddhism and Christianity, for example, see the long list of differences in Wach, 1951, pp. 125ff. My views on the diversity of religion are not shared by all scholars. Friedrich Heiler, for example, argues for seven general unifying principles of religion in his essay in Eliade and Kitagawa, pp. 142–152.

3. A different arrangement of possible options, more closely tied to individual thinkers' ideas, appears in Thomas, pp. 19–28. His seven alternatives can, I think, be reduced to my four.

Despite the problem's importance, little analysis of it exists, and less still that is informed and perceptive. Therefore, ideas in this area can be little more than proto-theories. For a good overview of earlier works on the question, see Joseph Kitagawa, "Theology and the Science of Religion," *Anglican Theological*

Review, XXXIX, 1 (June 1957), 33–52. Also see Wach, 1951, pp. 3–29, and, though they are usually occasional pieces, the essays in Wach, 1968, pp. 69–114 and 142–155.

4. On the distinctions among mystical experiences, one of the most important works is still Joseph Maréchal, *Studies in the Psychology of The Mystics,* trans. Alger Thorold (London, 1927). Also see R. C. Zaehner's *Mysticism Sacred and Profane, An Inquiry into Some Varieties of Praeternatural Experience* (Oxford, 1957). That work is valuable, if polemical and somewhat unclear both at critical points and in its general structure. An excellent review of both works in this area and problems in methodology is found in Frits Staal, *Exploring Mysticism* (Berkeley, 1975). Differences in the idea of "love" are even clearer. See the distinctions between, say, either Buddhist *karuna* and Christian charity or between love as understood today and Taoist love *(tz'u).*

5. The art of balancing statements is a notion developed, in a theoretical context, by Farrer, pp. 115–116. For some notions of the spirit's incarnation in matter in primitive religion, see Douglas, p. 13. For Buddhism spreading into very divergent cultural situations and assimilating them, see, for instance, Joseph Kitagawa, *Religions of the East* (Philadelphia, 1966), p. 210.

6. Two examples of Roman Catholic analyses that are well-intentioned but show little change in basic formulation are those of Piet Fransen and of Hans Küng in Neuner, pp. 25–119. The notion of a theology of religions has various meanings today. I use it here to refer to a position lying midway between, say, van der Leeuw and Schlette.

7. Quoted in Thomas, pp. 85; 90. For a modern example of a similar attitude, see W. C. Smith in Eliade and Kitagawa, pp. 34–35.

A statement like Troeltsch's can be viable when it is put in the first person. A religion's "primary claim to validity" may be its existence as "the only religion I can endure." This change, however, makes the point different. Newman's work on the indefectibility of certitude *(G.A.,* pp. 248–251) is relevant here, as is the cogent criticism of his position in Brunton.

8. *Ess.,* II, p. 336; also see pp. 340–341.

9. *U.S.,* p. 244; *Jfc.,* pp. 150–151; *Ess.,* I, pp. 288; 290–291. (For Newman's full analysis of superstition, see *U.S.,* pp. 117–118; 242–250.) Although the pluralistic point can be extrapolated from these quotations, certain interpretative difficulties remain. For instance, the reference to a limited fulfillment may be a rhetorical device; moreover, the last reference is to one tradition and in a time span that Newman thought showed continuities.

Another place where a pluralistic tendency appears is in the attitude to diversity that runs through the *Apology.* The tendency is evident both in Newman's emphasis on the need for plurality inside the Roman Catholic Church and in his feelings, after his conversion, toward members of the Church of England. (See *Apo.,* pp. 156–157; 219; 240; 296–299; and Dessain, 1966, p. 97.) The extrapolation from parts of the Christian community to different religions is, of course, large, but the point remains that people are saved in different religious communities and that Newman's own conversion is personal. For other relevant references, see *Mix.,* p. 159; *U.S.,* pp. 21; 33; *Ari.,* pp. 79–85; *Dev.,* pp. 84–85.

10. *Ward,* II, p. 492; also see *G.A.,* pp. 410; 413–416. The general question of first principles is discussed at the beginning of Chapter 4.

11. This formulation slides over certain questions raised by speaking of a similar experience that receives different conceptual articulations. Does an ex-

perience exist independent of an interpretative framework? Is the experience changed by the frame applied to it? This problem is vexing, but a reasonably safe supposition is that similar experiences are modified by divergent conceptual articulations. For the exposition of a contrary view see Richards. For an astute philosophic examination of this question, see Richard Rorty, "The World Well Lost," *Journal of Philosophy* (October 1972), 649–665. For some excellent studies of this problem, see Bryan Wilson, ed., *Rationality* (New York, 1971).

12. The historical question of the pluralism of Newman's society requires, of course, careful analysis. Moreover, Newman lived through a number of significant changes in that society, even if he was related to only certain aspects of them. Clearly, however, the combination of the society itself and Newman's relation to the society did not force upon him the pluralistic question.

13. Aspects of this question are also dealt with in examining Newman's view of conscience, in Chapter 1. A clear explication of this developmental model of human nature is found in Graham.

14. For Aristotle's point, see *Nicomachean Ethics,* 1095A11–1097A14. (For a discussion of the point, see W. F. R. Hardie, *Aristotle's Ethical Theory* [Oxford, 1968], pp. 28–67.) The notion of ultimacy is most prominent in Wach's argument. See 1961, pp. 30–37 especially, but also note 1951, pp. 32–33. On the relationship of ultimacy to the notion of a quasi religion, see especially 1961, p. 37. The idea of a religious perspective is developed well in Clifford Geertz's works; indeed, we are combining Wach and Geertz. See his 1968, pp. 97–98, and his 1973, pp. 87–125; 193–233.

15. On this general idea, see Alasdair MacIntyre's "The Logical Status of Religious Belief," in MacIntyre, ed., *Metaphysical Beliefs* (London, 1957), pp. 167–205. The point holds whether one speaks of "open" or "closed" views of religion, though it is clearly more germane to open views; see Smith. (Smith's article, incidentally, is relevant both to the question of the diversity of religions and to the difficulty of a "descriptive fulfillment" ideal, even one working only in the West.)

16. Newman reflects that part of the Western Christian attitude that argues that men must protest against death; see his treatment of the death of Julian the Apostate or his portrait of the gentleman who submits to death "because it is his destiny." (*Idea,* pp. 194–196, 210.) The general rationale for this attitude is well developed, though without a comparativist's perspective, in Karl Rahner, *On the Theology of Death,* trans. C. H. Henkey (London, 1961). See Phillip Ariès, *Western Attitudes toward Death: From the Middle Ages to the Present,* trans. P. M. Ranum (Baltimore, 1974), for a historical analysis that argues such a protest has been common in only part of the Western tradition. For an excellent exposition of a culture where such a protest is not prominent, see W. La Fleur, "Japan," in F. Holck, ed., *Death and Eastern Thought* (Nashville, 1974), pp. 226–256.

Related to this is the question of whether Liberal religion carries people above themselves. See Culler's criticism of Newman on this point, p. 227, and Vargish's analysis of the religious importance of Newman's idea of mind, p. 150. Clearly people are moved beyond themselves, but the ultimacy criterion is still not met because of the limitations in both quest and foundation.

17. Newman usually deals with this problem in psychological terms; for example, he unpacks the implications of the feeling he calls conscience, and he validates faith as a given of human nature by trying to show it is one among other human mental states. The philosophic cogency of his ideas rests on an Augustinian foundation, however.

18. See *L.G.*, pp. 121–123 on Liberalism as a religion of principles. A principle is an abstract idea under which various elements, such as a doctrine, may fall. For example, Newman will argue that mediation is a principle of Christianity but that the Incarnation is a doctrine, a specific and factual element. (See *Dev.*, pp. 178–185, particularly and, for one of many examples, *Ess.*, I, p. 367.)

19. *Faith and Speculation* (London, 1967), pp. 169–170. The philosophical argumentation that underlies Farrer's analysis is complicated, but the significant point here is only the religious need he points to. See *Ess.*, I, pp. 96–98, for what is, to my knowledge, Newman's only discussion of Schleiermacher.

Another modern option might be said to be the acceptance of religious positions that break either completely or substantially with the presuppositions of the Western tradition. Zen Buddhism, for example, represents an almost complete break. William James's religious views, for example, represent a substantial break. (On James, see William Clebsch, *American Religious Thought, a History* [Chicago, 1973], pp. 125–170, and Henry Levinson, "Science, Metaphysics, and the Chance of Salvation: An Interpretation of the Thought of William James," Thesis Ph.D., Princeton University, December, 1975.) To my mind, however, even this option fits within the three outlined here.

A Selected Bibliography

This list indicates the abbreviations for titles of Newman's works used in the notes. Abbreviations are those recommended by Stephen Dessain in *The Letters and Diaries of John Henry Newman.* Reference is to the uniform edition, Longmans, Green and Co.; publication information about that edition is contained in *The Letters and Diaries.* The original appearance date of each of Newman's works appears in parentheses after the title of the work, although in the case of collections this can be misleading. For fuller bibliographies of Newman's works, including manuscript sources, see John Coulson, *Newman and the Common Tradition: A Study in the Language of Church and Society* (Oxford, 1970) and Dwight Culler, *The Imperial Intellect: A Study of Newman's Educational Ideal* (New Haven, 1955).

Apo. *Apologia pro Vita Sua* (1864)

Ari. *The Arians of the Fourth Century* (1833)

Ath. *Select Treatises of St. Athanasius;* 2 volumes (1842)

A.W. *John Henry Newman: Autobiographical Writings,* ed. Henry Tristram (1956)

Call. *Callista, a Tale of the Third Century* (1855)

D.A. *Discussions and Arguments on Various Subjects* (1872)

Dev. *An Essay on the Development of Christian Doctrine* (1845)

Diff. *Certain Difficulties Felt by Anglicans in Catholic Teaching;* 2 volumes (I: 1850; II: 1866, 1875)

Ess. *Essays Critical and Historical;* 2 volumes (1871)

G.A. *An Essay in Aid of a Grammar of Assent* (1870)

H.S. *Historical Sketches;* 3 volumes (1872)

Idea *The Idea of a University Defined and Illustrated* (1852–1859)

Jfc.   *Lectures on the Doctrine of Justification* (1838)

L.G.   *Loss and Gain: The Story of a Convert* (1848)

M.D.   *Meditations and Devotions of the Late Cardinal Newman* (1893)

Mir.   *Two Essays on Biblical and on Ecclesiastical Miracles* (1826, 1842)

Mix.   *Discourses Addressed to Mixed Congregations* (1849)

Moz.   *Letters and Correspondence of John Henry Newman,* ed. Anne Mozley; 2 volumes (1891)

O.S.   *Sermons preached on Various Occasions* (1857)

P.S.   *Parochial and Plain Sermons;* 8 volumes (1834–1843)

Prepos.   *Present Position of Catholics* (1851)

S.D.   *Sermons Bearing on Subjects of the Day* (1843)

S.N.   *Sermon Notes of John Henry Cardinal Newman,* 1849–1879, ed. Fathers of the Birmingham Oratory (1913)

U.S.   *Fifteen Sermons preached before the University of Oxford* (1843)

V.M.   *The Via Media;* 2 volumes (I: 1877; 1837; II: 1830–1841)

V.V.   *Verses on Various Occasions* (1867)

Ward   Wilfrid Ward, *The Life of John Henry Cardinal Newman;* 2 volumes; London (1912)

Arendt, Hannah. *Between Past and Future: Eight Exercises in Political Thought.* New York, 1968.
Aristotle. *The Nicomachean Ethics,* trans. M. Ostwald. New York, 1962.
Barth, Karl. *Protestant Theology in the Nineteenth Century, Its Background and History,* trans. B. Cozen, J. Bowden. London, 1972.
Beer, John. "Newman and the Romantic Sensibility," in H. S. Davies and G. Watson, ed., *The English Mind.* Cambridge, 1964, pp. 143–218.
Berger, Peter. *Invitation to Sociology.* London, 1967.
Berger, Peter. *The Sacred Canopy: Elements of a Sociological Theory of Religion.* Garden City, N.Y., 1969.
Bettis, J. D., ed. *Phenomenology of Religion.* New York, 1969.
Boekraad, A. J. *The Personal Conquest of Truth According to J. H. Newman.* Louvain, 1955.
Boekraad, A. J., and Henry Tristram. *The Argument from Conscience to the Existence of God According to J. H. Newman.* Louvain, 1961.
Bouyer, Louis. *Newman, His Life and Spirituality,* trans. J. May. New York, 1960.
Brunton, J. A. "The Indefectibility of Certitude." *Downside Review,* 68, 284 (1968), 250–265.
Butler, Joseph. *The Analogy of Religion.* New York, 1961.
Calkin, A. B. "John Henry Newman on Conscience and the Magisterium." *Downside Review,* 87, 289 (1969), 358–369.
Cameron, J. H. *The Night Battle.* London, 1962.

Capps, Donald. "John Henry Newman: A Study in Religious Leadership." Thesis Ph.D., University of Chicago Divinity School, June 1970.

Cassirer, Ernst. *The Philosophy of the Enlightenment*, trans. F. A. C. Kelly and J. P. Pettegrove. Boston, 1966.

Chadwick, Owen. *From Bossuet to Newman: The Idea of Doctrinal Development.* Cambridge, 1957.

Chadwick, Owen. *The Victorian Church.* 2 vols., New York, 1966, 1970.

Church, R. W. *The Oxford Movement.* London, 1892.

Coulson, John. "Belief and Imagination." *Downside Review*, 298, 90 (1972), 1–15.

Coulson, John. *Newman and the Common Tradition: A Study in the Language of Church and Society.* Oxford, 1970.

Coulson, John, ed. *The Rediscovery of Newman: An Oxford Symposium.* London, 1967.

Coulson, John, and A. M. Allchin. *Newman: A Portrait Restored.* London, 1966.

Culler, Dwight. *The Imperial Intellect: A Study of Newman's Educational Ideal.* New Haven, 1955.

Davis, H. F. "Newman and Thomism." *Newman-Studien*, III, 157–169.

De Laura, David J. *Hebrew and Hellene in Victorian England: Newman, Arnold, and Pater.* Austin, Tex., 1969.

De Laura, David J. "Matthew Arnold and John Henry Newman: The Oxford Sentinel and the Religion of the Future." *Texas Studies in Literature and Language, 1964–65 and Supplement*, 573–703.

Dessain, Stephen. "Cardinal Newman and Uncreated Grace." *Clergy Review*, 47 (1962), 207–228, 269–288.

Dessain, Stephen. *John Henry Newman.* London, 1966.

Döpfner, Julius. "Das Verhaltnis von Natur und Übernatur bei John Henry Newman." *Newman-Studien*, IV, 269–330.

Douglas, Mary. *Natural Symbols.* London, 1970.

Eliade, Mircea. *Rites and Symbols of Initiation: Birth and Rebirth, The Religious Meaning of Initiation in Human Culture*, trans. W. R. Trask. New York, 1958.

Eliade, Mircea. *The Sacred and the Profane*, trans. W. R. Trask. New York, 1959.

Eliade, Mircea, and J. M. Kitagawa, eds. *The History of Religion: Essays in Methodology.* Chicago, 1959.

Evans-Pritchard, E. E. *Theories of Primitive Religion.* New York, 1962.

Farrer, Austin. *Reflective Faith*, ed. Charles Conti. London, 1972.

Geertz, Clifford. *The Interpretation of Cultures.* New York, 1973.

Geertz, Clifford. *Islam Observed: Religious Development in Morocco and Indonesia.* Chicago, 1968.

Graham, A. C. "The Background of the Mencian Theory of Human Nature." *Tsing Hua Journal of Chinese Studies*, New Series 6, 1–2 (1967), 214–271.

Harrold, Charles F. *John Henry Newman: An Expository and Critical Study of His Mind, Thought and Art.* London, 1945.

Harrold, Charles F., ed. *John Henry Newman: Essays and Sketches.* New York, 1948.

Holmes, J. Derek. "Newman's Attitude towards Historical Criticism and Biblical Inspiration." *Downside Review*, 89, 244 (1971), 22–37.

Hudson, Donald. *Ludwig Wittgenstein: The Bearing of His Philosophy on Religious Belief.* Richmond, Va., 1968.

James, D. G. *The Romantic Comedy.* London, 1948.

Kenny, Terence. *The Political Thought of John Henry Newman.* London, 1957.

Keogh, C. B. "Introduction to the Philosophy of Cardinal Newman." Thesis Ph.D., Université Catholique de Louvain, Institut Supérieur de Philosophie, 1950.

Kitagawa, J. M., ed. *The History of Religious Essays on the Problem of Understanding.* Chicago, 1967.

Kitagawa, J. M. " 'Verstehen' and 'Erlösung': Some Remarks on Joachim Wach's Work." *History of Religions,* II, 1 (1971), 31–53.

Küng, Hans. *Infallible? An Inquiry,* trans. E. Quinn. New York, 1971.

Lash, Nicholas. "Second Thoughts on Walgrave's 'Newman.' " *Downside Review,* 87, 289 (1964), 339–350.

Laski, H. J. *Studies in the Problem of Sovereignty.* New Haven, 1917.

Leeuw, G. van der. *Religion in Essence and Manifestation,* trans. J. E. Turner. 2 vols., New York, 1963.

Lubac, Henri de. *The Discovery of God,* trans. A. Dru. Chicago, 1967.

McGrath, Fergal. *Newman's University: Idea and Reality.* London, 1962.

Moeller, Charles, and Gerard Phillips. *The Theology of Grace and the Oecumenical Movement,* trans. R. A. Wilson. London, 1961.

Nédoncelle, Maurice. *La Philosophie Religieuse de J. H. Newman.* Strasbourg, 1946.

Neuner, Joseph, ed. *Christian Revelation and World Religions.* London, 1967.

Newman, J. H. *The Catholic Sermons of Cardinal Newman, published for the first time,* ed. Birmingham Oratory. London, 1957.

Newman, J. H. *On Consulting the Faithful in Matters of Doctrine,* ed. J. Coulson, London, 1961.

Newman, John Henry. *On the Inspiration of Scripture,* ed. J. Derek Holmes and Robert Murray. Dublin, 1967.

Newman, J. H. *The Letters and Diaries of John Henry Newman,* ed. Charles Stephen Dessain of the Birmingham Oratory. Vols. xi (October 1845) ff. London, 1961– (in progress).

Newman, J. H. *The Philosophical Notebooks of John Henry Newman,* vol. II, *The Text,* ed. Edward Sillem and A. J. Boekraad. New York, 1970.

Niebuhr, H. R. *The Responsible Self.* New York, 1963.

Otto, Rudolf. *The Idea of the Holy,* trans. J. Harvey. New York, 1958.

Pailin, David. *The Way to Faith: An Examination of Newman's Grammar of Assent as a Response to the Search for Certainty in Faith.* London, 1969.

Patterson, W. T. *Newman, Pioneer for the Layman.* Washington, 1968.

Pears, David. *Ludwig Wittgenstein.* New York, 1970.

Penner, Hans. "Is Phenomenology a Method for the Study of Religion?" *Bucknell Review,* xxxviii (1970), 29–54.

Prestige, G. L. *God in Patristic Thought.* London, 1964.

Przywara, P. Erich. *Einführung in Newmans Wesen und Werk,* vol. 4 of *J. H. Kardinal Newman Christentum Ein Aufbau.* 5 vols., Freiburg, 1922.

Przywara, P. Erich. *Polarity,* trans. A. C. Bouquet. London, 1935.

Rahner, Karl. *Theological Investigations,* various translators. 10 vols., London, 1960– (in progress).

Ramsey, I. T., ed. *Words about God.* New York, 1971.

Reardon, Bernard M. G. *From Coleridge to Gore: A Century of Religious Thought in Britain.* London, 1971.

Richards, I. A. *Mencius on the Mind: Experiments in Multiple Definition.* London, 1932.

Rickaby, Joseph. *Index to the Works of John Henry Newman.* London, 1914.

Ricoeur, Paul. "The Hermeneutics of Symbols and Philosophic Reflection." *International Philosophical Quarterly*, II, 2, 191–218.

Ryan, John K., and E. P. Bernard. *American Essays for the Newman Centennial.* Washington, 1947.

Schlette, Heinz R. *Towards a Theology of Religions,* trans. W. J. O'Hara. New York, 1966.

Seynaeve, Jaak. *Cardinal Newman's Doctrine of Holy Scripture.* Louvain, 1953.

Sheridan, Thomas. *Newman on Justification.* Staten Island, N.Y., 1968.

Sillem, E. J. "Cardinal Newman's Grammar of Assent on Conscience as a Way to God." *Heythrop Journal,* 5 (1964), 377–401.

Sillem, E. J., ed. *J. H. Newman, The Philosophical Notebooks,* vol. 1, *General Introduction to the Study of Newman's Philosophy.* New York, 1969.

Smart, Ninian. *Reasons and Faith: An Investigation of Religious Discourse Christian and Non-Christian.* London, 1958.

Smith, Jonathan Z. "The Influence of Symbols upon Social Change: A Place on Which to Stand." *Worship,* 44, 8, 457–474.

Streng, Frederick. *Emptiness, A Study in Religious Meaning.* Nashville, 1967.

Thomas, Owen, ed. *Attitudes towards Other Religions: Some Christian Interpretations.* New York, 1969.

Tierney, Michael, ed. *A Tribute to Newman.* Dublin, 1945.

Toulmin, Stephen. *Human Understanding,* vol. 1. Princeton, 1972.

Trevor, Meriol. *Newman, Light in Winter.* Garden City, N.Y., 1963.

Trevor, Meriol. *Newman, The Pillar of the Cloud.* Garden City, N.Y., 1963.

Triffin, John. "In Defense of Newman's Gentleman." *Wiseman Review,* 499–506 (1964/65–1965/66), 245–254.

Tristram, Henry, ed. *Newman, Centenary Essays.* London, 1945.

Vargish, Thomas. *Newman: The Contemplation of Mind.* Oxford, 1970.

Versfeld, Martin. "St. Thomas, Newman, and the Existence of God." *New Scholasticism,* 41 (1967), 1–34.

Vries, Jan de. *The Study of Religion, A Historical Approach,* trans. K. Bolle. New York, 1967.

Wach, Joachim. *The Comparative Study of Religion,* ed. J. Kitagawa. New York, 1961.

Wach, Joachim. *Sociology of Religion.* Chicago, 1967.

Wach, Joachim. *Types of Religious Experience Christian and Non-Christian.* Chicago, 1951.

Wach, Joachim. *Understanding and Believing,* ed. J. Kitagawa. New York, 1968.

Walgrave, J. H. *Newman the Theologian,* trans. A. V. Littledale. London, 1960.

Ward, Wilfrid. *The Life of John Henry Cardinal Newman.* 2 vols., London, 1912.

Welch, Claude. *Protestant Thought in the Nineteenth Century,* vol. 1, *1799–1870.* New Haven, 1972.

Wicker, Brian. "Newman and Logic." *Newman-Studien,* V, 251–269.

Willey, Basil. *More Nineteenth Century Studies.* New York, 1956.

Willey, Basil. *Nineteenth Century Studies.* New York, 1949.

Wittgenstein, Ludwig. *Lectures and Conversations on Aesthetics, Psychology and Religious Belief,* ed. C. Barret. Berkeley, 1972.

Wittgenstein, Ludwig. *Philosophical Investigations,* trans. G. E. M. Anscombe. Oxford, 1968.

Yaritell, V. R., ed. *A Newman Symposium.* New York, 1952.

Yearley, Lee. "Karl Rahner on the Relation of Nature and Grace." *Canadian Journal of Theology,* xvi, 3 and 4 (1970), 219–231.

Yearley, Lee. "Mencius on Human Nature: The Forms of His Religious Thought." *Journal of the American Academy of Religion,* 43, 2 (1975), 185–198.

Yearley, Lee. "The Nature-Grace Question in the Context of Fortitude." *Thomist,* xxv, 4 (1971), 557–580.

Yearley, Lee. "Newman's Concrete Specification of the Distinction between Christianity and Liberalism." *Downside Review,* 93, 310 (1975), 43–57.

Yearley, Lee. "Toward a Typology of Religious Thought: A Chinese Example." *Journal of Religion,* 55, 4 (1975), 426–443.

Zeno, Dr. *John Henry Newman, Our Way to Certitude.* Leiden, 1957.

Name Index

Subject Index